THREE CENTURIES
IN A CAPE COD VILLAGE

The Story of Chatham

Chatham Historical Society
Chatham, Massachusetts
2012

4880 Lower Valley Road · Atglen, PA 19310

Library of Congress Control Number: 2012930774

Designed by Marie Williams, WATERMARK, Chatham, MA
Type set in Adobe Garamond Pro

ISBN: 978-0-7643-4118-2
Printed in China

Schiffer Books are available at special discounts for bulk purchases for sales promotions or premiums. Special editions, including personalized covers, corporate imprints, and excerpts can be created in large quantities for special needs. For more information contact the publisher:

Published by Schiffer Publishing Ltd.
4880 Lower Valley Road
Atglen, PA 19310
Phone: (610) 593-1777; Fax: (610) 593-2002
E-mail: Info@schifferbooks.com

For the largest selection of fine reference books on this and related subjects, please visit our website at **www.schifferbooks.com**
We are always looking for people to write books on new and related subjects. If you have an idea for a book, please contact us at proposals@schifferbooks.com

This book may be purchased from the publisher.
Include $5.00 for shipping.
Please try your bookstore first.

You may write for a free catalog.

In Europe, Schiffer books are distributed by
Bushwood Books
6 Marksbury Ave.
Kew Gardens
Surrey TW9 4JF England
Phone: 44 (0) 20 8392 8585; Fax: 44 (0) 20 8392 9876
E-mail: info@bushwoodbooks.co.uk
Website: www.bushwoodbooks.co.uk

Cover image: *Northwestern View of Chatham, Massachusetts, 1839*, by John Warner Barber, *History and Antiquities of Every Town in Massachusetts*, Dorr, Holland and Company, 1839

Dedication

To all those who love Chatham

Preface

On this occasion of the Town of Chatham's 300th anniversary we are pleased to offer the first complete look at the town's fascinating 300-year history from the earliest days of pioneer William Nickerson, through the great days of sea captains, right up to the present day.

Several writers have tackled the town's history before now. William Smith, a founding member of the Chatham Historical Society, used early deeds and documents to publish his *History of Chatham* between 1909 and 1917. Yet Smith's work, while providing detailed and accurate information, essentially ends with 1816. Recent writers have turned their gazes to events of the 20th century. When planning began in 2008 for Chatham's 300th anniversary celebration, it was evident that an essential element of this occasion should be a new history, covering Chatham's entire past.

The obvious organization to sponsor such an endeavor is the Chatham Historical Society, founded in 1923. Therefore a group of potential writers gathered under its aegis to plan a new history.

The people involved in the discussions changed through the months until the group consisted of Dana Eldridge, Mary Ann Gray, Eric Hartell, Debra Lawless, Lynn Van Dine, Tim Weller and Spencer Grey. Among us are several journalists, a memoirist, a high school English teacher and an archivist. While we each bring a unique point of view to the table, what we share is a love of Chatham's history. Unwittingly we agreed on a plan that closely parallels that suggested by the late writer and Chatham historian Robert D.B. Carlisle in June 2008. He recommended that "the Chatham Historical Society... publish an illustrated book of essays and articles dealing with the town, its heritage, its life and its times."

In *Three Centuries in a Cape Cod Village* each of the seven contributors has painted vivid portraits of people whose lives most effectively evoke the essence of the roughly fifty-year period he or she has covered. We have relied on whatever historic records are available, many of which are found in the archives of the Atwood House Museum. We are indebted to committee member Tim Weller of Professional Writers & Editors for his fine editing of this book.

These selections, and the illustrations that accompany them, bring to life the people and their times over the course of 300 years in a special, yet typical, Cape Cod village. We hope you will enjoy our book.

Contents

1656-1712

Before Chatham: Monomoit and the Monomoyicks

By Dana Eldridge

Cape Cod, born of glaciers, was uninhabited for the first 10,000 years or so of its existence. Then for the next 10,000 years, hardy Native Americans trickled in to settle the longest peninsula on the East Coast.[1]

By the time of the Pilgrims, the Cape likely had fewer than 5,000 Native Americans spread thinly over this benign landscape. The land was blessed with bountiful natural resources which helped them adapt.

The most abundant – and most easily gathered – natural resource was shellfish. The inviting and warm shallow waters were home to acres of tasty oysters, quahogs, and steamers. The inhabitants lived in a cornucopia of readily available foodstuffs very near their campsites. And if they ever tired of seafood, with a little more effort deer, turkeys, waterfowl and small game were also easily available.

These Native Americans also learned to use fire to clear the land and to plant crops to augment their wild harvests. Pumpkins, squash, corn and a surprisingly varied list of crops were gathered seasonally, and in some cases stored for later consumption.

With ample foodstuffs and no apparent enemies, their lives were, by some measures, bucolic. Their 10,000-year occupation was by all accounts free of strife

A map of Port Fortune drawn by Samuel de Champlain in about October, 1606. *Voyages of Samuel de Champlain*, Prince's Society of Mutual Publication Edition, 1613.

and rancor. These "gentle and forgiving" people had stumbled on a near idyllic location to live out their lives.

One fall day in early November 1620, just after noon, white sails appeared on the ocean's horizon off Monomoit. They may have made the Monomoyicks – the tribe living on the Cape's elbow – nervous. What were those white smudges slowly ghosting south, so close by to their land? And why did they turn about a few hours later and move back across the ocean in the opposite direction, up past the Nauset tribe and out of sight along the coast?

We can speculate that the medicine men made much of this unusual happening, perhaps calling to their gods for answers. The Monomoyicks had seen other such sights – Bartholomew Gosnold had rounded Monomoy Point in the bark *Concord* and anchored in the bay in 1602, and in October 1606 the explorer Samuel de Champlain and his French crew were the first Europeans to land at Monomoit. While relations between the Native Americans and the Frenchmen were initially friendly during Champlain's three-week visit, a skirmish broke out that left four Frenchmen and untold Native Americans dead. Those particular smudges on that afternoon in 1620 were the sails of the tired little ship *Mayflower*. The strangers on board would change the natives' way of life for all time.

The Mayflower Comes Calling

On that November day the *Mayflower's* master, Christopher Jones, had been turned back by the fearsome, turbulent waters of Pollack Rip, just off Monomoy's eastern shore. He wanted to head south toward his destination at the mouth of the Hudson River. But Master Jones well knew that the twelve-foot draft of his ship was no match for the shallows fringing the sandy shore to the west. Yet "just when it seemed they might never extricate themselves from the shoals, the wind began to change, gradually shifting in a clockwise direction to the south," historian Nathaniel Philbrick writes in *Mayflower*. By 4:35 p.m., the *Mayflower* had sailed to the west of Pollock Rip; that night the ship drifted with the tide, four or five miles off Monomoit.[2]

The following day the *Mayflower* headed north and, after spending a night jogging off what is now Provincetown, sailed into a well-protected natural harbor where the ship lay at anchor while the settlers searched for a place to settle for good. By then the group on the ship had composed the Mayflower Compact, an important document of governance for Plymouth Colony. Before they disembarked on the morning of November 11, forty-one men signed the compact.[3]

Four passengers would perish while the ship was anchored in Provincetown. After about four weeks of exploring the Cape, the group found what they were looking for: another natural harbor, with ample fresh water and good rich soil, forty miles across the bay in Plymouth Harbor. On December 15 the Pilgrims departed Provincetown to begin their lives in Plymouth, and from there they spread out across the land, in some cases down the peninsula that was to become Cape Cod. Indeed, in the present day Cove Burying Ground in Eastham, three *Mayflower* passengers lie for all time.[4]

Mayflower passes Chatham.

Squanto dies and is buried in Monomoit.

1620

1622

Eventually these hardy newcomers discovered what the natives already well knew: That this land and the sea had bountiful foods ready to be taken. Fortunately for these newcomers, the Monomoyicks were willing to share with their new neighbors and teach them new harvesting tricks.

A Willful Man Used To Having His Way

When Monomoit's first white settler, William Nickerson, came to this land in the mid-1600s, he arrived with just his family. He dared what no other white man dared – to set up housekeeping in the midst of the natives' encampments, on land he had already purchased from them. In 1656 William bought a thousand acres of what would become modern-day Chatham from Mattaquason, the sachem of the region, "giving him a boat in payment."[5] Sixteen years of wrangling with the courts in Plymouth ensued before William took legal title to the land.

William has been called "the greatest speculator in wild lands the Cape ever saw" with the "soul of a pioneer and the tenacity of a bulldog."[6] William, who was a father of ten, "was the ancestor of all the great tribe of Nickersons that draw their origin from the Cape, and there are not many descendants of the other ancient families of this vicinity that do not, through the marriages of his female descendants, carry his blood in their veins," wrote Chatham native son James W. Hawes.[7] In fact by 1915, when William's descendants erected a memorial stone on the probable site of William's grave, William was estimated to be the "progenitor of fifty thousand descendants."[8]

The white man's history in Monomoit begins with this rugged individual and his stalwart wife Anne Busby, who was just as tough, just as resolute and just as determined as her husband.

The site of William Nickerson's homestead on the Nickerson Family Association's property at 1107 Orleans Road, Chatham. The property is a stone's throw from Ryder's Cove. *Photo by Tim Weller.*

Nickerson leaves England.

1636

Nickerson family migrates to Yarmouth.

1640

William, known to family genealogists as "William the Immigrant,"[9] was determined to stake out his claim in this new land. He had chafed at the strictures of the Crown Colony and the church in England. He bristled at the limitations of the Crown in Yarmouth. It seemed very likely he wanted a place he could organize and rule.

This area we now call Chatham was known then by a variety of names, as English ears tried to convert the natives' language into something the English could pronounce. "Mannomoiett," "Manomoy," and "Monomoit" are just a few of the English interpretations. The word "Monomoy" is still in use, a pleasant and concrete connection to times past.

A Weaver by Trade

William's story begins earlier, at his home in Norwich, England, where he was a well-established weaver. In 1636 he, Anne and their four children were hounded out of Norwich by religious zealots led by the Bishop of Norfolk. This forced the Nickersons to try life anew in the barely understood "new land" many leagues to the west across the Atlantic Ocean.

Such a daring move cannot be overstated. How desperate they must have been to chance the crossing! When they embarked, all they knew was that they would never again see family, friends, and the only land they had ever known.

What thoughts must have been going through their minds as the little ship cleared the English harbor on that blustery early fall day in 1637?[10] William was about 33; Anne was slightly younger at 28. Anne's parents, too, accompanied the family. Eventually William and Anne would be the parents of ten: Nicholas, Elizabeth, Robert, Thomas (who died in infancy), Anne, Samuel, John, Sarah, William and Joseph.

The trip itself proved uneventful. Two ships, the *Rose* and the *John and Dorothy*, captained by a father and his son, traveled together. In Salem the ships landed more or less on schedule and disembarked their passengers, William and family among them.[11] By 1640 the family had migrated to the outpost town of Yarmouth, and William found even that small frontier village a bit too restrictive. William decided to head east to find an area he could more easily tolerate, where the strictures of the Crown and Puritan religiosity were not as dominating. By all accounts he was a willful man used to having his way, and impatient with bureaucracy. To that end he eventually purchased or traded with the native peoples for nearly all of what is now Chatham. Little is known of the natives' understanding of land ownership, but certainly the natives and the English had far different ideas. All of William's transactions with the natives were verbal.

But before heading east, while still living in Yarmouth in 1656, William entered into an agreement with the sachem of the Monomoyicks, Mattaquason, known as "the Old Sagamore,"[12] for the first purchase of four square miles of what was to become a part of Chatham. The purchase price was "a shallop, ten coats, six kettles, twelve axes, twelve hoes, twelve knives, forty shillings in wampum, a hat and twelve shillings in coins."[13]

William Nickerson makes first purchase of Monomoit lands.

1656

The Monomoyicks taught the English how to plant their crops.
Illustration courtesy of Dana Eldridge and the Cape Cod National Seashore.

Later William made three more purchases. The second purchase included property in the vicinity of Oyster Pond and south to Stage Harbor. To enlarge his holdings to the west, he purchased most of what is today known as South Chatham, and some land slightly further west. Apparently not completely satisfied, he added a fourth, taking the land then known as Tom's Neck. This included lands east of Stage Harbor to the shore line. As far as is known, these transactions were all verbal agreements with only approximate understanding of boundaries.

When William headed east from Yarmouth, he was heading into barely known lands where no white man lived or had ever lived.

Learning to Live Off the Land

For the newly arrived Nickerson family, this land was a wonderful place to raise their rooftree, and William did so at the head of Ryder's Cove in what is now Chathamport.[14] There he found ample wood for building and for firewood, along with acres of land for gardens.[15] These pioneers were well used to gardening; harvesting food from the land was all but second nature to the English. They had brought enough seed to start their gardens and the natives were happy to share their own supply.

Cape natives lived in a conical shelter called a wetu, with a fire pit in the center.
Illustration courtesy of Dana Eldridge and The Cape Cod National Seashore.

William Nickerson moves to Monomoit lands.

1664

But these settlers knew nothing of the sea and its bounty. The Nickersons probably would not have made it through their first or second winters had it not been for the willingness of William to adapt his ways to those of his Native American neighbors – and for the natives' willingness to help. They showed the family how to jig for flounder in a small dugout using just a torch and spear, and by wading along the shallows. These techniques also worked for harvesting eels. In the spring alewives or herring choked the streams which flowed from fresh ponds into bays and the ocean. Herring are a bony fish, but their abundance in early spring, a time of scant rations, made them a welcome sight.

Striped bass were nearly a year-round catch, and the natives' methods of smoking and drying made preservation easy. One report from the mid-1660s said striped bass were so thick one could walk dry-shod across their backs. Hardly likely, but the point was made.

In times of inclement weather the settlers could nearly always scratch for shellfish; most shellfish will keep more than a week in storage, much longer in the colder months. Oysters, a shellfish they were used to back in their native country, adorned the rocks. Steamer clams and quahogs were abundant. One wonders if the Nickerson clan ever felt the pangs of hunger after they set up housekeeping. I'm equally sure that some of those Nickerson children were told the same thing that I (a direct Nickerson descendant) was told twelve generations later: Why don't you go down to the shore and get us some quahogs for dinner?

They did, and I still do today.

The Nickersons Settle In

After the difficult times of a persecuted life, this new land must have seemed like a slice of heaven. For many years this Nickerson clan was the only white family who dared live on this part of Cape Cod. William no doubt knew the natives inland were in upheaval, fighting a brutal uprising called King Philip's War (1675-1676).

But on the Cape no such confrontation existed. Because of this, "the Cape had become the colony's one oasis of safety."[16] While all the townships or population clusters were required to send men to help quell this uprising, relations with the Monomoyick remained routinely friendly.[17]

Mattaquason and William, despite their disparate upbringings, and despite the lack of a shared language, managed to bridge a divide of understanding and work out a relationship that could have been a working model for the entire nation to come. It's a working model we can envy even today.

While the Native Americans lived in conical shelters called wetus, with a fire pit in the center, the Nickerson home, built in about 1664, was a rude cottage close by the shores of Ryder's Cove, near a freshwater creek that empties into the cove. In those days few, if any, homes were more than two hundred square feet – and most were smaller. Nickerson soon enlarged the cottage to accommodate his growing family. This cottage was, by necessity, a most basic structure: oiled paper for windows that also let in some light, earthen floors, crude cots, and the all-important fireplace along one wall. This fireplace was the lodestone of the home. All cooking was done there and all heat – and evening light – emanated from it.

Resilient people, indeed!

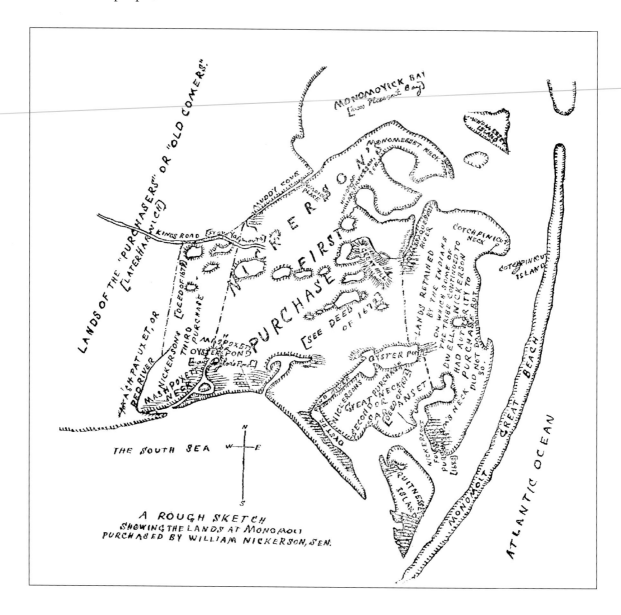

William Nickerson has free and clear title to his four purchases.

William Nickerson begins to deed out parcels.

1672

1674

A Typical, Difficult Day

What would a typical day have been like for the Nickersons?

Up at dawn, the family's immediate chore was to put food on the table. Perhaps breakfast was meat from some animal William had shot or trapped. Or perhaps it was smoked fish. Whatever breakfast was, it would have been rugged fare. With breakfast over, it was time to assign chores to the children. Chopping and splitting firewood was a continuous job. The maw of the fireplace allowed no slacking off of this chore. If they wanted heat, cooking fuel, and light in the evening, the firewood supply had to be replenished daily and stocked for the months ahead.

The nearby stream made washing clothes somewhat easier, but the big kettle over the fire took a long time to heat and the collected animal fat soap was not very sudsy. Cleaning clothes required much scrubbing on backyard rocks.

Very likely everyone grabbed whatever was available to eat during the day, probably smoked fish or meat hanging from hooks in some cool space in the cottage.

As head of the family, William was responsible for keeping his family fed, warm, and secure. He saw to it that the firewood supply was adequate, that the larder was well stocked, and the gardens and their crops were as they should be, ready to be harvested and stored for the winter.

To keep the larder stocked was no small task. Every calorie consumed by this family of hard workers came from the ground, the woods, or the nearby ocean. On any given day, the children were likely delegated to find food. Shellfish harvesting was an easy but cold project in the fall, winter, and spring. Still it was a chore that couldn't wait; it was an everyday job for the family. The ground had to be turned over, the seeds planted, weeds plucked, varmints kept at bay, and the crop harvested at the proper time. It was never-ending work.

The Nickersons' livestock also needed attention. William and his grown sons would scythe the abundant marsh grasses in the closest marsh. Not an easy task. Once cut, the grasses had to be dried – either on platforms on the marsh called staddles – or rowed to shore wet and spread out to dry. The animals didn't much like this salty grass but would eat it rather than starve. A steady diet of salt hay also prematurely wore down their teeth.

No matter the chore, these jobs required hard, physical labor. Anne's jobs would have been made worse because of the tedious nature of the work. William and the boys at least could draw some pleasure out of hunting, fishing or digging for shellfish.

When the interminable jobs were done for the day, the family would relax in the late afternoon. By early evening it was time to recount the day's events, probably over the evening meal. That completed and the daylight gone, it was time for rest.

Smallpox sweeps across Monomoit, decimating native population.

1679

William Nickerson dies at approximate age of 85.

1689

Highway surveyors chosen.

1696

William Sets Out to Build an Outpost

For William chores were just one facet of life. With all the land he had purchased, at some point he began to concentrate on building a town as he thought it should be.

William needed more people to make his proposed community a reality. Until he had undeniable title to his purchases, his chances of attracting people were slim to none. His solution? Deeding out some of his holdings to his growing family.

In 1661 William deeded about fifty acres south of Oyster Pond to his daughter Elizabeth Eldred, who had married Robert Eldred. This probably was the first written deed of Monomoit land ever executed.

This transfer of title was done despite the fact that his legal hold on the deeded land was in limbo. The deed is written as follows:

> To all Christian people to whom this present writing shall come, Know ye that I William Nickerson of Yarmouth in ye jurisdiction of New Plymouth in New England for divers good Causes & Considerations here unto moving Have given & granted & by these presents do give & grant unto my Daughter Elizabeth Eldred fourty acres of upland & ten acres of meadow out of ye lands that I purchased of ye Indian Sagamore Mattaquason at Manamoy & there about, part of ye lands lying & being by a swamp near to ye Oyster pond furlong.[18]

It finishes: *in ye thirteenth year of ye Reign of our Sovereign Lord King Charles.* This deed was witnessed by Sarah and William Nickerson Jr., siblings of Elizabeth.

The exact date that William settled permanently in Monomoit is uncertain, but it probably was around 1664 – during the Crown's lawsuit against him for dealing with the natives without the authority of courts. While the legal wrangling was ongoing, two more of his daughters married, one to Tristram Hedges, one to Nathanial Covell. William deeded out to these two daughters more fifty-acre parcels. Through marriage alone, this outpost of Nickerson's was growing!

After his Day in Court

Finally, in 1672, having survived all the various court proceedings, having paid a fine of £90 pounds, and having obtained written deeds from Mattaquason and his son John, William became sole owner of all he had negotiated with the natives, except, of course, the land he had deeded to his children. He was now able to sell off land and populate the growing village with an eye toward incorporation.

In 1674 he conveyed to John Downing, Teague Jones, and Thomas Crow (after whom Crows Pond was named) parcels of his domain in good and clear title. This meant that when

First full-time preacher hired (Reverend Vickery) dies at sea.

Church erected.

1697

1701

volunteers were needed to fight in King Philip's War, the Downing family was able to send three of its sons. One of the Nickerson boys also went. But about a year after it began, the war sputtered out.

In 1678 calamity sailed into one of Monomoit's many coves in the guise of a trading ship. The ship's young master was very sick and soon died. The cause of the untimely death was smallpox. Smallpox was a rapid and sure killer and worked its havoc on the natives.

Smallpox arrived with the new settlers and decimated entire families of these native peoples whose immune systems had no resistance to the white man's diseases. Even the white population suffered from smallpox. A previous epidemic in 1634 had taken a terrible toll in the Plymouth Bay Colony. The skin of the Native Americans "became so consumed with sores that their flesh adhered to the mats on which they slept."[19] The native population of Monomoit, as counted by the Reverend Samuel Treat of Eastham in 1693, totaled 505 Monomoyicks and 150 white adults.[20] But by 1698 the native population had dwindled to fifty-to-seventy adults and the English had increased their numbers. The natives were becoming irrelevant in their own time on their own lands.

It was the beginning of a steep decline in the native population. As the white population was increasing, the native population was in near final collapse.

Building a Meeting House

Every group of people has to find some governmental representation somewhere, and the Nickerson family was no exception. Initially the few residents of Monomoit hitched their fortunes to that of the town of Eastham, which was seven or eight miles away, a five hour ride on horseback or oxcart.

By 1679 this distance had become a barrier of no small consequence. It was proving to be a tedious proposition to be allied with the constablewick of Eastham, so William and his in-laws petitioned the courts to separate.

The court agreed to the separation with certain conditions: "That they put money aside to house a minister and build the meeting house." They promised to do so. With the concurrence of the courts the inhabitants could now meet together, raise money by taxation, and appropriate the same. They could choose a constable, grand juryman, and assessors. In short they were a separate entity though not quite yet a town. William's dream of creating a town of his own was inching along towards becoming a reality.[21]

Death of a Pioneer

In his old age William Nickerson was still leading his small family and the few hardy souls who had joined them. Every Sunday he gathered everyone and gave readings from the Scriptures. He was the undisputed leader of the small village.

Another full-time preacher found, Reverend Adams. He is told to find a more appropriate name for the area, decides on Chatham. Thirteen families move away.

Crown declares Chatham is a town with all rights of incorporation.

1711

1711

1712

This marker shows the site of Nickerson's home. *Photo by Tim Weller.*

John Taylor bought some land from William, land in the South Chatham area enclosing what came to be known as Taylor's Pond. In 1681 William is listed as a grandjuryman, a position of some responsibility. John Savage is listed as a constable. William's little outpost was growing.[22]

In 1685 events were looking better for incorporation as a township. More people had moved to this area, but they still hadn't built the meeting house or a parsonage. Newcomers included the Stewart family, Caleb Lumbert, and William Griffith.

As the fledgling town grew, people banded together to purchase a whaleboat to harvest the whales that appeared just off their shores. This substantial boat was owned in shares by the few pioneers. The residents of Monomoit were beginning to think not only as individuals but as a unit. Things were looking up for incorporation as a town.

By this time William had outlived almost all of his contemporaries by at least thirty years. Between August 1689 and September 1690, some fifty-three years after landing rootless in Salem, he died at about age eighty-five. His fierce will, his stamina, and his determination had taken this small, remote settlement almost all the way to becoming a town.[23] It remained for his family to carry on that quest.

The Drowning of Reverend Vickery

In 1690 William Nickerson, Jr., was appointed Inspector of Whales, a position of some importance. Even at this late date the budding town could not afford a minister and, as a result, could not be incorporated.

More meetings were held as the outpost continued to grow. At one such meeting it was decided that each householder should kill twelve blackbirds or three crows or be fined for not doing so.[24] The reason? These hungry birds had no trouble unearthing early spring plantings. This practice continued for many years with, very likely, negligible success.

A local militiaman, Lt. Nicholas Eldredge, was given some arms, powder, and bullets for safe keeping in the event of hostilities. The French privateers were a constant threat to the local populace.

Roads were becoming important. By 1696 highway surveyors were appointed to clear and repair the dirt roads. Travel was by oxcart or horse so the roads needed routine and regular maintenance to keep up with the daily wear.

Most importantly, the Reverend Nathanial Stone began serving as minister for a time, although his primary audience was in Harwich. Then in the spring of 1697, a lay minister, Jonathan

Vickery, came to the area to preach. And he preached with vigor. At the turn of the century he prevailed on the population to set aside funds for a meeting house. To that end he presided over numerous meetings. Village residents were ordered to bring support posts, planking and the necessaries for constructing a meeting house, which, in a community effort, they proceeded to do. This building was completed at last in about 1701 and Mr. Vickery gathered his flock to praise the efforts of the builders and volunteers. All seemed well for continued prosperity and incorporation. But these hopes were dashed on April 30, 1702, when a number of influential townsfolk drowned on a fishing trip, Mr. Vickery among them.[25]

1711: The First Emigration

In January 1703, Gershom Hall of Harwich agreed to preach, although he was not ordained. Still, this farmer and millwright had a gifted tongue.[26] Just three years later townspeople tried to hire a "coleg man as cheap as they can."[27] Their man was the Harvard-educated Reverend John Latimer, who boarded around among his parishioners. He stayed in town until 1709 and was followed by other preachers.

The idea of incorporation seems inevitable, but in 1711 thirteen families emigrated to what is now Smyrna, Delaware. That left just thirty families to support the all-vital church. Why did these thirteen families leave? One reason was the increasing fear of raids by French privateers. Also the distance from population centers proved difficult for many.

The remaining families (who had only seven male church members) found the Reverend Hugh Adams to preach for them, but there was still no parsonage to house him. It was at this time that the town changed its name to Chatham, after Chatham, England. "It is likely that Mr. Adams had as much influence as any one in the selection of the name" which "may have been chosen under the impression that the place might some day become a naval station like the English town."[28]

The families liked the name Chatham. It was far more pleasing to them than the name Monomoit. This was quite fitting; to this new land they brought along some of the old and familiar.

Now this "new" area had met all the crown's conditions for incorporation. It had a church, a parsonage was being subscribed, and Reverend Adams was the hired preacher. So on June 11, 1712, the crown brought William's idea to fruition, when Governor Dudley signed the following order: *"Ordered that the village or district now called Monomoit be erected into a Township and the Town be called Chatham."*[29]

Chatham became a bona fide town with all the legal powers of governance. Interestingly, "the incorporation of the village, at length attained thirty-seven years after William Nickerson Sen. first petitioned for it, appears to have been received by the people with no flourish of trumpets."

That would all change two hundred years in the future when William Nickerson's descendants joined with the descendants of old comers and new comers alike to celebrate the town's bicentennial.

The Search for Squanto

"I wonder if it's Squanto?" asked Donald Aikman, vice-chair of the Chatham Historical Commission, during a recent winter when yet another Native American burial was unearthed in North Chatham.[1]

Aikman voiced the question on many minds. Just about every time a shovel strikes a mysterious pile of bones buried in Chatham someone telephones the Chatham Historical Society to ask archivist Mary Ann Gray if the bones might belong to Squanto, from the Patuxet tribe, who died in 1622.

Squanto, also known as Tisquantum was, of course, the Pilgrims' guide, famous for his ability to speak English. Squanto lived for five years in England, Spain, and Newfoundland after he was taken captive near Plymouth in 1614. Back in Plymouth County during the Pilgrims' first winter and spring, he taught the newcomers to catch

An early image of Squanto.

eels and to grow corn by fertilizing the poor soil with herring. Even as he mediated the treacherous arena of Native American-Pilgrim relations he was thought to be hatching intrigues of his own, and the powerful Wampanoag sachem Massasoit came to hate him.

In November 1622, Squanto traveled with Gov. William Bradford from Plymouth to Chatham, then known as Monomoit, on a mission to trade with the Monomoyicks for eight hogsheads of corn and beans. Their sloop, the *Swan*, anchored in Pleasant Bay. The trip was a success but just before departure, Squanto fell ill, bleeding from the nose. He was placed in a Monomoyick's hut or *wetu*. "On the sea night descended, cold, green, and gray with winter. Tisquantum buried his face in a deerskin cape and made no moan as the 'Blood of Death' seeped into the woven mat."[2] So Elizabeth Reynard, a resident of Chatham 300 years later, poetically described Squanto's final moments.[3]

Now here's the kicker: After he died, Squanto was buried immediately. But where? Theories abound.

Warren Sears Nickerson (1880-1966) placed Squanto's death "at the Monomoyick head village where the *Swan* lay at anchor." This would be somewhere near present-day Jackknife Cove. About 150 years later – in 1770 or so – "an Indian skeleton was washed out of a hill between the Head of the Bay and Crow's Pond." Because this corpse was buried more in the manner of the Pilgrims than of the Monomoyicks, a theory rose that the bones were those of Squanto.[4] At another time, Nickerson suggested Squanto's body still lay under the golf course at Eastward Ho! Country Club, overlooking Pleasant Bay.[5]

Nearby, at the Nickerson Family Association at 1107 Orleans Road, is a 1955 plaque that says Squanto was buried "somewhere within gunshot." But where? The trouble is, until it was moved a few years ago, the plaque and its stone were planted across town at the Atwood House Museum on Stage Harbor Road.

"When I was president of the Chatham Historical Society, I was unhappy with the incorrect historical statement that 'within gunshot' of this marker was the place of Squanto's death," recalls Spencer Grey. "The logical location for the stone marker was the Nickerson Family property, which *is* within gunshot of the location of his death."

Wherever his final resting place, why do we remain obsessed with Squanto, dead now for nearly four centuries?

While any old gravesite is interesting, when we attach the name Squanto to it our imaginations have full play. We think of Squanto equally at home roaming the streets of London and lying in a wetu overlooking Pleasant Bay a good thirty years before William Nickerson set up shop here. Squanto was a true cross-cultural ambassador. He could explain his own culture to the Pilgrims while translating theirs back to his people. And he seemed to like the Pilgrims and their ways. It may be apocryphal, but lore has it that Squanto asked for a "white man's burial" because he wanted to "go to the Englishmen's God in heaven."[6]

Finding Squanto's bones would transport us all back to that far-off time, now largely lost in myth, when the Pilgrims were the new kids on the block and Native Americans pretty much ruled the land. It tantalizes.

And so the search for Squanto continues.

By Debra Lawless

1712-1775

The Exodus from Chatham

By Mary Ann Gray

I t's an old story: the minister doesn't approve of demon rum. But most feuds between ministers and tavern keepers don't result in protracted court cases, as did the one in the new town of Chatham, which was finally incorporated in 1712.

When William Nickerson first arrived in the area known as Monomoit in 1656, the region could not support a church of its own because its population was too low. Although churches had been established in Harwich and Eastham, the distance often made travel to services impossible. So when Monomoit was first settled, William served as a lay preacher, holding services in his home and later in the meeting house.

Following Nickerson's death in 1689 or 1690, a series of non-ordained men filled the role of minister, but it was not until the spring of 1711 that the Reverend Hugh Adams accepted the call to Monomoit. Adams arrived at an unfortunate time, just after what is called the first emigration (of an eventual four) that left the town with only seven male residents eligible for church membership. Although he tried, he failed to stop emigration by securing exemptions for the male citizens from the military and by having taxes reduced. Monomoit was, however, given the right to incorporate and did so in 1712, changing its name to Chatham.

Reverend Adams, who had arrived in Chatham in 1712, then tried to encourage the people settled in the area next to South Chatham to join with the people of Chatham to raise the number of male church members to fifty, the number necessary to establish a church. He did not succeed and in February 1715 he angered the citizens by preaching a sermon handling "those who differed with him without gloves," as Chatham historian William C. Smith puts it. Furthermore he specifically criticized Ebenezer Hawes, who owned the town tavern.[1]

And as for Hawes? "He was a man of intelligence and honor, a foe to bigotry, and a valuable citizen for any town," writes historian Henry C. Kittredge. "The esteem in which he was held by the townspeople was shown by their choosing him as selectman, an office which he filled with ability, and he was also captain of the military company. His taproom became the rendezvous for the best men of the village; many a bushel of corn and barrel of tar was bargained for over a friendly glass before his fire."[2]

John Stewart purchases Morris Farris's tavern on Morris Island and runs the tavern for twenty years.

1725

Clearly the popular Hawes was not a man you wanted as your enemy, and his number one enemy was now the good Reverend Adams. "This gentleman took exception to Hawes's public house, not because it was improperly run, but because it was a public house, and he took up arms against Hawes, not because the latter was an undesirable character, but because he sold rum."[3] One account has it that Adams's problems came about because "the tavern and the parsonage were too near together and Mr. Adams saw too much of what was going on."[4]

In any event, "parsons were formidable men, but when Adams attacked Hawes, he opposed a man who was quite as formidable as he was and just as strongly entrenched in respectability."[5]

Hawes declared that Adams lied in the February sermon that took the town to task. And the war was on. Adams sued Hawes for slander. The resulting trial decided that Adams should resign and a town meeting was called on June 13, 1715, at which the town "voted not to employ Mr. Adams in the work of the ministry any longer."[6] Adams fought for his salary by appealing to the Common Pleas Court in Barnstable. He wrote a treatise which he sent to the General Court in Plymouth. He appealed to the quarter session of the Inferior Court of Common Pleas at Barnstable in 1716. All this activity resulted in a second victory for Hawes although another appeal to the Superior Court at Plymouth resulted in a favorable decree for Adams. Damages of 10 shillings were to be paid to him. Among existing papers is one written on behalf of Hawes, signed by twenty-eight men of Chatham. The end result was that Adams advertised his "good Double House and a Barn" and about fifty acres for sale in May 1716 and hightailed it to Maine to preach.[7]

The New Town: Growing Pains and the More Squabbles

Life in the newly incorporated Town of Chatham was anything but idyllic. Its people, perhaps following the lead of their deceased founder, William Nickerson, tended to be litigious.

Early on, a long-rumbling dispute again broke out over common lands. As illustrated in the map, when Nickerson sold land to the families who followed his family to Chatham, he granted rights of pasturage and of cutting wood (for heating and building) in the common lands. As time went on Nickerson sold portions of the common lands to the newer settlers, thus reducing the acreage of land set aside for the common good. Eventually residents began to demand that the common lands be divided and opened up for settlement.

Shortly after Nickerson's death in 1689 or 1690, the issue of dividing the common lands became more pressing. Two groups were involved. The first were those who claimed they had the right to be given a portion of the common lands due to their original purchase of land from Nickerson; they were called "proprietors." The second included those who had been granted rights or privileges by Nickerson as he sold additional land and then granted privileges to the new owners to use the remaining commons; they were called "privileged men."

This dispute was settled in court by a test case in which Nickerson's son, William Jr. (a proprietor), brought suit against Daniel Hamilton (a privileged man). William Jr. accused Hamilton

Money is raised to add a gallery to the meeting house until a larger house can be built.

The ship *George and Ann* lands on the shores of Monomoy. Poorly treated passengers are immigrants from Ireland whose original destination was Pennsylvania.

1727

1729

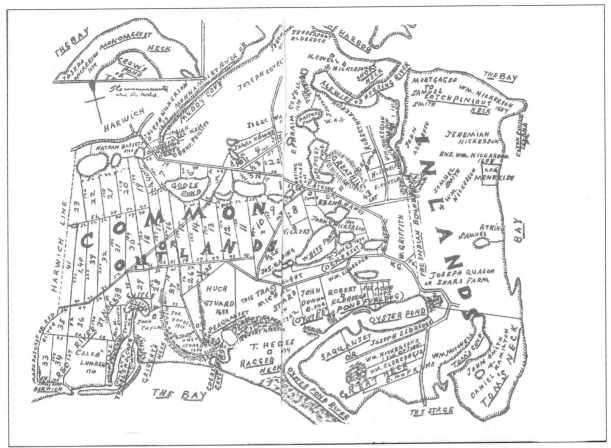

On this map the division of the common lands can be seen, stretching form the Harwich line on the west to White Pond on the east. From a sketch on pages 132-133 of William C. Smith's book, *A History of Chatham, Massachusetts.*

of cutting wood on the common lands. In 1710 the court decided in favor of William Jr. Daniel appealed the decision to the Superior Court of Adjudication and the case was tried before a jury. The result of that trial favored Hamilton and reversed the lower court's decision, thus establishing the rights of the "privileged men."

    With the common lands now in private hands, there was less open space for either new families or members of the larger families.

    In 1712, with the help of the Reverend Adams, the proprietors agreed to survey the common lands and lay them out into lots of equal value. These lots were then divided among all the freemen. The privileged men would get three-eighths of the lots and the proprietors would get the remaining five-eighths. The lots of the proprietors were distributed by a lottery system. Common lands no longer existed.

A new, larger meeting house is built on the site of the old one.

Monomoy is no longer used as a site for grazing cattle or home sites, only for mowing lands.

1730

1733

But the equitable division of common lands was not the only problem plaguing residents of this infant town. Lands that had been farmed for many years began to yield fewer crops, making it more difficult for farmers to feed their large families. As a result more men turned to the sea to earn their living by fishing. The fish stocks then began to decrease and many of the fishermen sought fertile fishing grounds off the coast of Nova Scotia. The years from 1725 to 1775 were a time of exodus from Chatham, and the town struggled to maintain and even add to its population. A lack of available land and opportunities compelled scores of young men, many with families, to pack up and leave.

Complicating the problem for the settlers was the tendency for their families to be very large. An agrarian society required many hands to cultivate and care for the crops and animals. In a society in which the environment and lack of adequate medical care led to a high rate of infant mortality, it seemed only practical to have a large family. William and Anne Nickerson had a family of ten children, nine of whom lived to adulthood. Each of their children had large families. William and Anne's grandchildren numbered seventy-six. It doesn't take much imagination to see how quickly the land, if just divided among his progeny, would have contained lots of such small acreage that they would not support a family.

Life in the newly established communities was hazardous, especially for those depending on the sea for their income. Often families were faced with the death of the husband or several sons due to accidents at sea or risks related to farming. Farming, fishing, and whaling were just about the only occupations during this period. Aside from a town blacksmith, carpenters, coopers, shoemakers, a tannery, and the local tavern, not many worked outside their farms. There were no merchants until Elisha Hopkins opened a general store near Stage Harbor in 1735. And "there were no villages such as there are today," Smith writes. "The centre of the place, so far as there was any centre, was in the vicinity of the church and cemetery.... Here was the sun dial to give the correct time, the pound for stray cattle, the tavern where people met to make trades and to hear the news, and the windmill where their products were ground into meal."[8]

Like the Native Americans, the early settlers preferred the area away from the seacoast, near today's Old Queen Anne and Old Comers Roads, the site of the town's oldest cemeteries.

Joseph Lord Called to Chatham

While many histories are divided into periods of war, or kings, or presidents, Chatham's early history was divided up into ministries, and it often seemed that each minister's time in the pulpit was marred by scandal. Participation in church life was anything but voluntary, and each citizen was taxed a certain amount to keep the church afloat. (It would not be until the 19th century that the finances of church and town parted ways.)

While Reverend Adams had carried on like an early version of Carrie Nation in the tavern, the Reverend Joseph Lord took after a neighboring minister accused of philandery. Lord, who arrived in March 1718, conducted a "long and bitter controversy" with the Reverend Samuel Osborn, who had a taste for hanky-panky.[9]

Dr. Samuel Lord, son of the Reverend Joseph Lord, begins his medical practice in Chatham.

1735

Elisha Hopkins opens the first general store in town in the vicinity of Stage Harbor.

1735

The town called Lord to preach for six months beginning in 1718. He followed Gershom Hall, a lay preacher. Lord, the son of Thomas and Alice (Rand) Lord of Charleston, was baptized on June 26, 1672, and graduated from Harvard College in 1691. He had taught school in Dorchester, and by 1695 had joined a group organized to establish a church of the Puritan faith in South Carolina.[10]

He was ordained pastor of the South Carolina church on October 22 and on December 5 set sail for Charleston with the members of the new church. While on a trip back to the Cape to recruit new members, he married Abigail Hinckley, the daughter of Thomas Hinckley, the last governor of the Massachusetts Bay Colony. The couple would eventually have eight children, including a pair of twins. Abigail's hometown was Barnstable, and in 1717, Lord began to preach in Eastham. However, he was not called to that church.

Lord's call to Chatham came at a time when Chatham was at a turning point. Immigration from other parts of the Cape and Massachusetts had slowed; the exodus of residents to Duck Creek, Delaware, and elsewhere had removed twenty-four families from the rolls. Most of the land had been farmed or cleared of wood.

If the town was to survive, it must begin to develop its educational and religious institutions and consolidate its government. In 1718 the town voted to extend a temporary call to Lord and set about acquiring a house and land for his use. In October of that year, his call was extended for six months and his salary was fixed at £35 for six months. A vote toward the end of that year extended a call as permanent pastor and residents at town meeting in June 1719 accepted the terms of the settlement. He and his family were to use the house purchased for the ministry, and repairs on the house would be made at the town's expense.

Lord's service began in earnest and he, like Adams, set about trying to organize a separate church for the town. In 1720 he was ordained by the church council and installed as pastor. June 15, 1720, is also the date the church, today known as the First Congregational Church of Chatham, considers its "formal gathering" date.

To help the church grow, it adopted a system of a halfway covenant. This would allow members of the community who had not yet professed their adherence to the full covenant to have their children baptized and participate in all of its activities except communion. The number of males in the church remained at seven, the same number as under the Reverend Adams in 1711. (The church also had between twenty-one and twenty-eight female members.) This halfway covenant procedure, not accepted by all seven of the males, became the practice in the Chatham church. However the plan proposing to annex the "South Side peoples" of Harwich was not successful when it was proposed again in 1722.

In 1725 Lord's wife died. He would wait eighteen years before he married Mrs. Bethiah Smith of Eastham in 1743. She had been a member of Lord's church. Twice widowed, her first husband was Lt. Isaac Hawes of Chatham and her second husband was John Smith of Eastham.

In 1732 Lord's salary was raised from its original £80 to £90. Over time a few families moved into the area; at the end of Lord's ministry in 1748, about 100 families were living in Chatham.

Seafaring becomes the major occupation with about a dozen fishing vessels and many local residents commanding ships sailing from Boston.

1740

Get Your Hands Off Me!

Now, let us return to what historian Smith calls "The Great Osborn Controversy"[11] in a chapter-long account in *A History of Chatham, Massachusetts*. Smith's narrative and another by Gustavus Swift Paine[12] titled *Ungodly Carriages on Cape Cod* read like soap operas as they describe the events that took place when Samuel Osborn was called to minister at Pochet Church in Eastham.

The story goes like this: Osborn arrived in 1707 from Ireland and settled in Edgartown, Martha's Vineyard. Based upon letters of reference brought with him, he was hired as a school teacher. Three years later he married Jedidah Smith, the daughter of one of the town's leading citizens.

A few months after his marriage, "charges were preferred against him by a young lady of the place, which it should be said he persistently denied on all occasions, although admitting that he had been foolish and indiscreet in some of his actions with her."[13] The court in 1711 found him guilty of the charges but he refused to admit that he had committed any wrongdoing. He left the island and moved to Sandwich, where he obtained another job as a teacher. In 1713 he taught in Harwich and by 1717 was teaching in Plymouth when he was invited to preach in Eastham.

In the spring of 1718 the Eastham church sought, as was custom, the rest of the churches' consent to engage him as their permanent pastor. The churches, knowing of Osborn's conviction in Martha's Vineyard, did not wholeheartedly endorse his appointment. In spite of this, Eastham hired him, and thus began a controversy that ran until 1738, when Osborn was asked to leave the church in Eastham after twenty years of what Smith dubs "guerilla warfare against Mr. Osborn."

The debate was fueled by Chatham's Reverend Lord, the Reverend Nathaniel Stone of Harwich, and a member of the Eastham church, Hannah Doane. "They did not consider Mr. Osborn, even if he had repented, a suitable man for the ministry, and they believe the Bible sustained them in their attitude."[14] The church council finally asked Osborn to leave because his beliefs differed from the tenets of mainstream churches.

In 1742 Osborn moved to Maine where he also was unsuccessful. Weirdly enough, he returned to Chatham the following year. Around this time he lost his wife, the former Jedidah Smith, and married the widow Experience Hopkins, whose late husband had been a well-to-do merchant in Chatham. By two years later, he had changed careers and began practicing medicine on Nantucket. By 1756 Osborn had separated from Experience, as she was again living in Chatham. Finally Osborn moved to Barrington, Nova Scotia[15] in 1762, where he joined his sons and most likely some of the Chatham residents who were proprietors in that town. He died in Boston in about 1774.

Second major emigration from Chatham takes place. Residents leave for Connecticut and the Oblong.

The Reverend Joseph Lord dies and the Reverend Stephen Emery is employed to take his place.

1747

1748

The Death of the Reverend Lord

When the Reverend Lord died on June 6, 1748, he had been preaching in Chatham for thirty years – a generation. After so much time his death must have jolted the town, as he acted not only as minister, but also doctor, lawyer, and judge. During his ministry he baptized 492. And impressively, at the conclusion of his ministry the church boasted more than forty male members.

In looking to replace Lord, the town hired several ministers to fill the pulpit, finally asking Stephen Emery to become a candidate for a permanent position. In October 1748, Emery came to an agreement with the town that included £800 as a settlement to be paid in two installments. In addition his annual salary was to be £170; one half was payable on May 21, the second half on October 21 of each year. He was to have four loads of salt hay delivered in September annually. In lieu of a parsonage he should have £20 paid annually; one half in May and one half in October. He was to have twenty cords of wood delivered annually by the first of November (sixteen in oak and four in pine). He was installed on May 17, 1749.[16]

Emery was the son of Reverend Samuel and Tabitha (Littlefield) Emery of Wells, Maine. He was born in 1707 and graduated from Harvard in 1730. His first ministerial position was at Nottingham, New Hampshire, in 1742. He married Hannah Allen, daughter of The Reverend Benjamin Allen of Falmouth, Maine, and he was living in Exeter when the Chatham church called him.

When Emery arrived the town had apparently turned the corner; it had a population of about five hundred, consisting of one hundred or so separate families. He arrived to find a church that had been well organized during the period of Lord's ministry. The first few years of Emery's pastorate were uncharacteristically uneventful. This was, however, before what is known as the third migration to Nova Scotia decimated the population.

The Four Great Emigrations

As we have seen, some residents of this fledgling town sought to find a home elsewhere. On four major occasions, residents emigrated from Chatham. The story of what happened to those individuals has not been told in great detail, but it shows the profound effect Chatham men and women have had on diverse parts of our country and Canada.

1711: Bluer Skies in Delaware

Just a year before Monomoit incorporated and changed its name to Chatham, thirteen families packed up and moved to Duck Creek, Delaware, on the Delaware River. (The town, situated in Kent County, later changed its name to Smyrna.) Eleven other families also left Chatham at the same time, but their names and destinations are unknown. The families that went to Duck Creek included Jeremiah Nickerson and Robert and Samuel Eldredge. This first emigration probably resulted in only thirty-three families left in the village.

Joseph Atwood builds a home on the Stage Road.

1752

Town meeting decides that non-adherents to the town church should not be taxed for its support.

1755

1747: Greener Grass in the Oblong

Thirty-six years later, in 1747, at least twelve adult males, later joined by another, moved to the Oblong during the second emigration. The Oblong was an area of land that adjoined the town of Ridgefield, Connecticut; at the time it was in Dutchess County, New York. The county later became Putnam County.

The Oblong was a strip two-and-a-half miles wide along the Connecticut border, and was ceded by Connecticut to New York in 1731 in exchange for land along Long Island Sound. A guarantee of title and low prices attracted young families who were dissatisfied with their prospects on the Cape. Families from Yarmouth and Harwich had gone as early as 1740, but Chatham did not participate until 1747.[17]

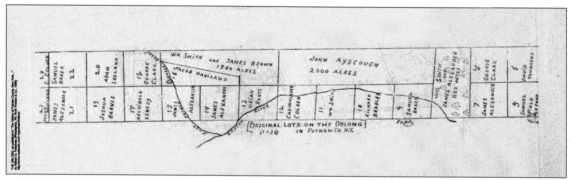

This sketch depicts the area known as the Oblong, situated between Connecticut and New York.

NICKERSONS DEPART CHATHAM FOR OBLONG

A fourth generation Nickerson, **William Nickerson**, settled first in Ridgebury, Connecticut, and then moved to Danbury in 1781. His children by his third wife, Sarah, were all born in Connecticut. After William's death, his widow married David Rockwell in Ridgebury.

Nathaniel Nickerson was William's brother. He was born in 1709 and died in 1769 at Philipse Patent. He was married to Hannah Hamblin. He moved from Chatham to Ridgefield, Connecticut, then emigrated over the state line to the Oblong. He sold his claim there and bought land in the Croton River area in Dutchess County, New York. Before 1747, he had moved to Poughkeepsie.

In 1769 Nathaniel deeded his property to his son, Nathan. His widow was made executor of his estate at the same time. Nathaniel had nine children, all born in

Third emigration from Chatham occurs with about fifty families moving to Nova Scotia.

1760 to 1763

Connecticut – some in Fairfield and some in Danbury. William and Nathaniel were sons of Thomas Nickerson.

Also a fourth generation Nickerson, **James Nickerson,** was born in 1704 in Chatham. His parents were William and Deliverance (Lombard). James moved to Ridgefield in 1747 and died a decade later in Danbury. His estate mentions his wife, Dorcus and seven children (all born in Chatham). Also included in the will was Thomas Nickerson, who had married James's daughter, Mary. Dorcus was named guardian of the three minor children and Joseph Nickerson was appointed guardian of Elizabeth in 1757. Dorcus died in 1803 at more than 90 years and was living at that time in Danbury.

Seth Nickerson was a fifth generation Nickerson who was born between 1720 and 1725. He married Mary Smith of Chatham. In April 1748 he moved to Ridgefield and appears on the tax list of the Southern Ward, New York. Later he lived in the South Precinct where he was appointed to road commissioner in 1773. The 1790 census places him in southeast Dutchess County with a family of two males over 16 and two females. Eventually he and his wife had nine children, all born in New York state. Seth died before April 1798 in Franklin, New York.

Thomas Nickerson was born in Chatham and married Mercy Nickerson in 1762. He served in the Revolutionary War for New York. He was a farmer living in the Oblong. In the 1790 census he lived in Rhinebeck, Dutchess County, with a family of three males over 16 and three females. He and his wife had six children all born in New York. Two of his children also served in the Revolutionary War and died due to insanity following the war. He died before December 29, 1801, in Clinton, New York.

1759-1760: Tastier Fish in Nova Scotia

This third emigration of 1759-1760, coming a decade into the Reverend Emery's pastorate, was the largest from Chatham. Approximately fifty families or about three hundred residents moved to the areas of the southern Nova Scotia seacoast now called Barrington and Liverpool.

So who were the first settlers to Barrington? They probably shared the general expectation of stabilizing the British possession of the coastline, but their main idea was to establish their homes in a place more convenient than Chatham to carry out their livelihoods of catching fish for food and lighting oils, and bartering or marketing the animals they hunted. This emigration was less well written about, probably because the small vessels which were used to transport them brought only a few families at a time.

One whose boat washed ashore at what was later called Howe Snow's Point, with 1,000 dry fish and a deckload of oil – all lost – was **Eldad Nickerson**. Eldad was one of the very first émigrés to

Nova Scotia. He carried freight and passengers in his schooners *The Sally* and *The Roxbury*. He was a justice of the peace, and his first lot was No. 12 opposite the Sherose Island (a small island off the south shore of Nova Scotia), but he lived at Fish Point where he had an additional lot. He died there before 1784. Nickerson was married in 1744 to Mary S. Reuben Cahoon and they had at least eight children who seemed to have all left Barrington, probably during the Revolutionary War.

Others who went to Nova Scotia to fish seasonally sometimes chose not to return home to Cape Cod in the fall. These included: Solomon Smith, Archelaus Smith, Jonathan Smith, and Thomas Crowell. They went by boat to Barrington and landed where a store was later built. In the meantime the families of Thomas Crowell and Archelaus Smith had arrived in August and built a log house.

On October 2, 1761, a few others left Chatham and were at sea for eight days. This group under the charge of Captain Eldad Nickerson included the families of Solomon and Jonathan Smith. They were followed shortly, in November 1761, by others from Cape Cod, chiefly Chatham and Harwich.

The Chatham list of "ratables" for 1755 contains the names of twenty-seven members who left for Nova Scotia. These people must be given credit for breaking their ties with old associations and planting their homes in such a desolate area. By 1762 more arrived from Cape Cod as well as from Nantucket. Many, if not most, of the Nantucket settlers were Quakers who took advantage of the offer for all religions to settle in this new territory.

The difficulties in moving from Cape Cod to Nova Scotia are almost inconceivable. This was particularly true for the women and children of these families. It meant exile for those leaving their established homes and little prospect of ever seeing their families again. The motives for moving must have been extraordinarily strong. Separation from family and friends was heartbreaking.

TWO WHO MOVED TO NOVA SCOTIA

Archelaus Smith (1734-1821) was born in Chatham, the son of Stephen and Bathsheba Smith, and married Elizabeth Nickerson, daughter of William and Sarah Nickerson. Archelaus had the distinction of being one of the two first families to emigrate to Barrington. He was a fisherman, tanner, shoemaker, surveyor, and a magistrate.

When no preacher was available, Archelaus would officiate at religious occasions. Elizabeth was known as having an energetic temper and was described as a tall, masculine woman.

Archelaus sailed for Cape Cod to bring his wife to Barrington, and, by coincidence, on that same day Elizabeth sailed to Barrington. Their vessels pursued different passages and did not pass at sea. An early winter prevented Archelaus's return, so Elizabeth had to find shelter in the old meeting house. According to tradition, she would have been capable of making the trip to Barrington with her children if only to surprise her husband; Mrs. Thomas Crowell, who accompanied her, could have been easily persuaded to keep her company as a recent bride venturing to meet her husband.

At the time of the Revolutionary War, Archelaus moved his family to Cape Island. There he and his descendants occupied the shore facing the Passage. His own house was near the shore. James Smith, son of Archelaus, had the distinction of being the first male child born in Barrington.[18]

Sarah Nickerson was the daughter of Absalom Nickerson, the eldest son of William Nickerson and Sarah (Covell) Nickerson. She was born in Chatham in 1748, one of three children. According to family stories, Absalom was away at sea a great deal of time and his whereabouts not known for long periods.

It is unknown how Sarah got to Nova Scotia, but she married Richard Nickerson before 1767, when her first child was born in Barrington. Richard is recorded as the owner of Lot No. 14 in 1761. Sarah and Richard had five boys between 1767 and 1789. When Richard died in 1774, Sarah returned to Plymouth rather than Cape Cod, and the records indicate she married a man by the name of Spinks (Spenks). That marriage must not have lasted long, but we know it occurred, as Sarah signed two documents as Sarah Spinks, copies of which are in the collection of the Chatham Historical Society.

Sarah returned to Nova Scotia where she married for the third time in 1786. Her third husband was Samuel Penny, a soldier of English parentage. According to the Nickerson genealogy[19] Sarah had three children with Samuel: David, Sarah, and Irene. In 1789 Samuel Perry was fishing with Sarah's sons Richard and Seth when their boat was upset by a squall and all three drowned. Also in 1789 records indicate that Sarah Penny, now a widow, gave power of attorney to her son Moses who would have been age twenty at the time.

The Nickerson genealogy states that she supported her two children by her loom.

Summing up Sarah's life reveals some of the difficulties she faced. As a child, her father was absent most of the time. She outlived three husbands. Two sons were lost at sea before the ages of 15 and 18. She moved from Chatham to Nova Scotia to Plymouth to Nova Scotia over the course of her lifetime. Finally she had to support her three youngest children by weaving and managed to live until the age of eighty, having been a widow for forty years.

The Complicated Business of Settling Nova Scotia

The history of the settlement of Nova Scotia is complicated. Originally inhabited by the Micmac Indians, it was later settled by the French and, in 1713, by the English. In 2005 Canada dedicated a new bronze plaque at Horton Landing, Hortonville, and Kings County, Nova Scotia. The monument is dedicated to the New England colonists, known as planters, who settled in Nova Scotia in 1759. The plaque, inscribed in both English and French, reads:

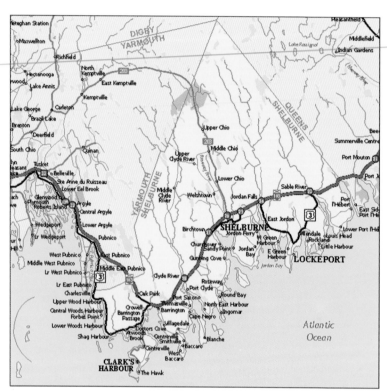

Detail of the Minas area in Nova Scotia which was settled by Cape Codders in 1759 on the lands of displaced Acadians.

"In 1759, New England farmers and fishermen sent agents to Halifax to discuss with Governor Lawrence the settlement of the undeveloped areas of the province. Substantial immigration began in 1760 and, by late 1763, several thousand settlers were established throughout Nova Scotia. They were particularly successful in the Minas Area, where they took up the fallow lands of the displaced Acadians. By 1780, Edmund Burke could describe the province as 'formed by the overflowings of the exuberant population of New England.' This influx was to have a significant effect on the character and development of Nova Scotia."[3]

By 1753 Governor Charles Lawrence had taken over the province and sought Protestant settlers to replace the Acadians (former French colonists) who had been driven from their homes when England gained control of the province. After an unsuccessful attempt to attract English citizens with the offer of homesteads, the provincial government turned to a group of Protestants who were from the German/Swiss/French areas of Europe. Most of these individuals accepted that offer and entered Nova Scotia by way of Halifax and Lunenburg. They were farmers who found the land not easy to cultivate, so many returned to their homelands.

Governor Lawrence then turned to New England, whose fishermen had for years fished off the coast of Nova Scotia and were familiar with these waters and the shoreline.

"I have every reason to believe from the earnest desire I perceive in the people of Cape Cod to settle there [Cape Sable], that a considerable tract of land is now under actual improvement and the other French settlements on the Cape are more highly calculated for a flourishing industry than any part of the coast of Nova Scotia we are yet acquainted with," Lawrence wrote to the Lords of Trade in England.

His later publications spelled out the terms of the grants to be offered to those who chose to accept.

"That 100 acres of wild woodland will be allowed to every person being master or mistress of a family, for himself or herself, and fifty acres for every white or black man, woman or child....

"That the grantees will be obliged by their said grant to plant, cultivate, improve or enclose one third part of their lands within the space of 10 years, another third part within the space of 20 years, and the remaining third part within the space of thirty years from the date of their grants. That no one person can possess more than 1,000 acres by grant, on his or their own name."

This proclamation further ensured that the people accepting the offer would, as soon as their township reached fifty families, be entitled to send two representatives to the General Assembly and the Courts of Justice. Individuals were to be allowed full liberty in the matter of religion regardless of whether they were Protestants dissenting from the Church of England, Calvinists, Lutherans, Quakers, or under whatsoever denomination, and promised the liberty to build meeting houses for public worship. The only religion excluded was "Papists" (Roman Catholics).

The government would also establish forts to provide for security. Even though two grants had been issued for the erection of a Township of Barrington, only a few individuals arrived. It may have been those original grantees who encouraged the Cape Cod and Nantucket families who eventually settled there.

The Planter's Monument at Horton Landing, Hortonville, Kings County, Nova Scotia, is dedicated to the New England colonists, known as planters, who settled in Nova Scotia in 1759. The plaque, inscribed in both English and French, reads: "...substantial immigration began in 1760 and, by late 1763, several thousand settlers were established throughout Nova Scotia..."

1760: Bigger Logs in Liverpool

At about the same time, another group of Chatham residents went to Liverpool, Nova Scotia. Liverpool is on the banks of the Mersey River, southwest of Halifax. The town was founded by New Englanders. At first it was just a fishing settlement, but the settlers soon discovered the huge pines and spruces of the inland plateau and began milling logs. The best white pine became ships' masts not only for the local trade but for export to distant shipyards.

Besides its safe harbor and access to the back country, the little settlement had another advantage. It was halfway between Halifax and Cape Sable, where ships entered the Bay of Fundy and the Gulf of Maine. In later years this town became the privateering capital of Canada.

In 1760 the list of names of persons coming from Chatham to Liverpool included Collins, Eldredge, Snow, Bea, Bearse, Crowell, Godfrey, Harding, Hopkins, Knowles, Nickerson, Smith, Tripp, and Young.

Many of these men were among the original grantees of Liverpool. Ten left Liverpool within a few years and some went back to Cape Cod.

The most interesting person appears in the publication *Nova Scotia Immigrants to 1867*. His name is Alexander Godfrey and he entered Nova Scotia at Liverpool with his father and his mother Eunice. The stories of Godfrey and Enos Collins, the grandson of Joseph Collins who also immigrated to Liverpool in the 1760s, are told in a book titled *Bandits and Privateers* and serve to substantiate the claim that Liverpool was the privateering capital of British North America.

GODFREY, COLLINS AND THE HALIFAX ELITE

Alexander Godfrey, born in Chatham, married Phoebe West in 1791. He was the captain of a ship named *Rover* and his first mate was Enos Collins. In the 1780s, the *Rover* sailed to the Caribbean and returned in less than a month with valuable prizes: a ship with a hold filled with Madeira wine and another carrying 1,100 barrels of sperm oil. His next trip became the foundation of the legend that made Alexander the hero of a book by Thomas H. Raddall titled *The Saga of the Rover*. The introductory lines to that book are:

Come gather round the capstan, lads, an' lend an ear to me,
　　For I've a tale o' the days o' sail, when England won the sea:
Of loss an' gain on the Spanish Main, o' powder, beef and an' beer;
　　O' fightin' Alex Godfrey an' the Rover privateer.
Big Alex was the kind that breeds in the Nova Scotian air,
　　A fathom neat in his naked feet, an' strong as the northern bear.
His taut an' trim slim-waisted brig (save guns and the galley stove)
　　From jollyboat to sprits'l yard was built at Herring Cove.

The poem ends with the following two verses:

He slipped away to the Carolines wi' two score knaves an' fools,
　　His fear o' the Lord went overboard along o' the book o'rules
If a neutral hold revealed no gold he sent her into port.
　　And blood? His owners sweated it—in the Admiralty court!

The Rover's lost an' gone, my lads, these hundred years an' more,
    Among the bones in Davy Jones, or rottin' on the shore,
But when the lights are lit o' nights, she puts to sea again—
    The Carib fisher sees her ghost along the
Spanish Main!

As the poem suggests, Alexander died from yellow fever in the Caribbean in 1805.

Enos Collins, Godfrey's first mate on the maiden voyage of the *Rover*, was born in 1774 in Liverpool, the son of Hallet C. Collins and the grandson of Joseph Collins who emigrated to Nova Scotia in the 1760s.

Collins was best known for his role in the ownership of a schooner that he had outfitted to serve as a privateer, changing her name to the *Black Jack*. The ship, captained by Joseph Barss, set off in 1812 on a series of voyages, capturing American ships and most notably took eleven vessels off the coast of Cape Cod in one week. In a single day he made prizes of nine fishing schooners with a cargo valued at $50,000.

He sailed home to Liverpool to be refitted. On his next voyage he captured eight or nine more ships with values to $90,000. Barss continued in this manner for some time. He was captured at Portsmouth, New Hampshire, where he was jailed for months before being allowed to return to Liverpool.

All of this prize money made Collins rich and he married into the Halifax elite. He eventually founded the Halifax Banking Company in 1825, a bank that is now known as the Canadian Imperial Bank of Commerce. The original solid granite building he built for the bank still survives with the carved title "BANK" over its front door. His estate today is the site of Saint Mary's University. Collins died in 1871, a very wealthy man.

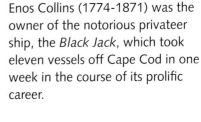

Enos Collins (1774-1871) was the owner of the notorious privateer ship, the *Black Jack*, which took eleven vessels off Cape Cod in one week in the course of its prolific career.

1790: A Deeper Quiet in Maine

The fourth and final emigration from Chatham began a decade after the American Revolution in 1790 and took place over a period of several years when residents moved to the unsettled lands along the Penobscot and Kennebec rivers of Maine. Again the names of the emigrants are familiar. They included: Collins, Hopkins, Nickerson, Fowler, Freeman, Godfrey, Doane, Kent, Smith, Young, Eldredge, Ryder, Taylor, Bearse, and Covel.[27]

"Send these, the homeless, tempest-tost to me"

The residents of Chatham may have been accustomed to shipwrecks off the town's treacherous elbow, but the ship that arrived in 1729 carried a ghastly cargo: upwards of one hundred starving and dehydrated Irish immigrants crying out for food and water. When one parched man was given water he "drank to that degree that he soon after died," historian Smith wrote about the incident.[28]

On October 4 a ship off Monomoy sent out a distress signal. When a Captain Lothrop, who happened to be sailing by, climbed aboard the ship to investigate, he found a grotesque scene: desperately thirsty passengers who wanted, after five months at sea, to set foot on land. Any land. Over a hundred of their fellow passengers had already died of starvation and disease during the extended sea voyage from Ireland.

The *George and Ann*, a boat of about ninety tons, had left Dublin on May 20, 1729, and reached the Azores on July 5 with a Captain Rymer at the helm. By then ten children and three servants had died. Much worse was to come.

The expedition was organized by Charles Clinton, a wealthy man who persuaded many of his relatives and friends to emigrate with him. The passengers intended to disembark at Philadelphia, drawn by offers from William Penn to settle there. Unlike many of the later Irish settlers who fled Ireland at the time of the famine, these passengers were relatively well-to-do descendants of families who had fled from Scotland to Northern Ireland to escape religious and political persecution.

Smith speculates that before reaching the Azores "some terrible epidemic broke out." When they left the Azores the ship tossed through severe storms. Worse, instead of bringing the ship to port, "it is also charged that the captain roamed aimlessly about the sea, hoping that all would die and their large possessions fall into his hands." The passengers claimed they had to bribe Rymer to bring them toward the coast. By the time the ship reached Monomoy, at least 101 passengers had perished. Besides the master and first mate, only three sailors were still alive.

Lothrop was on a trip from Boston to his home on Martha's Vineyard when he spotted the ship's distress signal. On the ship, the passengers pleaded with him to pilot them to the closest port. Lothrop sailed into Wreck Cove on Monomoy and from there passengers were transported to Stewart's Tavern. The tavern, run by Joseph Stewart for a clientele of sailors, was the only building

Small pox epidemic leaves thirty-seven dead and many ill.

1765
to
1766

on that part of the island and served as a safe haven for the many sailors from ships that wrecked just off the coast. Since the tavern was small, the passengers were transported to Chatham and Harwich homes where they lodged for the following winter.

The story of the *George and Ann* was published in the *New England Weekly Journal* of November 10, 1729. Records seem to indicate that Captain Rymer was taken to Philadelphia, tried, and returned to England where he was sentenced to be hanged.

In the spring, the small group of *George and Ann* survivors sailed along the coastline until they selected and purchased a site for a colony in a place in Ulster County, New York, which they called Little Britain. The rest of the group joined them there in the spring of 1734, with the exception of an orphan boy, James Delap. He was the last surviving member of his family after his mother, who was still living when Captain Lothrop boarded the ship, but died shortly thereafter, when food was distributed and she choked to death on a biscuit. James was apprenticed at Barnstable to John Bacon, a saddler and blacksmith. Eventually Delap had his own blacksmith shop, married, and had a family of ten children. In the spring of 1775, due to his Loyalist beliefs, he moved to Nova Scotia where he died in 1789.

Interestingly, Clinton would father a son, George (1739-1812), who became the first governor of New York, and was later chosen vice president of the United States, serving under Presidents Thomas Jefferson and James Madison. His brother, James (1733-1812), became a revolutionary war general. DeWitt Clinton (1769-1828), George's nephew, became a U.S. senator, mayor of New York City, and governor of New York, and under him the Erie Canal project was carried out.

To Arms! The French and Indian Wars

During the last twenty years of this period, many residents were called into service to fight the French and Indian Wars. First they were sent to Crown Point, a French port on Lake Champlain. This expedition failed. In 1758 the men of the town were enlisted to proceed against Ticonderoga and Canada.

By 1759, another group of men enlisted under General Ambrose to invade Canada. In 1760 a complete company was raised from Chatham and Harwich to join forces against Canada and, it was hoped, complete its defeat. The war ended in 1763 with the Peace of Paris by which Canada, Nova Scotia, and Cape Breton were conceded to England.

At the time of its fiftieth anniversary in 1762, Chatham had suffered not only the loss of many of its citizens to Nova Scotia, but the loss of men in fighting.

Nonresidents are prohibited from taking shellfish from town waters.

Schooner *Abigail* is found adrift on the Atlantic side of the Cape with all crew except Ansell Nickerson dead. He is accused of murder and tried in Boston, defended by John Adams and John Quincy Adams.

1768

1771

The Smallpox Epidemic of 1765-1766

And then came the epidemic.

In December 1765 and January 1766, an especially virulent strain of smallpox raced through the town. By the time the epidemic was over, sixty-one people had contracted the disease and thirty-seven were dead.

The epidemic was believed to have started in the family of Deacon Paul Crowell. Contemporary theories speculated that the disease arrived in a bale of cotton imported from the South or arrived in a package of clothing from the West Indies. Garments in the package were washed in the Crowell house.

Smallpox was present in most major European cities by the 18th century. Boston suffered seven major outbreaks between 1721 and 1792. The Cape had two doctors who were pioneers in the practice of vaccination, but their practices were limited to Falmouth; there is no indication that any of Chatham residents had been vaccinated at the time of the outbreak of 1765.

The hero of the Chatham epidemic was Dr. Samuel Lord, the town's physician who cared for the sick until he became ill and died on January 12, 1766. Dr. Lord's ties to Chatham had begun when his father, the Reverend Joseph Lord, came to preach in Chatham. There is no evidence that Dr. Lord had any special training in the care of the sick.[29] Lord lived on

The gravestone of Dr. Samuel Lord, who cared for the town's sick during the smallpox epidemic and eventually died of the disease, can be seen on Training Field Road near Crowell Road *Photo by Spencer Grey.*

a farm near Burying Hill and was listed in the 1755 rate list as having 1 poll and 2 real (two pounds value of real estate). He never married.

A tombstone on Training Field Road was erected in his memory by the Town of Chatham in 1941 with the inscription: "Here lies buried Dr. Samuel Lord who died of smallpox after devoted service to the citizens of Chatham in the epidemic of 1765-66."

There is no record of another medical doctor living in Chatham after Lord's death until the Revolutionary War.

The first to die in the epidemic was Paul Crowell Jr., followed shortly by others including almost the entire family of John Ryder.

The second meeting house is repaired and enlarged.

1773

The Smith family lost Stephen Smith and his wife Bathsheba as well as two unmarried daughters, Betty and Bathsheba. That family also lost the wife of their son Elijah.

In the collection of the Chatham Historical Society is a letter written by Chatham residents George (son of Stephen Sr.) and Barbara Smith to George's half-brother, Stephen, a resident of Liverpool, Nova Scotia. On April 19, 1766, they asked Stephen to please send a letter of power of attorney to allow somebody to act on Stephen's behalf to sell the property that belongs to the estate of the Smith Family.[30]

In the letter George asks that "God will give us Grace to serve him more acceptable then ever as yet we have dun *[sic]* for his great goodness to us when in great danger of having the small pox that he has kept us from." This comment was made in spite of the death of George's parents and sisters.

To avoid spreading the disease, families omitted funeral services and often buried family members on their own farms. Some of these graves, marked by stones, were visible many years later. The Town of Chatham does have a cemetery dedicated to the smallpox victims and it can be visited via a path off Old Comers Road. It is marked by a sign on the side of the road.

Another smallpox cemetery is nearby at the end of A Leonard Way (on the mound by William Nickerson's memorial marker) and includes stones for six members of the Ryder family. As both of these cemeteries are in the center of Chatham, near the current Riverbay development, this suggests that the epidemic was confined mainly to this part of town.

The town appointed Barnabas Eldredge to ask the General Court for assistance in paying the costs associated with care of those afflicted. Eldredge also asked for care of those now left indigent. There is no record that the petition was heard, but the lack of response spurred the town to appoint a representative to the court to speak on its behalf in the future.

This time Joseph Doane, agent for the town, was heard and the province director was instructed in 1768 to confirm to the requests in the petition asking for the remittance of the sum of £98, 7 shillings and 9 pence which had been the amount of province tax on Chatham for the year 1766.

Neighboring towns as well as churches raised monies. A committee led by John Hawes received the gifts and the selectmen distributed the funds. The town voted to give the monies "for the relief of those that had been sufferers in the town by the small pox of late and should be disposed of to defray the charges of those poor people among us which had been exposed to great charges and had little or nothing to pay the same and to help some others that had been exposed to so grat *[sic]* charges by said sickness that they could not pay the same without selling great part or all of their inheritance and had families which they could not comfortably support, if they so did."[31]

"The Estate of Hezekiah Eldredge charged off the following items, house and barn taken down of necessity by reason of the small pox and appraised at £17."[32]

The Eve of the Revolution

During this period leading to the American Revolution, the new town was merely treading water. Four emigrations, the French and Indian Wars and a smallpox epidemic decimated the population. On the other hand, under the final minister of this period, the Reverend Emery, the meeting house built in 1729 was enlarged. In 1774, glass was placed in its windows and the walls were plastered. When it was finished, as resident Levi Atwood later reminisced, it was "a plain building of good size with no steeple, with a red roof and yellow walls."[33]

After the Revolution, as the town neared its centennial, life began to look rosier.

1775 – 1812

Revolution, Recovery and Rehabilitation

By Lynn C. Van Dine

As the American Revolution issued call after call for soldiers and provisions, Chatham's supply of both ebbed to critical lows.

With a population seriously depleted by the 1760s migration of three hundred residents to Nova Scotia, followed by a smallpox epidemic that killed at least thirty-seven, Chatham was already in a severely diminished state at the beginning of the American Revolution.

And things would only get worse before they got better.

Heeding either a sense of patriotism or a need for the £20-30 bounties offered to those who enlisted, many of Chatham's men went off to fight, leaving their women, children, and the elderly to run their farms or businesses. (See "Chatham's Patriots: The Young Family," in this chapter.)

The town was on guard because of the ongoing threat of raids by British ships and privateers who lurked in the waters off Chatham. Ships, schooners, and whalers were hidden so they could not be seized by the British. More than once, the locals bravely fought off invaders (See "The Battle of Chatham Harbor," this chapter).

The monies and provisions sent by the town to support the Revolutionary troops further diminished Chatham's scant resources until, by the time the troops returned, there was neither money nor crops to pay the war-worn soldiers. Farms were ill-tended, and fishing and commercial shipping had been utterly disrupted by the British blockade and privateers.

At the beginning of the war Chatham had thirty vessels and two hundred men working on them. By the end of the war only four or five remained in the harbor.[1]

Chatham must have seemed bleak to the returning soldiers.

But as Chatham's sons came home and their wounds healed, so did the town.

Families grew. Fishing and shipping brought the docks to life. Shops opened. Schools were built. And growing prosperity brought with it progress and promise.

Fishing industry dominates economic base of Chatham. It is a leading cod fishing town on the Cape.

Barnstable County organizes a company of men from Chatham, Harwich, and Yarmouth for defense of the sea coast.

Chatham forms a town militia. Benjamin Godfrey is named captain.

1775

1775

1775

The American Revolution

Soon after December 1774, when the Provincial Congress resolved to cease the drinking or use of British tea after March 1, 1775, Chatham's military company was reorganized: Lt. Benjamin Godfrey (whose windmill still stands in Chase Park) was named captain; Richard Sears

The headstone of Capt. Benjamin Godfrey, who led the defense of the town in the Battle of Chatham Harbor, in the Old Burying Ground on Old Queen Anne Road. *Photo by Lynn Van Dine.*

was appointed lieutenant, Joseph Crowell as ensign, and John Emery as military clerk. Later that year, on June 17, Capt. Godfrey would fight at the Battle of Bunker Hill during the Siege of Boston.[2]

To defend the sea coast, a company of men was formed with volunteers from Chatham, Harwich, and Yarmouth. Among them was Hiat Young, a veteran of the French-Indian War[3] (see related story, this chapter).

Most of the Chatham men recruited joined the local coast guard, and almost all of them served on privateers that sought to interrupt British commerce, supplies, and reinforcements. [4]

Later that year, in the fall, the schooner *Williams*, belonging to a Tory refugee from Halifax, Nova Scotia, was seized by armed cruisers and brought into Chatham Harbor. Another sloop, the *Elizabeth*, which was making its way from the West Indies to Halifax, was captured by an armed brigantine and also brought into Chatham Harbor as a prize of war in August 1776. In the spring of 1777 the privateer *Wolf* was seized by a crew of Chatham and Harwich men, and later awarded by the Colony to Capt. Nathaniel Freeman of Harwich, whose second officer was Joseph Doane, Jr., of Chatham.[5]

The luck of Freeman's Chatham and Harwich sailors did not hold, however. They were captured by a British man-of-war disguised as a merchantman and taken to New York where they were thrown into prison and were later exchanged for British prisoners.[6]

Answering the Continental Army's frequent calls to enlist soldiers and finding the money to pay them was an ongoing concern for Chatham throughout the war. In August 1776, the town

---

Chatham votes to raise enlistment bounties to £20 per man. The town also agrees to take care of the families of enlisted soldiers. In 1777, ten men signed up for three years; twenty men for eight months.

Sgt. Hiat Young serves at the Valley Forge encampment.

Town votes to raise £150 for seven soldiers for the state and two more to guard General John Burgoyne.

1777

1777

1778

raised £32 to pay a bounty to soldiers who enlisted and £9 14 shillings for gunpowder for the town's use.[7] To encourage enlistment, on May 19, 1777, the town voted to increase the bounty to £20 for each man who enlisted for service through January 10, 1778. For the men that enlisted for three years, or through the end of the war, £20 was paid at the time of muster. The town also agreed to take care of the families of soldiers, certainly an appealing offer for men of small means.[8] In September of that year, the town voted to divide the town into twenty sections, and each section was to furnish one soldier. At the same time four men were appointed to raise money to pay the men.[9]

As the number of volunteers dwindled the town realized it had to up the ante, so, in March 1778, it voted to increase the bounty to £40 for ten soldiers to guard Gen. John Burgoyne, who surrendered at the Battle of Saratoga in October 1777. In April 1778, the town voted to procure the material and clothing called for by the Continental Army and, two months later, voted to raise money "to hire five men for the Continental Army and four for the state."

But that still wasn't enough. In July 1778, the town voted to raise £150 for seven soldiers for the state and two more to guard Burgoyne, making the soldiers' wages £40 a month for six months of service.[10]

But the town could not sustain the cash payments. By July 1779 the town sent Capt. Godfrey to find the men required and negotiate how much they would be paid in grain. In July 1780, the town voted to pay the wages in produce. By April 1782 little or no grain or produce could be mustered and no men "would go into service under any terms."[11]

Recovery from the War

After the war Chatham's people began pulling themselves up by their bootstraps through innovation and industry.

Cleverly using the resources at hand – wind, sea and their own determination – residents developed various means to make a living with what little they had.

By 1790 the population had grown to 1,140, according to the U.S. Census, up from 929 in 1776. And it kept growing: in 1800 it rose to 1,351.[12] There were four houses of more than one story in the town of 158 dwellings.

Also, after considerable legal wrangling, Strong Island was separated from Harwich and officially declared part of Chatham. The re-establishment of the boundaries also took the southern part of Eastham and incorporated as the town of Orleans.[13]

There were more signs of progress. In 1798 a post office was opened in the home of James Hedges, and by 1804 the mail was carried to and from Yarmouth on horseback. Chatham's first schoolhouse was built at the corner of Barcliff Avenue and Old Harbor Road. Previously smaller schools operated in homes throughout town, but only for three-month sessions. By 1800 there were five school districts in town, each with a small schoolhouse or place for educating children.[14]

But breathing life back into a war-ravaged Chatham would not be easy.

Chatham votes to support the Massachusetts Constitutional Convention.	Capt. Godfrey recruits the men required by the Continental Army and, because the treasury was depleted, negotiates how much they would be paid in grain.	Massachusetts constitution, drafted by John Adams, becomes effective. John Hancock elected governor.
1779	1779	1780

"Not a fruit tree grows in Chatham, and not more than 65 acres of woodland are left … and consists principally of pitch pine," wrote Reverend James Freeman in an account of his travels in 1802.[15] "Very little English hay is cut, but the marshes yield salt hay enough for the use of the inhabitants. Butter is made in the summer, but butter for winter and cheese are procured from Connecticut, Rhode Island and Boston. Beef and provisions for the fishermen are brought from the last mentioned place. … As the land, particularly in the centre and south part of the township is every year growing worse, by the drifting of the sand, there is little to encourage the agriculture industry."[16]

Monument to Revolutionary War soldier Hiat Young as designed by his son, Joseph Young, who also fought in the war. Joseph is buried at People's Cemetery. *Photo by Lynn Van Dine.*

The people of Chatham, Freeman wrote, pass "the flower of their lives at sea, which they do not quit till they are fifty years of age, leaving at home none but the old men and small boys to cultivate the ground.

"A few of the young and middle-aged men are engaged in mercantile voyages and sail from Boston, but the great body of them are fishermen. Twenty-five schooners, from 25 to 70 tons, employed in the cod fishing… On board these schooners are about 200 men and boys, most of whom are inhabitants of Chatham; and they catch, one year with another, 700 to 800 quintals [one quintal is about 100 pounds] to a vessel. Besides these fishing vessels, there are belonging to the town five coasters which sail to Carolina and the West Indies."

Shellfish, especially quahogs and clams were plentiful, Freeman noted, and the oysters in Oyster Pond were excellent, although they sold for the high price of $1 a bushel.

The area surrounding Old Harbor bustled with businesses related to fishing and shipping – bait sellers, block and barrel works, and sail makers. In addition, the commercial drying of fish on flakes became an established source of income in Chatham.[17] In fact, Old Harbor Road is named after its destination – the Old Harbor.

Those who follow the road to its end near the water can get a sense of what the area must have been like when the water was deep enough to support a bustling port.

New fishing techniques also evolved. Cod fishermen switched from single baited lines to traps and then to multi-hooked handlines.

By 1800 seven windmills had popped up in Chatham and Chatham Port, the oldest one built in 1796 by Captain Benjamin Godfrey on Crocker Rise Inlet Road, which now stands in Chase Park. Another owned by the Crosbys operated around 1800, grinding bark for their tannery at Old Harbor.[18]

Sgt. Hiat Young is present at the hanging of Major John Andre, who assisted Benedict Arnold in the attempted surrender to the British at West Point, NY.

1780

Chatham votes to pay its soldiers in produce.

1780

Richard Sears is elected deputy; serves 19 years.

1781

About this time Reuben Ryder came up with the idea of making salt from sea water by evaporation, using a series of large, shallow boxes, called a saltworks. Sea water would be pumped into the first compartment by windmill and the water would evaporate by the sun in a series of lower boxes. The system was so successful and profitable that, by 1809, twenty more saltworks were in operation in Chatham.[19]

One of the larger saltworks was operated by the charismatic Richard Sears (see related story, this chapter) who also ran a substantial general store next to his home on the corner of Seaview and Main Streets. [20]

Ezra Crowell, nicknamed Squire Crow, operated another sizable general store at what was then the center of town on the east side of Old Queen Anne Road just west of the old cemetery, where a marker indicates the location of the town's Meeting House.[21]

Nearby a widow named Hannah Doane Knowles ran a tavern just by Great Hill, where the town fathers would adjourn from their meetings to swear in new officers. Paul Mayo ran a blacksmith shop near Mrs. Doane's tavern, and did a thriving business making everything from nails to tools to plows.[22]

As the town and its harbor prospered and bustled, the need for a lighthouse became evident (see related story, this chapter). In 1806 Congress appropriated $5,000 for a twin-lights station in Chatham.

Yet just as Chatham was beginning to thrive, global politics struck a blow to its mainstay industries – shipping and fishing.

The Embargo Act of 1807, enacted during President Jefferson's administration, severely impacted Chatham's economy. The law restricted American ships from departing for a foreign port, especially British ports, whose ships had been harassing U.S. vessels by impressing sailors thought to be British.

New England in general and Chatham in particular opposed the Embargo Act, citing its disastrous impact on the local economy. The impact was so severe that young men driven away from seafaring left for Rhode Island and other inland locations to work on farms.[23]

When the Embargo Act led to the War of 1812, the majority of the town voted against the war.[24]

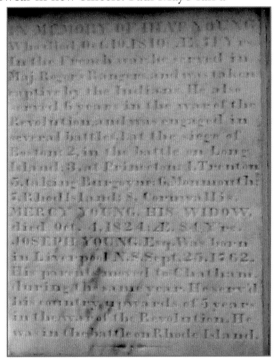

Detail of the monument to Hiat Young, listing the battles he fought in, including the Siege of Boston, the battles of Princeton and Trenton, and the winter at Valley Forge. *Photo by Lynn Van Dine.*

Town reports that with little or no grain or produce to pay soldiers "no men would go into service under any terms."

1782

Siege of Chatham Harbor.

1782

September 3: U.S. and Great Britain sign the Treaty of Paris, ending the war.

1783

Commercial drying of fish on flakes comes to Chatham.

1784

Chatham's Patriots: The Young Family

Many Chatham names can be found on the rolls of officers and soldiers who fought for America's independence: Doane, Nickerson, Eldredge, Godfrey, Bassett, and Ryder among them.

The Young family of Chatham can boast an exemplary patriotic tradition of military service. During the American Revolution, three Young men enlisted and one lost his life. They were part of history as it unfolded – at Valley Forge, the imprisonment of Benedict Arnold, the Siege of Boston, and the Battle of Trenton. In the years to follow the name Young would be found among those who battled in the War of 1812 and America's Civil War.

This legacy began in July 1775, when Hiat Young (also spelled Hyat, Hyatt and Hiatt), a veteran of the French-Indian War, signed up to join Barnstable County's military company as a sergeant for defense of Chatham's sea coast, under the command of Captain Thomas Hamilton.[25] At 36, Hiat was married to Mercy Hinckley; together they had four children.[26]

"He was extremely poor with a large family of children, but the blood of the brave soldiers who fought through the French war leapt through his veins at Liberty's call, and so he must," wrote his son Joseph Young. "On the day he left, there was not a dollar of money or a barrel of provisions in the house. Only the corn in the shed." Joseph was 13 at the time and was left to help his mother.[27]

Times were hard in Chatham in 1775. The thriving fishing industry, which boasted twenty-seven vessels in Chatham's cod fishery in 1774, was decimated as British privateers cruising the coast sought to capture or scuttle American ships.[28] The promise of a military bounty to be paid by the town may have contributed to Young's decision to enlist.[29]

In January 1776, General George Washington issued a call for soldiers and Sergeant Young joined Captain Benjamin Godfrey's company, which consisted mostly of Chatham men. Among them were 1st Lt. Thomas Hamilton, Ensign Joseph Doane, and John Hawes.[30]

Sgt. Young fought at the Siege of Boston from April 1775 to March 17, 1776, considered the opening of the American Revolution, when the Continental Army surrounded the city to weaken the British Army garrisoned there (the British finally withdrew and headed to New York, an event now called Evacuation Day).[31]

In August 1776, Young fought in the Battle of Long Island (also called the Battle of Brooklyn Heights), the first battle of the Revolutionary War after the signing of the Declaration of Independence. The British defeated the Continental Army after General Washington withdrew his troops from New York.

Young fought at the Battle of Trenton in December 1776 after General Washington crossed the Delaware, leading the Continental Army to capture almost the entire Hessian force. Young served in Captain Peter Harwood's light infantry company at both Trenton and the Battle of Princeton (New Jersey) in January 1777, where Washington defeated the British forces.[32]

Young travelled from Princeton to Valley Forge, Pennsylvania, where he served in Colonel William Shepherd's light infantry under Geneneral Washington during the winter of 1778. There he

Two major fishing disasters: ◆ Ten Chatham men are lost at sea with all hands on board a New Haven schooner bound for the Grand Banks; ◆ Capt. Josiah Hardy, in a schooner bound for Boston with two men and a boy, sees a storm rise quickly. The party is found dead from exposure the following April in Great Pamet, Truro.

U.S. Constitution signed.

1786

1787

suffered the dismal conditions of the encampment, as the Continental Army of 12,000 bunkered for the winter to prevent British movement in Pennsylvania.

Among those soldiers was Hiat's nephew, John Young of Chatham, who fought alongside his uncle under Captain George Webb in engagements that preceded the surrender of Burgoyne at Saratoga in October 1777. Soldiers waited months for the replenishment of troops and resources. John Young was among the approximately 2,500 soldiers who died of exposure, malnutrition, or disease there, after serving only ten months in the army. He was presumed to be 17 or 18 years old.[33]

Yet when the British moved away from the area toward New York, Valley Forge was considered a victory "not of weapons, but of will."[34]

After Valley Forge, Young re-enlisted in the Continental Army and the town of Chatham voted to find provisions for his family.[35] He was assigned to Tappan, New York, where he guarded the imprisoned traitor Benedict Arnold[36] and was present at the hanging of Major John Andre, the spy best known for assisting Arnold in the attempted surrender to the British at West Point, N.Y. He last saw fighting at the Battle of Cowan's Ford at Yorktown, where fewer than 1,000 Americans defeated 5,000 redcoats, leading to the surrender of the British Army at Yorktown in February 1781.[37]

Local legend has it that when Hiat was discharged in 1781, he returned "to his little home, without a cent, weary and footsore, have suffered many privations and hardships, he left his footprints in blood upon the freshly scrubbed floor, and that they never could be erased while the house remained standing."[38]

Even as Hiat made his way home from the war, his son Joseph, not yet 16 when he enlisted, was fighting with the Continental Army. In 1778 Joseph Young tried to conceal his young age in order to join the fighting. "I was so very small and short of stature that I had to resort to stratagem in order to pass the very yielding eye of the enlisting officer. I put on a pair of my Father's big cowhide boots and filled under my feet all I could to raise me up. Then I put on all the clothes I could to make me look stout. When I went before the examining officer, I stretched all I could, and was accepted," he wrote in a brief memoir.[39]

Joseph served for about five years. "I was at the Battle of Rhode Island under General (John) Sullivan and in many other scrimmages, one at Morristown, another near Redden between Valley Forge and Philadelphia, and many others, in which we stood our ground bravely and were not daunted to see a Redcoat," Young later wrote.[40]

"I stayed until peace was declared," he wrote. "I was discharged … without a cent to pay my expenses home, which I reached after many privations, to find my father and family in distressed circumstances as neither of us had received any compensation for our services. At this time, Continental script was of such depreciation in value that a month's wages would not buy a bushel of corn."

His father Hiat also was not paid the bounty due him, amounting to £30, according an old memorandum.[41]

Massachusetts becomes sixth state in the union.

U.S. Census reports Chatham population of 1,140 (193 families). Between 1790 and 1830, Chatham has the fastest growing population on the Cape with a growth rate of 174.5 percent.

Captain Benjamin Godfrey builds the town's first grist mill.

1784

1786

1796

"I travelled to Boston to secure our wages, which the government was paying by issuing notes, and found that Lieutenant Hamblin of the Fourth Regiment, who was paymaster, had disposed of our notes and run away to Canada with the proceeds, so that was the last I ever heard of our wages."[42]

Despite his lack of means, Joseph set about building a life. He married Anna Nickerson over her Tory family's protests. At first he made a living as a fisherman, rising from deck hand to master seaman, and then becoming a successful ship owner. He was elected selectman in 1804, a position he held for ten years. Young's fortunes stumbled during the embargoes of France and Great Britain in the early 1800s when his ships' movements were severely restricted; some even had to lay idle.

His father Hiat was frail and thin. "A faint recollection of him … (was of) a tall, gaunt looking man, then much enfeebled, and near his end. His actual grave remains unknown, not withstanding a persistent search was made for it in the ancient Parish burying ground (on Old Queen Anne Road)."[43] Hiat died on Oct. 10, 1810, at the age of 71.

During the war of 1812 one of Joseph Young's vessels was captured within twenty-four hours of home. Aboard were two of his sons, Joseph Jr. and Reuben, who were captured and sent to Dartmoor Prison in Devon, England. They were released at the end of the war.[44]

Once the war ended, Joseph Young quickly built up his shipping business and began accumulating property. He built a woolen factory in Chatham and a cotton factory in Harwich. He also started a block factory (for block and tackle), where the Isaac Bea Young house now stands on Main Street (and is inhabited by Hiat Young's descendent Janet Whittemore). In the meantime Joseph and Anna raised six daughters and three sons.[45]

Joseph became a prominent citizen in Chatham and held a seat in the state Legislature for several years.[46] A firm believer in the doctrine of universal salvation, he contributed substantially to the building of the first Universalist meeting house in Chatham.

As his health failed and he neared death in 1848, Joseph had one last mission to see through. He was determined to erect a fine monument to the memory of his father. He had the stonecutters work on the monument in his front yard where he could see it from his sickbed, to be certain that they made no mistakes. Joseph died a week after its completion. The large monument stands near the center of the People's Cemetery (formerly the Universalist cemetery). Joseph is buried where the stone stands alongside a number of his children and grandchildren [47]

For a time Hiat's legacy was kept alive by the Daughters of the American Revolution, with the Chatham-Harwich group named the Hiat Young Chapter of the D.A.R., but the chapter is no longer active.

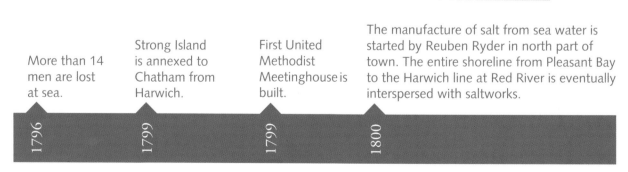

More than 14 men are lost at sea.

1796

Strong Island is annexed to Chatham from Harwich.

1799

First United Methodist Meetinghouse is built.

1799

The manufacture of salt from sea water is started by Reuben Ryder in north part of town. The entire shoreline from Pleasant Bay to the Harwich line at Red River is eventually interspersed with saltworks.

1800

THE BATTLE OF CHATHAM HARBOR

Chatham Harbor was invaded on June 20, 1782, when a British privateer entered under cover of darkness and took possession of one of the few boats anchored there, a brigantine. After sending sailors to board her and hoisting a British flag the privateer attempted to leave with the brigantine and several smaller vessels in tow.[48]

But the privateer's captain had not reckoned on the swift response of Colonel Godfrey and his company. When the British flag was raised on the *Joseph, Peter and Wells*, an alarm gun was sounded and a flag raised on the hill opposite the harbor.[49]

Colonel Godfrey, Joseph Doane, Richard Sears, and a number of other armed men, members of the town's militia, gathered at the top of the hill and then headed for the beach. By the time they reached the brigantine the privateers had unloaded her cargo onto a sloop to lighten her enough to get out of the harbor. Led by the British privateer, the brigantine and sloop began to sail out of the harbor.[50]

But Colonel Godfrey and his band of fifty men had reached the beach and launched a hail of gunfire at the privateer, which immediately returned fire. Once the privateer had sailed out of range, the Chatham men peppered the brigantine with constant gunfire. The men aboard the brigantine returned fire with grapeshot and small arms. But the brigantine ran aground on the bars and listed to one side. The crewmen abandoned ship and fled in small dories back to the privateer, chased the entire way by Chatham men in their own small boats. Col. Godfrey and Doane boarded the brigantine, struck the hated British flag and hoisted the Continental flag.[51]

Not long after the privateer disappeared from view, four Connecticut coasters laden with provisions were sighted about three miles outside the harbor. Doane, as head of the militia, ordered some men into a boat to warn them of the danger. Two pilot boats were then sent out to lead them to the safety of Chatham Harbor.[52]

Not long after they secured the coasters, a large British cruiser and the British privateer were spotted approaching the harbor. The cruiser anchored beside the bar and the privateer continued on in. The recaptured brigantine fired an alarm and Captain Doane ordered two cannons to the beach and mustered the militia. After one or two warning shots, the privateer turned about and made a speedy departure, along with the cruiser. "It was claimed that one of the British was killed and two wounded, but no casualties are reported among the militia."[53]

To service the needs of the growing fishing industry, there is a ropewalk opposite the Cow Yard on Old Harbor Road, where ice makers walked back and forth with fiber to make ship packing.

1800

The population of Chatham is 1,351 of which 90% are related to William Nickerson.

1800

There are seven windmills in town.

1800

HOW THE MOONCUSSERS BROUGHT A LIGHTHOUSE TO CHATHAM

As shipping and fishing boomed in the waters off Chatham in the early 19th century, so did the business of mooncussers – men (and some women and children) who would go out on the beaches, dunes, and bars on dark nights and, with the use of lanterns, deceive ships into running aground on the shoals. Once the ship ran aground and the cargo washed ashore, they stole and sold the goods. They were called "mooncussers" because they operated on nights when the moon was not shining. Another name for them was "wreckers."[54] And the false lights were called "Judas lights."

Adding to the hazards faced by mariners off Chatham were the constantly shifting bars of sand, strong currents, and ever-changing rips, especially off South Beach. "Not only do the bars alter, but the mouth of the harbor also is perpetually varying," wrote Reverend James Freeman in 1802.[55] "At present, it is gradually moving southward by the addition of sand to the point of the beach. The beach has thus extended about a mile within the course of the past 40 years."

Many ships ran aground or wrecked off Chatham. "Nowhere on the Cape's shorelines has the sea kept busier at her handiwork than among these storm-bitten sands. Directly to the south of the bluff, Monomoy lies beckoning like the bony finger of death which it has been to countless ships," wrote Josef Berger in *Cape Cod Pilot* in 1937.

Off Chatham hundreds of ships grounded, wrecked, or sunk. In the early 1800s there was an average of two wrecks every month during the winter.[56]

To protect vessels from the treacherous waters and the treachery of the mooncussers, Congress appropriated $5,000 for a twin-lights station in Chatham in 1806. A second appropriation of $2,000 was made in 1808.[57]

Chatham Light was built nine years after Highland Light was erected in Truro. So mariners could distinguish the Chatham Light from the Highland Light, the station was fitted with two fixed lights. Two octagonal wooden towers each forty feet tall and about seventy feet apart from each other were built on moveable skids about seventy feet apart. A small dwelling house was also built with only one bedroom. President Thomas Jefferson appointed Samuel Nye as its keeper.

The original structure lasted little more than thirty years, when a Coast Guard inspector described the towers as "very much shaken and decayed." In 1841 the towers were rebuilt with bricks.

25 vessels employed in cod fishing; each vessel is 25 to 70 tons with 200 men on board, most of them from Chatham.

Six saltworks in the town and six windmills in operation.

Four shelters are built for sailors who might be washed ashore in Chatham; one on the east side of Monomoy and three on the Outer Beach.

1802

1802

1802

Richard Sears: The Squire of Chatham

One of Chatham's most charismatic citizens in the late 18th and early 19th centuries was Richard Sears, Esquire, commonly called "Squire Sears."

Indeed he was a squire in the old-fashioned sense of the word – landed gentry and a proprietor of a number of businesses in town. He was said to have the largest land holdings in the town, including a large farm with many head of livestock that included the land where the Chatham Bars Inn and the neighboring Seaside Links are situated. He owned a saltworks and engaged in shipping and fishing enterprises.[58]

Painting said to be of Richard Sears, the Squire of Chatham. *Courtesy of Leslie Ray Sears, III, Sears Family Association.*

And he carried himself in accordance with his title.

"Mr. Sears was tall and of great dignity in manner; calm in speech and action; civil and attractive in his intercourse with his fellows. He was a conscientious Christian man and a strong supporter of the church."[59]

But he also was a bit of an odd duck when it came to the fashion of the day. "Mr. Sears was a gentleman of the old school with a sort of pompous air and wore his hair tied up in a queue behind."[60] "His attire, up to a short time before his death, was of the late Revolutionary period – he wore long hose, shoe and knee buckles, and ruffled shirts at all times."[61]

Born in Chatham in 1749, Sears lived in the family mansion built by his grandfather, Daniel Sears, at Seaview and Main Streets, where he also ran a general store attached to the home.

He held many important positions in the town and state: Sears was appointed town clerk and treasurer in 1775 and 1776; coroner in 1781; state senator in 1804; justice of the court in 1814; justice of the peace in 1814; and representative of the town to the General Court for a number of terms between 1781 and 1814.[62] He also served in the 1st Company of Chatham's Militia during the American Revolution.

While serving in the Legislature, Squire Sears would ride his horse to Boston where he would stay during the session at the Beacon Street home of his brother, David Sears, considered to be one of the wealthiest men of the city at that time.[63]

He also brought a number of esteemed gentlemen to Chatham for fishing and shooting including Noah Webster, James Otis, and Josiah Quincy.[64]

Sears married Mehitable Marshall in Framingham in 1778. They had six children: Sarah, Richard, Daniel, Hetty, Ebeneezer and Fear. The son of Daniel and Fear Freeman Sears, the Squire was a direct descendent of Richard Sears, "The Pilgrim," who was an early settler at Plymouth Colony and the Massachusetts Bay Colony.[65]

The Squire died in 1839 in his bed at his Chatham home at the age of 90.[66] He was buried in the Union (Congregational) Cemetery.

In April, the U.S. Congress appropriates $5,000 for a twin lighthouse station.

President Thomas Jefferson appoints Samuel Nye as keeper of the two lard-burning lighthouses erected in Chatham. Seamen rounding the Cape to Boston would see one light on the tip of Monomoy, two at Chatham and three (the Three Sisters) at Nauset.

1806

1808

1812-1862

New Ventures at Home and Abroad

By Spencer Grey

Already angered by the Embargo of 1807, which prohibited foreign commerce and placed restrictions on coastal trading, the citizens of Chatham were strongly opposed to the War of 1812 because it would further disrupt their primary source of income.

This opposition was expressed at town meeting of that year, and the majority also expressed abhorrence toward any alliance with France. Many of the young men who were driven from their seagoing ventures sought employment in Rhode Island and other farming communities. But everyone in Chatham suffered from the presence of British warships that entered or cruised near the harbor and threatened to fire upon the town.

In its issue of May 30, 1888, the *Boston Globe* printed an interview with 94-year-old Rhoda Howes, widow of Collins Howes, in which she displayed a clear memory of that time when she was 18 years old:

The War of 1812. Yes! Yes! I remember them Britishers. One of their big ships anchored off here and plagued us dreadfully. She hung around here a long time and when a storm came up she would get away for a time, as she drew too much water to come into the harbor. Then our fishing boats would run out. But she would soon come back and our packets couldn't run, so we couldn't get fish or coin either. Once in a while a fishing smack would slip out and in, but fortunately she never got hold of one of our boys. There was old Squire Crow, he was a Tory and sympathized with the Britishers. He killed a creetur and carried the beef over to the ship to make friends with them. He owned a top sail schooner then, and she was bound this way and they thought she would run in here on her way to Boston. They did come in and the Britishers caught site of her and chased her and drove her ashore and burned her, not stopping to find out who she belonged to. Most of them thought it was good enough for him and he did not get much sympathy in town.

Town meeting expresses abhorrence of an alliance with France and votes against the War of 1812.

First stage coach service established.

1812

1814

Isaiah Nye then had a small store down near the harbor and he used to watch nights for fear of a boat's crew landing and setting it afire. They threatened to bombard the town, because we would not pay tribute, but there wasn't much of any town then to fire on. The men were always on the watch and used to have training days to keep them in condition to repel any land attack. After the ship had got away, I went over to Nantucket in a sloop with Uncle Josiah Gould to visit my grandmother. In a few days to our astonishment that Britisher came up in front of the harbor and anchored. We wanted to go back home dreadfully after a while, so in the dead of night we started out, and we succeeded in getting by her, arriving home the next day.

The Copy Book of Levi Atwood
From Student to Educator and Editor

In 1839, the homes of the children and grandchildren of Sears Atwood[1], son of the builder of the Atwood House, lined the street from the Oyster Pond to Bridge Street. Accordingly it was called Atwood Street until the name was changed to Stage Harbor Road in 1945. While the surname of most of them was Atwood, other names, such as Godfrey, Taylor, Emory, and Mayo also could be found among the residents on that street, as men of those names had married Atwood women. To own a house in this area one had to be an Atwood by birth or marriage.

Although Captain Solomon Atwood undoubtedly lived on Atwood Street, the location of his house is unknown. With his wife Lucy Smith, he had six children: Sears, Mary, Solomon, Levi, Lucy and George.

Levi was born March 25, 1824, and in 1839, when he was 15 years old, he kept a copy book which is in the archives at the Atwood House Museum. All school children at that time kept copy books which were used to copy some of their favorite stories and practice their penmanship and mathematics. Some students also used their books to keep a journal. Although sporadic, the journal entries that Levi made during 1839 provide a clear picture of life during that time, especially as experienced by a young boy.

Beginning in January 1839, he recorded his daily experiences on a few days in January and February and later in December. Here is a selection of his journal entries, presented exactly as he wrote them, including his own spelling and almost total lack of punctuation.

First Methodist Meeting House built for $900 where Chatham Ford now stands.

Two stoves are placed in the Meeting House, with the town to pay for their support.

A road is laid out to shorten the distance between the Meeting House and the Twin Lights.

1820

1823

1824

Journal of the weather and nesisary afairs

January 1839

      Begins these 24 hours early in the morning fine weather and calm the night previous Joseph Atwood staid with me we got up early in the morning and scrached around and made up a fire and then went to the barn fodered the cattle with salt hay and scattered out some stalks for their foddering and then went over to the swamp to cut ice for them to drink and then we walked about and took a sort of observation and then went into the house and in a few moments we had brecfast and after brecfast we went directly to uncle Josephs and turned out the cattle and fodered them then we went to school but when we got as far as unkle Elnathans we stoped to slide a spell and when we got to school it had just begun we went in and read in first class book and attended to the duties of the school and when it came time for resess we went out and played ball untill the school master knocked for us to come in There is now a little breeze to the South It is quite clear and fine we have about 35 schollars to day. We went in and staid untill the school was done then we went out and played ball a little more and then I went home and got a little dinner and went along to school but had another stop at Elnathans pond I got to school and red in first class book it clouded up very sudden about 11 O clock and before 12 it began to hail and about 1 it began to snow it came on quite fast for a spell it being moderate and light breeze in all directions the weather being thick I attended to the school untill reces when I went out about 5 minutes and came in and staid till the school was done when I went home and attended to my cattle and then went and got in peat fetched water and eat my supper there was to be a singing school that evening

---

Joseph Young establishes a factory to produce wooden blocks for rigging.

A new Congregational Meeting House is built at Union Cemetery.

The town and church separate.

1828

1830

1831

but wether to go or not I could not tell but at last I concluded that I would go the weather was quite squally some times raining and then snowing and hailing but still moderate when the school was done it was cloudy and some stormy I went home and had a very fine time after all and soon went to bed very well contented with the evening soon got to sleep and sleeped pretty well all night so ends this Journal all well

Dec 3 1839 Tuesday: Commences winds from the N E blowing freash the appearance of a storm got up early in the morning made up a fire and after breakfast watered the horse and went to school got there before it began and when Mr. Conant came went to get a grammar lesson went out at resess and staid a few moments and went in again and went to work a scyferring [ciphering] a spell and then said my lesson and then the school was done went home to dinner and went back to school again the wind blew a gale and the night of the 2nd there was a schooner ashore on the Monomoy point loaded with cole she struck and went to peaces pretty soon the Crew got in shore all but one by swimming all but one who was drowned the master Mr. Conant came in the afternoon I studied Mathematics in the afternoon until it was time to spell and then we had a new contest about spelling that was the one that was up to the head the most had a piece of money or he had to have it divided amongst them that was up to the head the least was to have the least money after this preceedure the school was done I went home did my things got my supper and went to the lyceum and got a ticket for admittance but there was not any Lyceum the weather was so bad that the people could not come so I went down to Snows and made that the Evening and got home about 9 O clock in the Night and went to bed

Dec 7th 1839 Satterday: Commences Winds from the N. E. moderate and cloudy some appearance of a storm got up about sunrise and went to work cutting and splitting a load of wood before brecfast and then went to work helping cut up the hogs getting up Sea Weed[2] and towards night went to grind the bones went home did my things eat my supper and about 10 O clock Went to bed so ends these 24 hours

Dec 11th Wed: Commences winds first part moderate and cloudy got up about Day light eat my brecfast carted up some sea weed

Packets run between Chatham and Boston, leaving from Josiah Hardy's stage at the foot of Water Street.

1834

and went to school the school had not began then it had cleared of very pleasant with a light breeze from the N W the Steemer Bangor was of the back side and was expected to come up under the Neck and if she did I and several others expected to go on board of her at resess we went up on the hill there by Capt David Eldridges and to our great joy we saw her this set us all upon our upper leathers we went to school again and at noon I went home and cut up a half bushel of pumpkins for the cows and eat my dinner as quick as possible and went over to Uncle Elnathans and staid around there a spel and we got considerable of a fleet together and had considerable talk about going [on] our voyage we had no boat to go in but Mr. Mayo's little one he sed he was very willing for us to have her but he was afraid we would get upset we did not know what to do it was getting to about 2 O clock at last we concluded to go down and take a look at the boat and went down and got her into the water and we could not see why she would not do we concluded to go at enny rate and we ballest her pretty well the weather was fine with a light breeze to the W we started with plenty of crew with 3 oars without enny sail Our crew's Names were John W Atwood Joseph Atwood Levi Atwood Ephraim Taylor Alpheus Mayo Stephen Eldredge we rowed of pretty fast until we got to Hardings beach point where we came into a pretty bad sea the wind blowed pretty fresh we had a pretty hard row and at last we got of and staid about 15 minutes took a look at the boat and then came on shore we came quick before the sea and wind without any sail we did not take in much water and got on shore finely I went home did my things eat my supper and about 9 O clock went to bed so ends these 24 hours

Dec 12th Thursday: Commences Winds first blowing from the S. E. Blowing fresh came on to rain a little while after Day Light got up considerable while before sunrise eat my brecfast and staid in the house untill school time because it rained so hard with the wind to the S E I went to school and staid till noon when I went home eat my dinner and went back to school again the wind by 1 O clock had got S. W. blowing freash and hard Stoped raining and by 3 O clock it had cleared of considerable I went home at night did my things and went up to Sam Emerys after some candles I came back eat my supper and went over to John Atwoods and staid a little while and then went up George Taylors where the party was staid around ther a spell then I went to J. A. again long Jon and the rest then we went up to the party again then we went

Twenty-eight small windmills are in use for pumping water to saltworks.

1835

over to sams but he was not open we staid around there considerable while then we went up to the post office and staid a whoping while then the stage came I got the paper and went home and went to bed so ends this....

Dec 16 Monday: Commences Wind from the N E got up early in the morning and went to the shore to get the boat up through the bars the tide was so high that she was thumping up against the fence after this I went to the house and cut up some Wood eat brecfast and went to school we had a pretty hard squal of rain before the school began but before it was done it came on a pretty hard storm of rain and hale I went home when the school was done got my dinner and went back to school again it stormed considerable and blowed heavy at night it was a strong storm I made out to get home and found a Pidgeon in the porch set upon the Wood to get out of the storm I did my things eat my supper and it came on to snow and blow I went to bed that night so ends this…

December 19 Thursday: got up eat my brecfast and went down to the shore and anchored of a way and then I went to school staid until noon when I went home got my dinner and went to school I went home at night did my things eat my supper and cracked some Wallnuts and went to Uncle Joseph's and then to Dr Carpenters to get some books out of the library then I went to the post office and got the paper then I went home and after a while I went to Bed So ends this…

December 21 Sat: got up in the morning very cold eat my brecfast there was no school that day I did my things and went over to the wind holes and scated a spell then I went home fixed my skates then I went up to the store then I went and scated a little before dinner after dinner I went over to the wind holes and skated till night then I went home did my things eat my supper and went to bed in the evening so ends this…

Dec 23 Mon: got up in the morning the wind NE blowing freash with rain and snow I went to school staid until noon when the school was over it rained pretty hard and it was dreadfull windy I went home got my dinner and went back to school I staid until night when I went home and went to Bill Hamiltons and from there to aunt Emorys

Enough residents live on Monomoy Point to support a school and a tavern.

1839

Eighty saltworks produce 27,000 bushels of salt annually.

1840

One of two original wooden lighthouses falls over the eroded bank.

1840

so home in the rain I got my supper and read in a book most of the evening about George Robert's Twelve Hens then I went to bed so ends this…

Levi Atwood's journal entries end at this point. It is a bit surprising that on December 23rd there is no mention of Christmas coming, as one would expect from a boy of 15. It may be that Christmas was less of a holiday at that time.

The Student Becomes Teacher, Storekeeper and Editor

As so often happened in those days, as soon as Levi completed his own education in local schools, he became a teacher in those same schools, probably around 1845. The school records for 1848 note that he had taught the winter term in District IV. The report indicates that "43 students attended and good order was maintained. … School appears to have been commendably still, studious and profitable. It is to be regretted that the ill health of teacher cut short the term two weeks."

But "ill health" did not prevent Levi from opening a small store on Pond Street (now Stage Harbor Road) in 1849. The store prospered, making it possible for him to marry Phoebe Mason in 1850 and build a house for her next to the barn that housed his store. Atwood Store eventually outgrew its original location, and Levi moved it to Main Street where it soon doubled in size and was operated by the family until 1964.

Besides operating his business, Atwood served on the school committee for many years, beginning in 1856. He was active in the Congregational Church, where he sang in the choir for fifty years and was superintendent of the Sunday school for forty-five years. For many years he was town clerk and town treasurer.

From 1875 until the end of his life he was editor of the *Chatham Monitor*. Clearly the bright young man reflected in his early journals had the intellectual curiosity, the energy, and the social conscience that made him one of Chatham's foremost citizens of his century. [3]

New brick twin lighthouses erected.

Joshua Nickerson establishes Granville Academy.

1841

1842

ALPHEUS HARDY: CHATHAM'S SHIPPING TITAN

Alpheus Hardy was born in Chatham on Nov. 1, 1815, the son of Captain Isaac and Betsey (Eldredge) Hardy. He attended the village schools until he was 12 years old, at which time he began working in his father's store that was located on the beach a few hundred yards north of the twin lights, on the wharf that was then at the foot of Water Street.

Young Alpheus was so ambitious that, when he was 16, he went to Boston to work in a store in the city. It wasn't long, however, before he had an accident that crushed one foot, making it impossible for him to continue working. But being unable to work did not diminish his ambition, for he decided while recuperating to continue his education and gained admittance to Phillips Andover Academy. There he made rapid advances in his education, but he studied such long hours that he became seriously ill and had to withdraw from the academy. Not one to remain idle any longer than necessary, he went to sea for three months.

When Hardy was 19 and had finished his stint as a mariner, he became an agent for the Philadelphia and Southern Packet Line, where he quickly acquired knowledge of shipping, to the point where he decided to form his own company in association with two friends, Captain Ezra H. Baker and Charles J. Morrill, under the name of Hardy, Baker & Morrill. Fortunately he had by then become a close friend of Joshua Sears, a leading merchant in Boston, who provided him with contacts in the business and with financial backing.

Alpheus Hardy as a young man in Boston.
Courtesy Chatham, Massachusetts Historical Society.

Town meetings are held in churches until town hall is built in 1851.

1843

Daily mail service begins.

1848

Levi Atwood opens Atwood's Store on Stage Harbor Road.

1849

An International Shipping Concern

Hardy, Baker, and Morrill were first successful in the coastal trade, and they decided to expand to international trade by buying the 150-ton brig *Otho*, which was small and fast. The ship succeeded in sailing to the Mediterranean and back so quickly that they captured much of the business for goods from that area, especially fresh fruit and wine. With this success at international trade, the firm of Hardy and Baker prospered and grew.

It was not long before Hardy's reputation for strict financial integrity, trustworthiness, and mercantile ability produced great confidence among investors and other businessmen. With such backing the firm rapidly acquired many ships that sailed all the oceans of the world. When that partnership was dissolved, Hardy continued on his own as Alpheus Hardy & Company.

On the occasion of the celebration of the 200th anniversary of Chatham in 1912, his son, Alpheus H. Hardy, made the following introductory remarks:

> In 1853 I crossed the Atlantic in a little 300 ton barque, officered and manned by Chatham boys. The captain, Elisha Harding, was one of Nature's noblemen and I have always kept him in affectionate remembrance. The mate was Horace Taylor, who as captain of our ship Wild Rover brought to Boston Joseph Neesima, afterwards fitly called the Apostle of Japan, I remember among the crew Freeman Burgess, possibly a younger Harding, but most of them rose to hold commands, through the hawsehole and not by way of the quarter deck.
>
> In the years when we when we still owned ships, so far as possible, we chose Chatham or Cape men as masters. Among them was John Paine, to whom was gladly paid a higher wage if he would take his wife with him; David Nye Nickerson, Thomas Crowell, Thomas Sparrow, Andrew Reynolds and others. The choice was based upon the confidence and belief in the character and ability of the men. In connection with this, let me mention an incident which occurred this morning. Captain Ephraim Smith told me that my father told him when he had chartered him for a special voyage, "I have not chartered your vessel, but you." It was not the ship, but the man he wanted. I recall the unwillingness to let the now Reverend S.S. Nickerson go to sea in command of the Heroine, which he had chartered, because of his extreme youthful appearance, until he learned that he was a Chatham boy. That settled it, and he made a successful voyage.[3]

Between 1840 and 1865 Hardy's fleet grew to include as many as fifteen vessels, at least thirteen of which were at one time or another manned by Chatham men as captains and crews.

Chatham Captain Justus Doane makes a record voyage to San Francisco in 92 days, 20 hours.

1852

The village center has five stores, three schools, a sail loft, and a mill.

1856

Captain Warren Crosby

One of the Chatham men hired by Hardy was Warren Crosby, whose story of his life at sea was recorded by Alice Wight while her son Frederick painted his portrait. Crosby begins his account by explaining that he exchanged his first name, Abijah, for his second, Warren, so that his school mates would not call him Bijah or something worse.

Like so many Chatham boys in the 19th century, Crosby first went to sea when he was 12 as a cook on coastal vessels. When he was 16 he signed on for his first international voyage on the *Oxenbridge,* bound for India, Melbourne, Le Havre, and Liverpool. During that voyage he was promoted to second mate and then to first, before the ship returned to Calcutta, Singapore, and Burma to pick up bags of linseed to take to Hull in the North Sea. On the way there the vessel was caught in a gale, resulting in a leak that made the linseed so wet that the ship was crippled and barely made it to safety on the island of Santa Helena. There it was abandoned and the crew was taken by a whaling ship to New Bedford.

By the time he arrived back in Chatham, Crosby was 20 years old and had grown from a beardless boy, too young to shave, to a mature man with a black beard and a weathered face. Before embarking on that four-year voyage, Crosby had a spat with his girlfriend, Annie Nickerson, but time and maturity had healed old wounds, rekindled the romance, and strengthened their love so that they married soon after his return.

The *Bounding Billows* was one of the several clipper ships owned by Alpheus Hardy & Company. *Courtesy Chatham, Massachusetts Historical Society.*

When Warren was promoted to captain, Annie joined him on his next two voyages, but after that he refused to let her accompany him because she had the uncanny ability to predict oncoming storms.

Warren Crosby later became master on two of Hardy's clipper ships, the *Daniel Webster* and the *Bounding Billows.* Because of their unusual speed, these clipper ships often were used to carry fruit from the Mediterranean to Boston.

When he was captain of the *Bounding Billows* returning from Valencia, Spain, with a cargo of oranges, the ship ran into headwinds that decreased its speed so much that the crew became sick

The graded school and first high school opens behind the present Community Center.

1858

with scurvy. But loyal to the owner, Captain Crosby refused to allow them to break into the oranges on board.

Undoubtedly the most famous ship owned by Alpheus Hardy & Company, at least in the annals of Chatham, was the *Wild Rover*. Built in 1853, she was captained by Chatham men from her launching until Hardy sold it in 1870. Those captains, three of whom were brothers, were:

1854: Benjamin Taylor
1855-1856: Horace S. Taylor
1857-1858: Benajah Crowell, Jr.
1859-1861: Thomas Sparrow
1862-1864: Simeon Taylor
1864-1869: Horace S. Taylor

The Apostle of Japan

In 1864 when Horace Taylor was captain of the bark *Young Greek,* he was ordered to sail her to Shanghai, where she was to be sold, and to wait there for his brother Simeon to arrive on the *Wild Rover*, at which time Horace was to take over command.

While the *Wild Rover* was in Shanghai taking on cargo and preparing for trips to other Asian ports, a 21-year-old Japanese man named Neesima Shimeta made the bold decision to leave his homeland, undaunted by the decree that made it a capital offense for any male to leave the country. Determined to learn English and study Christian doctrine, he traveled to Hakodate, an open port frequented by American vessels.

There he learned that the brig *Berlin* from Salem was about to leave for Shanghai. The captain, William Savory, was so impressed by Neesima's determination to go to the United States that he agreed to hide him in a store cabin if he could board the ship without being apprehended. Neesima did so by hiding under a pile of ship supplies in a small boat that was loading the *Berlin*.

When Captain Savory reached Shanghai he learned that the *Wild Rover* was scheduled to return to Boston within the next few months. Because the *Berlin* was returning to Japan, he persuaded Captain Horace Taylor to sign on the stowaway as his cabin boy. When Captain Taylor asked the young man for his name, he found he could not pronounce it and said, "I think I had better call you Joe."

After traveling to Hong Kong and Manila to load cargo, the *Wild Rover*, with all sails set, headed for Boston on April 1, 1865.

Many years later, Neesima Shimeta wrote of this voyage to Boston.

It took us four months to reach Boston. We did not stop on the way, as we had plenty of provisions. During the voyage my business was to wait upon the captain at his meals, and keep the cabin in order. I often pulled the ropes when I was free from the captain's service.

Rufus Smith begins stage coach service between Chatham and Yarmouth.

1858

The most enjoyable part of the voyage was my daily calculation of the ship's position with the captain. He was extremely kind to me, and treated me as if I were a brother. Everyone on board treated me pleasantly.

When the *Wild Rover* arrived in Boston, Captain Taylor went to 4 Joy Street, the home of owner Alpheus Hardy, to tell him of his most unusual passenger, the first Japanese man ever to arrive in the United States. Hardy was immediately interested and asked Taylor to bring the lad to his house. When he met him, Hardy was so impressed with Neesima's intelligence, determination, and courage that he unofficially adopted him, giving him the name Joseph Hardy Neesima, which he retained throughout his life.

The *Wild Rover* was captained by men of Chatham throughout its ownership by Alpheus Hardy. Under the command of Horace Taylor, who commissioned this painting, it brought Neesima Shimeta to Boston. *Courtesy Chatham, Massachusetts Historical Society.*

Post offices open in South Chatham and Chathamport.

1862

As a trustee of Phillips Andover Academy, Hardy had no difficulty getting Neesima accepted there, where he quickly proved to be an outstanding student, becoming proficient in English and science. From there we went to Amherst College, where Hardy also was a trustee, as the first Japanese person to be enrolled at any college or university in the country. Upon graduation from Amherst, Neesima fulfilled his lifelong dream of becoming an ordained Christian minister by completing the course at the Andover Theological Seminary.

During his years as a student, Neesima sometimes visited with the Hardys in Boston, but he spent more of his vacations in Chatham at the home of Horace Taylor and family on Kendrick Road. In a letter to Mrs. Hardy he told of one of those visits.

> *I was received by Captain Taylor's father's family kindly and welcomely. They are all pleasant and social people and they treat me as their own family. I do not read much this vacation but I read the Book and a few pages of geography every day. I love study dearly, so that I cannot leave it entirely. Now we have quite [a] number in the family. The sum of them is 12. We went to the seashore yesterday and dug out one bushel of clams and we shall go to the woods tomorrow to get blackberries if it be fine weather...*

Neesima Shimeta, who took the name of Joseph Hardy Neesima in honor of Alpheus Hardy. *Courtesy Chatham, Massachusetts Historical Society.*

Always mindful of his ambition to found a Christian school in Japan, Neesima obtained funds to help fulfill his dreams from Hardy and other fellow philanthropists. Because of his success in fund raising, he was able to return to Japan in December 1874. With $5,000 in hand, he opened a school in Kyoto named "Doshisha." The school began with six students, but within ten years its enrollment had increased to 250 and included both men and women.

Although Neesima did not live to see the fulfillment of his ambitious dreams, his followers carried on with the expansion of Doshisha. Today Doshisha is not only an internationally recognized university of some 30,000 students, but it also provides schooling from kindergarten through graduate school.

Following his historic around-the-world voyage of from 1862 to 1865, Horace Taylor embarked on a second such trip in 1866. Upon arriving back in Boston in 1869, he was in such a hurry to get off the ferry taking him from Boston to East Boston that he fell between the ferry and the dock and was crushed, dying at the age of 40 and at the peak of his career.

Changing with the Times

In the years following the Civil War, Alpheus Hardy began to feel that shipping, especially in sailing ships, was declining, at least partly because of the development of the railroads. With that decline in mind, he gradually began selling his ships and devoted more time to other interests, such as expanding his involvement in finance and railroads.

While it is clear that Alpheus Hardy was a major player in the world of 19th century shipping, hundreds of other men in Chatham followed the sea throughout the century.

Among those who did not command Hardy ships but were famous for their worldwide travels was Joshua Eldridge, who spent so many years trading in China that he acquired the name "China Josh."

In 1866, he was captain of the brig *Alma* that carried a crew of eleven when, while sailing between Yokohama and Hong Kong, he was attacked by Chinese pirates in two junks off the Ninepin Islands. At about seven in the evening, the lookout reported the two pirate junks approaching from astern. Because the *Alma* was becalmed, the junks, which were being rowed, soon overtook her.

Captain Eldridge fired on the pirates, killing a number of them and wounding even more, but they still managed to board the brig. After the Chinese killed two of his crew, Eldridge realized that he was overpowered. With the remaining eight crew members, he forced his way through the horde of pirates and fled in one of his boats, which he had lowered before the attack in anticipation of just such an emergency.

アルヒユウス・ハーディ

(Alpheus Hardy)

Alpheus Hardy in his later years.
Courtesy Chatham, Massachusetts Historical Society.

Through skillful seamanship and a touch of luck, they reached Hong Kong the next morning, and Captain Eldridge notified the authorities. In time, the *Alma* was found — the pirates had set her adrift when they had finished sacking her. Eldridge and his men were able to resume their trading along the Chinese coast.

Although most of the international shipping on sailing ships came to an end by about 1890, villages like Chatham benefitted from the worldliness that their mariners acquired during their travels. As Henry C. Kittredge explains in the concluding pages of his *Shipmasters of Cape Cod*:

> *Here were men who had lived in foreign cities for months on end, weathered typhoons, put down mutinies, smashed records, and taken tea with kings. They had seen life in half the seaports from St. Petersburg to Hong Kong; they had shivered through February*

snowstorms on the North Atlantic and sweltered through pongee and pith helmets in Ceylon. They had dined with Chinese merchants whom they had learned to trust and had been shamelessly cheated by Yankees whom they believe to be their friends. They had eaten caviar in Russia, drunk claret in Bordeaux, and smoked opium in Singapore. And when they came back to [Chatham], they brought with them something more than camphorwood desks and strangely inlaid card tables; they brought a perspective so true that they could distinguish between the important and the unimportant and could laugh at much that loomed large in the narrower minds of the few of their brethren who had stayed at home[4].

The Wives of Captains

While Kittredge speaks of the men who became learned and cosmopolitan from their travels, many of their wives joined them on voyages, acquiring even more culture.[5]

Almira Crowell, wife of Benajah Crowell, kept extensive diaries. On Nov. 1, 1860, she wrote in her journal that, while in London, they "…lived part of the time on board ship and part of it at America Square, at a hotel where Americans board; visited all the chief objects of interest, went to the houses of Parliament and saw Queen Victoria and Prince Consort."

Beside visiting national monuments around the world, she and her husband read extensively during their voyages.

Not only did these captains' wives experience the cultural centers of the civilized world but they also saw some of the most exotic parts of the Pacific, as clearly described in a letter from Emma Crosby Eldredge, wife of Walter Eldredge, the captain of the bark *Stillman B. Allen.*

> *Java Sea, Nov. 10th 1876*
> *Dear Uncle,*
> *Thinking perhaps a few lines from me might prove exceptable,*
> [sic] *I will write you a few lines informing you that we are all quite well at present, and hope this will find you and yours enjoying the same great blessing. We are now on our way from Cheribon, with a cargo of sugar, to Batavia, shall stop there to get water, and then proceed to Falmouth, England for orders. I assure you we are not sorry to leave Java. It has been very hot and quite sickly. We have all had an attack of Java fever, however it was nothing serious. I went on shore last week and stopped at the Hotel for a few days and had quite a pleasant time, although I find it far more comfortable on ship, as we layed about three miles from the shore, consequently we got the sea breeze, which made it much cooler than on the land. I enjoy myself quite well at Singapoor; plenty of fruit and quite cheap too. Bananas eight for a cent, oranges one cent each, pineapples*

four cents, and coconuts two cents, and there was a kind of fruit called mangorteen, and as I think you never saw any, I will describe it.

It has a shell similar to the pomegranate, and the inside has a flavor between the peach and grape. It is the most delicious fruit I ever ate, and is considered very healthy. The day we arrived at Singapoor before we came to anchor there were about twenty-five boats and sandpams came along side. The Malay merchants came on board with their servants bringing their guide for them. The merchants looked very clean, and some of them dressed up quite gay, with ten or twelve yds. Of muslin around their head for a turban with red skirt and white jacket, some had silk, cashmere shawls and cloaks, other had embroidery, braided slippers and smoking capes, precious stones, sandalwood boxes, monkeys and birds, shells and coral and different kinds of fruit. For about two hours the ship resembled a variety shop. Then Ho Ah Chung the tailor came marching along, his long braid flowing out behind, with samples of cloth under his arm all ready to take your measure for a suit of clothes, and Ho An Cheen the shoemaker came tripping behind with samples of leather for your boots and shoes. Some of the Malays are very intelligent looking, and are always ready for a trade, but will cheat if possible. The Java men seem a lower class, care nothing about trade or anything else except sleeping. They live in bamboo huts, eat with their fingers, and seem to be a degraded race of people. Their huts have no furniture except for a bamboo bedstead, a straw mat, a small charcoal stove and two or three dishes. The Dutch people that reside at Cheribon do nothing themselves but have the natives perform all the labors for very low wages, as their wants are few, only a little rice and a bit of calico. I attended a marriage fest at Cheribon, which I would like to describe, also their manner of fishing, but as I am limited for time, I must close. Give my love to Aunt Ann and the children. I trust her eyes are no worse. My love to Aunt Mary and family. Tell them to write me at Falmouth. I suppose they have received my letter from New Castle. How is Grandpa? Give my love to him; tell him I shall write him from England. Also remember me kindly to his family. Hoping this will find you all enjoying good health and every other blessing.

I remain your affect. Niece E. C. Eldredge.

With experiences such as these, many of the people living in Chatham were far from provincial.

The Mariners of Chatham

Most of Chatham's "mariners" were engaged in coastal shipping, traveling up and down the east coast from Boston to Salem to Nova Scotia, and down to Philadelphia and Baltimore.

The more adventurous sailed to ports in the Caribbean, where they could trade for valuable goods, such as sugar, rum, and molasses. In the 19th century most of the stores in Chatham and other Cape towns had a special area for what was termed "W.I. Goods."

In most cases, "W.I. Goods" was a euphemism for rum, which was the cargo of choice from the Caribbean. In 1864 Captain Luther Eldredge of Chatham sailed to the West Indies for a load of liquor with his brother Anthony as his first mate. Because of Anthony's rough treatment of the crew, there was considerable ill feeling among the men when they reached the islands.

It wasn't long after the ship arrived in port that it was loaded with rum and ready for the return voyage. When Captain Eldredge went ashore to secure clearance papers from port authorities, the crew rose up against Anthony.

When the captain arrived back onboard, he found his brother lying dead on the deck.

It was evident there had been a severe struggle, and the captain soon learned the men had been in a fierce fight with Anthony. Captain Eldredge had the men placed in irons and taken ashore, where they were put in prison. After reporting the incident to the consul, he raised a new crew.

Realizing that authorities would come on board to retrieve the body, the captain encouraged the crew to drink about half a cask of rum – and then placed Anthony's body in the cask. When local police boarded the ship looking for the body, the men were too drunk to give them any information.

When the authorities went ashore, Captain Eldredge immediately set sail and left the harbor with his brother's body resting safely in the barrel of rum.

When the vessel arrived in Chatham, Captain Joseph Atkins helped Luther Eldredge remove the body from the cask. They found it was well preserved. Anthony was buried in Chatham's Seaside Cemetery in Captain Eldredge's lot.

Coastal trade continued to flourish during the 19th century, employing most of the mariners from Chatham. While the most frequent cargoes were coal and lumber, the coastal traders also brought millions of bales of cotton from Alabama and South Carolina. The mill towns of Lowell, Lawrence, Fall River, and New Bedford depended on these coastal vessels to provide cotton for uniforms, blankets, and tents for the Union army. Following that war the mills grew so productive that they depended even more on the coastal ships to supply their needs and distribute their goods.

Giddings Ballou at Whitewash Village

In the early years of the 1840s, Giddings Hyde Ballou of Roxbury, Massachusetts, was advised to live either on the sea or near it because of his poor health. Young Mr. Ballou, then about 20, decided to settle near the seashore.

In his younger years he had been schooled by his father, Hosea Ballou, who had opened a private school for boys in his home. Because his father was intellectually demanding, young Giddings received an education that qualified him for college, but his deep interest was in painting.

As a Universalist minister, his father became the first president of Tufts University, and his biographer notes that Giddings chose not to attend college but instead, "with a passion for brush and palette, he painted industriously."[5] With this dedication to his art, he trained himself to paint with considerable skill.

Following his doctor's advice, Ballou set out for a life on Cape Cod that would be supported by his ability to paint portraits. Sailing from Boston to Provincetown on a packet boat, he recounts the experience in an essay that was published by *Harper's Magazine* in 1864[6]:

> *We well remember how blankly we stared when many years ago, on a bitter December morning, after a wave-tossed sea-sick night, we staggered up the cabin steps of the little packet and fish-dinghy, Success, on its return trip from Boston to Provincetown. A raw lad, it was our first experience on salt-water, and as we gazed across the ruffled waves toward Race Point, and saw naught but a huge assemblage of sand heaps from whence the cold sunlight was pitilessly reflected, our curiosity was quenched in disgust, and we hastily tumbled down into the bunk for consolation*

Apparently he settled in Truro for a time, because in 1841 he was paid $10 by Isaac Small of that town for painting a portrait of him. It was not until six years later that he settled in Brewster, boarding for several years in the home of a local lawyer, George Copeland. During that time he supported himself by painting portraits of a number of Brewster residents.

His connection with Chatham is first noted in 1849, when he painted a portrait of local dentist Dr. Joseph Atwood. On January 1, 1856, he drew a small portrait of Atwood's baby daughter Nina Modesta Atwood. Both of these works are now on display in the Atwood House Museum.

This same year, Ballou was hired by the town of Chatham to teach the three-month winter semester at the school on Monomoy Point for a monthly salary of $35, a position he maintained through the winter of 1861and 1862. His 1864 essay in *Harper's* describes life in Whitewash Village. The article is liberally illustrated by his drawings.

When Ballou took up residence there in 1856, the village was well established and flourishing after thirty years of development.

In the early years of the 19th century there was such a profusion of cod, mackerel, and lobster around the end of Monomoy Point that fishing vessels in great numbers frequented the area.

Lobsters were so plentiful that a good-sized one could be had for two cents, while small ones and large culls were one cent each. These fishing boats needed a safe harbor and support, such as supplies of lines, hooks, nets, as well as places to repair and service the craft.

At that time, the tip of Monomoy curved like a fish hook to the northwest, creating a large and deep harbor called the Powder Hole, which provided a safe anchorage for as many as forty vessels. By 1825 enterprising Chatham entrepreneurs began to meet those needs by building wharves, one on the south side of the harbor owned by J. Reed and David Lewis, and another on the north side operated by Anthony Thatcher, Isaac Loveland, and Daniel Webster Nickerson. In addition there were other small wharves, chandleries, shops, and general supply stores.

"Whitewash Village," illustration by Giddings Ballou for his article "Monomoy," *Harper's New Monthly Magazine,* 1864.

Originally these enterprises operated only during the summer but the fishing business was so profitable that a year-round community quickly sprung up. Prosperous families built substantial and sizeable homes, while smaller and less pretentious houses were built by the fishermen. Eventually the village boasted a church, a school, and a lodging house, all of which Giddings Ballou describes in his *Harper's* essay. The contrast between Giddings, urban-born and highly educated, and the villagers on Monomoy is evident in his amusing depiction of them, as in this drawing of "A Monomoyer."

About a mile beyond the Monomoy lighthouse stood Whitewash Village, composed of storage sheds, shacks and houses for the residents, and Monomoy House, which Ballou describes as "a weatherbeaten, barracky, amphibious structure" where he would find lodging. The building had a fishermen and coasters' fitting store on the first floor, and sleeping accommodations on the second.

The settlement received its name because of the generous use of whitewash on the larger buildings in its more prosperous years, but, by the time that Ballou arrived, most of the whiteness had washed away. In the following excerpt from his essay, he explains his use of the term "amphibious" in describing Monomoy House.

"A Monomoyer," illustration by Giddings Ballou for his article "Monomoy," *Harper's New Monthly Magazine,* 1864.

We designated the Monomoy House as 'amphibious'. The term was not applied unadvisedly. At certain rarely occurring winter tides the sea comes part way up the front stairs, and the inmates go a visiting by boats. At lesser and frequent floods the boys wade to school and carry the girls.... In fact, the little territory dotted by Monomoy village is a battle-ground between sand on the one side, and wind and water on the other. At flood the sea rushes up in long tortuous creeks, and almost touches the lighthouse fence on the eastern shore, and the dwellers in the cottages thereby might well look to their anchor-tackle, when going to bed of a stormy night, and make all fast, lest they should find themselves adrift in the morning.

Because the residents of Whitewash Village were fishermen and seafarers, they all spoke in seafarer's language, including their children. One incident observed by Ballou illustrates this custom. A bright-eyed lad name Bill committed an act sufficiently heinous to enrage his mother to the point where she took after him with her broom. As was so often the case on Monomoy, the wind was blowing a gale, which, because of her voluminous long skirts, propelled her at such a clip that she was rapidly overtaking the offender. Seeing his plight, Bill's young friend Big Hugh called out to him "Luff, Bill, Luff! Take her on the wind." Bill took a sharp turn to windward, while his mother "shot past him like a man-o-war with all sails set," and, before she could check her speed, Bill had raced well beyond her reach.

According to Ballou he went to Monomoy "...to induct the delights of literature into the minds of the hardy young Monomoians. One would have deemed these sands a mighty uncertain bed wherein to sow the seeds of learning." As a somewhat sickly and sensitive artist from the city, he seems an unlikely person to maintain control of a classroom of burly young men whose real interest was in fishing and the sea.

When asked if he had trouble with these potentially tough students, he replied "Not very. None of 'em over six feet, except Big Hugh, and he's tolerable good-natured. Not many of 'em can lick me – perhaps not." He goes on to explain that usually they were orderly and attentive, but when word was spread, as it was often, and the cry of "wreck, ho!" was heard, his students jumped to their feet to join the other "Pointers" in running at top speed to be among the first to salvage the bales of cotton, bags of potatoes, barrels of rum, or whatever cargo may have been spilled from the wreck.

Maintaining order in the classroom and keeping his students attentive to their lessons was not the only difficulty he encountered during his three years as schoolmaster. From a letter to the town selectmen written in December 1859, it is clear that there were some shortcomings with the facilities:

"Luff, Bill, Luff! Take her on the wind," illustration by Giddings Ballou for his article "Monomoy," *Harper's New Monthly Magazine*, 1864.

> *I mentioned that affair of an outhouse to you last winter, but you remarked that so much money had been spent on school houses that it was best to defer the thing, but an outhouse is <u>needed</u>. Estimated cost 7 or 8 dollars, the people here will set it up.*

Apparently his pleas fell on receptive ears. In the Town Report of 1860-1861 is the item, "F. B. Rogers for new privy – $8.50. Reed and Lewis – labor $6.30."

In his leisure time Ballou enjoyed the company of the Monomoyers who gathered evenings at Monomoy House, as described in the following passage:

> *Many a pleasant eve had Pedagogus* [his pseudonym in this piece] *spent on the long bench which ran behind the rusty stove in the at once sitting-room, dining-room, and kitchen of the Monamoit House… listening, while he toasted his thin legs, to many a tale of adventure in seas of the Old World, or in Pacific whale-ships, or amidst the semi-piratical resorts of the Gulf or the Spanish Main, the wreck fire sputtering blue or yellow, or flaming up spitefully, as though infested with troublous ghosts of Malay, Portugee, or Buccaneer…. and there was genial comfort within, though the blinding storm howled against the window-panes, and cased them thick with snow.*

As Ballou explains, this simple inn was a welcome refuge for many a ship-wrecked and frost-bitten sailor, who after struggling through wind and snow reached its sheltering rooms "…to warm his life-blood behind the stove of 'mine landlord' the 'Captain' of Monamoit House fame."

The heyday of White Wash Village reached its end after a hurricane in 1861 washed away the northwest point and filled in the harbor with sand. Many residents were forced to move back to the mainland, some leaving their houses to decay but others rafting them to new locations in town. The school was closed for lack of students, and the only remaining year-round residents were Asa Nye and his family, who tended Monomoy Light.

Ballou's closing words in his *Harper's* essay most effectively express this end to an era:

Drawing of a Monomoy wreck by Giddings Ballou for his article "Monomoy," *Harper's New Monthly Magazine, 1864.*

"At the Monomoit House," illustration by Giddings Ballou for his article *"Monomoy," Harper's New Monthly Magazine, 1864.*

But the golden era of Monomoy has passed away. Light-houses and light-boats, and careful charts and longshore pilots multiply, and harvest of hulk and cargo is not as it used to be. And the sand is sweeping about the entrance to the little harbor; and its habitants, mindful of the encroaching wave, have begun to forsake the beach for the main, taking with them even roof-tree and hearth-stone.

ENTERPRISING ZIBA NICKERSON

Ever since founder William Nickerson and his family settled in Chatham, conditions here have made it necessary for residents to adapt.

They first supported themselves by farming, with marginal dependence on fishing and shell fishing. But by the middle of the 18th century residents had largely depleted the soil, forcing them to adopt fishing as their primary means of putting food on the table.

By the early years of the 19th century the vast majority of Chatham men were mariners, and a substantial number of those were deep sea sailors.

But life on the high seas is not an easy one. Many took the first opportunity to find some occupation to stay on shore. Being able to make a living on shore required them to be enterprising and adventurous.

One such enterprising person was Ziba Nickerson, most famously known for being one of the first telegraph operators on the eastern seaboard, if not in the country. But before taking up that occupation he sampled a few others.

Born in 1823, he first signed on for a three-year hitch on a voyage that took him to ports throughout the Pacific and as far as the Orient. But unlike most other Chatham youths of his day, Ziba decided that one stint at sea was enough and looked around for a means of support that would keep him in Chatham.

In 1848, this short, stocky young man with a full beard and bright twinkling eyes caught the eye of Sarah Payne, who quickly accepted his proposal and married him on Nov. 28, 1848.

The 1858 Graded School House that was championed by Ziba Nickerson. *Courtesy of Chatham, Massachusetts Historical Society.*

A Leader in Education

At the time, Ziba was the teacher during the winter term at the school in District VI, the Old Harbor District in North Chatham. The report of the School Committee in May 1848 praises the school as one that has maintained a high rank among the town schools. The report singles out Ziba Nickerson for special praise, saying that "he is a competent teacher and true to his trust." The report expresses the belief that "teachers themselves must be in the pursuit of knowledge, to awaken a desire for improvement in their pupils – Mr. Nickerson we believe is one of this class; we commend his example to other young men."

There is no record of how many years Ziba taught school, but he continued his deep interest in learning throughout his life, serving for many years as a member of the school committee. He also was the driving force behind the proposal to build a central graded school. This effort required great determination on his part because it was strongly opposed by the many less enlightened voters of Chatham who derided it as "Ziba's folly."

Nevertheless the handsome building of two full floors above a spacious basement opened in September 1858, on the rise slightly behind the present Chatham Community Center. In a story about the school's dedication, the *Barnstable Patriot* reported that "the music, which was excellent, was under the leadership of Mr. J. W. Atwood and Ziba Nickerson." Ziba reportedly had an excellent singing voice and conducted the singing school.

A Successful Merchant

In 1851 he opened a store in his house on the corner of Main Street and Mill Pond Road and continued to operate it for more than fifty years. Like so many stores in Chatham during the time, his carried a wide variety of goods. According to an advertisement in the *Barnstable Patriot,* his store offered "choice family groceries, flour, paper hangings, and a variety of the most popular patent medicines." Among the medicines available there was one called "Shilos's Consumption Cure," which claimed to treat not only consumption but also "coughs, hoarseness, asthma, whooping cough, and all lung or throat troubles."

Ziba Nickerson in front of his house and store. *Courtesy of Chatham, Massachusetts Historical Society.*

Besides those basic commodities, the store carried boots, shoes, various styles of rubber overshoes for men, women, girls and boys, as well as boots and men's hip boots. The same advertisement ends by listing "crockery ware, etc. etc." and adds the caveat that all are "sold at reasonable prices. Our Motto — More Cash — Less Credit. Better for Buyer and Seller.**"**

Ziba also found time to serve as the clerk and treasurer of the Universalist Parish for forty-eight years, superintendent of the Sunday school for thirty-three years, and Chatham postmaster for twenty years. Beginning in 1855 he became the first telegraph operator in Chatham – and possibly in the entire country.

An Early Telegrapher

It was in that year that Brewer and Baldwin, one of the many small companies that preceded the Western Union Company, built a line to Chatham. Recognizing the importance of this early form of rapid communication, Ziba, always a quick study, learned the code of dots and dashes that Samuel F. B Morse had begun developing in 1836.

The company set up an office in Nickerson's store, and from then until well into the 20th century, the constant clicking of the telegraph sounders was a noticeable feature there. At first the use of the telegraph was not well understood. Ziba reportedly said that on his first day on the job, he had only one customer, who came in and bought 1 cent worth of telegraphing. Later in his life Nickerson recalled those early days, telling an interviewer, "in the old days we operators were required to do the line repairing between our offices, which meant lots of hard work to keep communications established in winter time when poles would blow down by the score after seeing long service, and the rusty old wires were in a most unserviceable condition to withstand the northeast blizzards."

But after 1861 as the Civil War heated up and battles became more frequent, the telegraph office became a hub of activity. It was there people would first hear the news.

In an interview in 1901, Ziba explained, "we had a flagstaff in the rear of the office, and when good news came recording the success of our boys in blue that flag went up quickly, when everybody would hurry to the telegraph office. Then those doubting copperheads would exasperate us by doubting our dispatches and say, 'wait till the newspapers come and you'll hear a different story about your brave soldier boys, as you call them, who are trying to deprive southern people of their rights.'"

Most of Nickerson's time as a telegraph operator was spent as a marine observer from the tower on top of his house, where he and his son William stationed themselves throughout the day. Using a powerful telescope, they recorded all passing vessels and barges. They reported their sightings to ship owners in Boston so that they could prepare for off-loading cargo. Equally important were their reports of grounded or wrecked vessels. Ziba carefully noted all this activity in log books that also recorded weather conditions for each day.

Family Tragedy

In August 1863, Sarah Nickerson's brother, John Payne, launched the bark *Madelia,* which was owned by Payne and others from Chatham. Captain Payne offered Ziba and Sarah's 18-year-old son, George, the position of third mate, and he readily accepted. Payne invited his wife, Reliance, to join him, and they decided to take along their 16-year-old daughter, Madelia, for whom the vessel was named, and their 2-year-old son John, whom they doted on.

Shortly before they sailed, John Payne visited his friend Captain Nathaniel Snow and entrusted him with a tin box, saying "I'm going to China. I'm going to take my wife and oldest daughter and little Johnny. If I never return, I want you to fix up my affairs." On Nov. 12, 1863, they departed from Boston.

From a letter from Reliance Payne to her sister, Emily Doane, dated June 12, 1864, it is clear that the *Madelia* reached Hong Kong safely and had been there for several days while off-loading cargo:

My Dear Sister

It is seven months to day since wee Sailed from Boston and it seems to have been a much longer time than that to me, but with you time has passed away I presume much quicker, winter and spring has passed and you are now having warm weather at home the Same as it is here all the year around, it is healthy here and not extremely hot as yet, wee lay off about two miles from shore have a nice breeze most of the time which makes it very comfortable there is not anything very attracting on shore So I Spend most of my time on board, sewing and reading

Thin clothing is cheap here, checked Summer Silks 40 cts per yd I bought Me one the other day if I new you would like one I would get one for you, crape shalls mantillas grass linen Ivray ware, and all kind of chinese goods are cheap compared with prices at home there are Several English stores here there goods are all imported from England and the prices higher than Boston, this is a beautiful munday morning I can imagine Myrick getting up soon as the first peep of day and starting off for the point & you a washing....I suppose you see my little girls quite often I long to see them I do not worry about them for I know they are well cared for, I am going to send you Johneys and Delias miniature It is not very good for he would not stand still a second at a time after you look at it you will send it to fathers, I shall not have time to write father this morning I shall write some of you every mail as long as wee lay here wee have nothing to do yet. Freights are very dull for American vessels. Write me when you receive for if wee leave the letters will be forwarded to us.

Wee are all well so good Morning,

At some time after this letter was written, the *Madelia* left Hong Kong bound for San Francisco, but nothing more was heard from her. On Jan. 3, 1865, the following article appeared in the *Barnstable Patriot:*

> *Serious apprehensions are entertained for the safety of the bark* Madelia, *of Boston, commanded by Capt. John Payne of Chatham. She was bound from Hong Kong to San Francisco, and at the present writing has been out one hundred and seventy-five days—forty days being the average time occupied in making the passage. A son of Ziba Nickerson, Esq., of Chatham, is third mate, and the captain has his wife, oldest daughter and a son with him. The greatest solicitude is felt by the relatives and friends of those on board, as well as by the entire Chatham community, and it is fervently hoped that the noble bark, which was on her first voyage, will yet be reported as having safely arrived at her destined or some other port.*

Unfortunately the *Madelia* never reached any port. Apparently the bark was struck by a violent monsoon and foundered not long after setting out for San Francisco, taking all hands with it. Other vessels reported being caught in such a storm at that time.

Service to the Town

As difficult as it must have been to lose a young son in this way, Ziba and Sarah continued their active life and dedicated service to the town for more than forty years, with the telegraph business taking up more and more of his time.

His son, Will, learned the trade and helped with the increasing activity. They felt this responsibility so strongly that they had an additional sounder and key set up in their dining room so that they would not miss any activity on the wire during their waking hours.

Their dedication is illustrated by a doubly sad day on Oct. 14, 1904, when they were observing the foundering of the schooner *Wentworth* during a powerful storm.

Ziba and Will spelled each other at the telegraph key so that they could report the fate of the ship while sitting up with Sarah, who was on her death bed. By the next morning the *Wentworth* went down and Sarah succumbed.

As he became increasingly frail, Ziba Nickerson resigned from many of his positions. But there is no indication that he ever gave up his post at the telegraph key.

The man who was honored on his 78th birthday as the "oldest active telegraph operator in this State, if not in the country," lived until he was a month away from his 89th birthday. He died at noon on Aug. 1, 1912, while the 200th anniversary of Chatham was being celebrated. When his death was reported to the hundreds assembled for the occasion, everyone observed a moment of silence and sang a hymn of farewell.

When Gold Rush Fever Came To Town

The Story of the Chatham Mining Company

When word of the discovery of gold at Sutter's Mill swept through the United States in 1848-49, hundreds of thousands of men and women dropped everything to seek their fortunes in California – and some of those "Forty-niners" came from Chatham.

At first the news of gold nuggets waiting to be discovered in the rivers near Sacramento seemed fantastical. But when the *New York Herald* published confirmation of the report by President James K. Polk in an address to Congress, gold fever seized the country.

As newspapers reported his announcement, farmers, fishermen, doctors, lawyers, and people from all walks of life left their homes and their families in a mad dash to get to California in the hope of striking it rich. With 300,000 swarming in a frantic dash to California, the Gold Rush was second only to the Civil War in its transformative effect on the United States in the 19th century.

In Chatham, some saw an opportunity in transporting goods and people to California and then mining for themselves.

This 19th century cartoon illustrates the degree of the gold rush fever that affected people throughout the world, but especially on the Eastern Seaboard. *Courtesy Chatham, Massachusetts Historical Society.*

There were three possible routes to California at that time: overland; by ship to Panama, overland across the Isthmus and then by ship to San Francisco; or by the ocean route around Cape Horn. By spring of 1849 the effects of a heavy winter in the west had made the overland route extremely difficult; crossing the Isthmus was an expensive journey that only the wealthy could afford; and a voyage around the Horn was lengthy and fraught with danger from stormy weather. But for many of those who lived in the ports along the East Coast, rounding the Horn was a familiar experience.

By spring of 1849 gold mining companies were being organized in nearly every seaport along the Atlantic coast, including the Chatham Mining Company. In 1849 as many as 102 such companies were incorporated in Massachusetts alone and, from 1849-50, more than one hundred vessels sailed from Massachusetts ports bound for the California gold fields

Because so many Chatham men were mariners who had sailed around the Horn, it is not at all surprising that, in June 1849, eleven of them, mostly in their mid-thirties, decided to follow the hordes that were leaving weekly from Massachusetts ports to seek their fortunes in California. On July 10, ten of that group gathered in Boston to create the by-laws and regulations of the Chatham Mining Company.[7] They were: David H. Crowell, Elisha E. Atkins, Kimball R. Howes, Jr., Alvah Ryder, Stephen V. Smith, Mark H. Crowell, Samuel P. Newcomb, Richard Smith, Reuben A. Snow, and John Crowell.

John Quinn was to join them upon their arrival in California. They agreed to "become Co-Partners in the Trading and Mining Expedition to California, and such other ports and places as is most advisable and profitable for the interest of the Company," to be known as "The Chatham Trading and Mining Company."

Capital for the company came from cash paid by the incorporators of $250 each ($7,300 in 2012 dollars), the maximum payment as provided in the by-laws. The resulting $2,500 ($73,000 in 2012 dollars) in capital was to be used for provisions, cargo, "such implements as the Company may think best, and a suitable house for the Company to live in, at California."

Further, each of the stakeholders was expected to "give his personal attention, and devote his time, during reasonable hours of business, and labor wholly to the interest of the Company, … and during this agreement neither of the said parties shall engage in any speculation or be in any way interested in any other business …"

Realizing that the venture could be dangerous, the partners specified that neither sickness nor disability would deprive any of them from his share of the profits, and if anyone should die before the vessel reached California, his heirs would be entitled to his share. It was further stipulated that the co-partnership would remain in full force and be considered binding for a period of two years from July 10, 1849.

The company owned the brig *William Penn* and agreed to sail from Boston as soon as the vessel could be fully provisioned. David H. Crowell was designated master of the *Penn*, as well as president and treasurer of the company, for which he was to receive two percent of the net stock. It is evident from the full name of the company that they planned to trade along the way in addition to mining once they arrived in California. They also supplemented their funds by carrying freight, as evidenced by two entries in the ledger for July that show payments by John Tyler and Charles Blake totaling $571.50 for their shipments of freight.

In addition to the cash invested by the partners, seven men paid for passage, with all paying $150 ($4,500 in 2012 dollars), except Ensign Nickerson, who paid $200, possibly for better accommodations, and Dr. Vale paying only $50, perhaps because the balance would be paid by his serving as the ship's physician. The other passengers were Isaac Cushing, Levi L. Lincoln, John McGovern, Ebenezer Darling, and David Shepherd. Alpheus Hardy, whose company owned a number of ships at the time, paid $117.50 on account for shares in the company

These men were not alone in considering taking cargo to sell in the event that gold mining might not be as profitable as many believed. In a letter written on February 3, 1849, Richard Meade of Londonderry, New Hampshire, made a similar proposal to Captain Richard Taylor of Chatham. Meade asked Taylor if he was inclined "…to fall in with the prevailing spirit of the day and go out to the land of promise, California, where gold may be had in any quantity for less almost than the trouble that one might be put to in asking for it."

Meade's plan was to form a company of between twenty-five to seventy-five men who each would contribute an amount between $300 and $1000 to create sufficient capital to cover the cost of a ship, the requisite provisions, the crew, and other expenses incurred during a voyage around the Horn to California.

Meade planned to "…take such articles as would answer for the California market, and at the same time for some other markets – Oregon, Canton, Sandwich Islands, Sumatra, or Calcutta… to guard against a failure at California." He went on to say that besides selling their cargo, they could pick up such goods as spices in the Far East and ivory or gold dust in Africa during the voyage to sell when they returned home. In this way they would be assured of financial success even if gold proved to be elusive or nonexistent.

Captain Taylor was a part owner and the commanding officer of the bark *Helen Maria*. Richard Meade proposed that if Taylor would assume responsibility to command the ship, hire a crew, and obtain provisions for such a voyage, he would find the investors. He wrote, "I can get any amount of men in this vicinity – men of means and respectability – capital R – to engage in such an enterprise."

While the letter from Richard Meade is in the archives of the Chatham Historical Society, there is no record of Captain Taylor's response to the proposal and no knowledge of a voyage by the *Helen Maria* to California in 1849 or 1850. Nevertheless, the letter provides another case of Chatham men being tempted to go to the gold fields.

We know, however that the ten men who signed the agreement forming the Chatham Mining Company immediately began to provision their vessel and to prepare to embark as quickly as possible. On July 13 the company paid Ensign Nickerson $5.23-½ for one pick ax, one shovel, spars and poles, and tools. Other necessities bought in preparation for the trip were six wash basins, a dozen plates, six pails, a wash board, and a portable furnace.

Reuben Snow sold the company a rifle for $15, a pistol for $10.50, and two canisters of powder for $1.25. Apparently they carried no other weapons, unless they were personal arms not mentioned in the ledger.

Fully provisioned and carrying the ten partners, seven passengers, ten crew members, and a cargo of building materials, the *William Penn* sailed out of Boston Harbor on July 28, 1849. They soon were enjoying the warm waters of the Gulf Stream, but when they reached its southern end on August 4, disaster struck in the form of a violent hurricane. Although it lasted but a short time, the storm dismasted the ship and set it on its beam ends. In order to right the vessel, the crew cut away the topmasts and rigging and returned to Boston under a jury rig.

After several weeks of repairs and after taking on more provisions, the *William Penn* sailed for the second time on August 29, 1849.

While the *William Penn* was making its second voyage, another Chatham native, Thomas Dodge, was departing from Boston as master of the *Civilian,* carrying the members of the Cochituate Mining Company that had been organized by Joshua Hayward, Jr., of Salem, who had mortgaged his home for seed money. When Captain Dodge embarked, the company consisted of six crewmen and fifty-three passengers, forty-eight of whom were shareholders in the mining company. They reached St. Catherine's, just south of Rio de Janeiro, on Christmas and departed five days later to navigate the Straits of Magellan, which they accomplished without incident. But as they proceeded up the Pacific, they encountered a violent storm and limped into Valparaiso, Chile, on February 14. They finally arrived safely in San Francisco on April 5, 1850

Fliers advertising ships bound for the Gold Rush were common the East Coast between 1848 and 1850. The quality of the vessel and the name of the Master were important factors in attracting passengers. *Courtesy Chatham, Massachusetts Historical Society.*

Meanwhile on February 21, the *William Penn* arrived in San Francisco after a trip of 154 days. Apparently some of those on board either had been injured or had been taken sick, because the first item in the ledger for that day is $15.40 paid to the hospital for eleven men for six months and 25 days.

By the middle of March the brig had sailed up the river to Sacramento, the city nearest to the gold fields. Captain Crowell remained on the ship and opened a bakery that sold cookies to the miners for 50 cents a dozen, a steep price because flour in the area of the mines sold for 21 cents a pound. Being a sharp businessman, he began providing room and board for the members of the company under the name of Atkins and Crowell & Company.

As was their intention from the beginning, they had a house built for themselves near the gold fields, where it seems some of them periodically boarded. The ledger also shows that sickness was prevalent among the men in the company, as there are several entries for payment to Dr. Hart, and others for "sundries while sick." David Crowell joined in panning for gold in the nearby mountains, but his entire find was so meager that he brought it back in a bottle containing small yellow flakes that he kept for the rest of his life.

By July 1850 the ship had been sold, but the new owners continued with Captain Crowell in command, sending him on a voyage to the Sandwich Islands and Panama. When he returned to San Francisco, he learned that the owners had failed, owing him $1,400 that never was paid.

San Francisco Bay was packed with ships, many of them abandoned after delivering passengers to the gold fields.

A typical miner during the Gold Rush.
Courtesy Chatham, Massachusetts Historical Society.

Captain Crowell made a second voyage to California in 1851 as master of the bark *J.J. Cobb,* carrying thirty passengers, mostly women and children, who were going there to join their husbands and fathers who had preceded them in their quest for gold. Fortunately for these passengers, the bark experienced smooth seas and fair winds that brought them safely through the Golden Gate in just 130 days. Crowell then returned to Boston in the *Cobb,* making trading stops at the Chincha Islands off the coast of Peru and Baltimore.

With the outbreak of the Civil War, David Crowell enlisted in the United States Navy and in 1861 was assigned to the *USS Tuscarora,* which sailed from New York under orders to London, where she was put at the disposal of the American ambassador, John Quincy Adams, to bring him safely home in the event

David H. Crowell in retirement. He is shown in front of his house which still stands on Orleans Road at the beginning of Crowell Road. Courtesy Chatham, Massachusetts Historical Society.

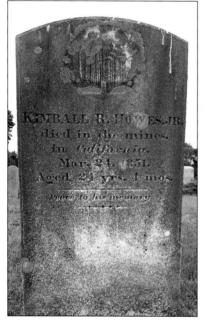

When Kimball R. Howes, Jr. died in a mine in California, this stone was erected in his memory in the Universalist Cemetery, now People's Cemetery in Chatham. *Photo by Spencer Grey.*

that England should declare war against the Union. The *Tuscarora* remained in European waters for a year and a half, defending American ships that ventured into the area. After that tour of duty Captain Crowell was forced to retire from the Navy because of sickness.

Back in Chatham he was an active member of the community for the remainder of his life, serving for nine years as the superintendent of schools and for eleven years as postmaster of Chathamport, where he operated a general store that housed the post office.

Kimball Ryder Howes, Jr., continued to search for gold for nearly a year, but he died in the mines in California on March 24, 1851. There is a stone in his memory in Chatham.

Alvah Ryder returned to Chatham and served as a corporal in the Union Army, discharged for disability on November 26, 1862.

Richard Smith, Mark Crowell, Samuel Newcomb, and Reuben Smith all continued going to sea after their adventure in California, most of them becoming captains before they retired from the sea.

Ensign Nickerson settled in San Bernardino and did not return to Chatham until August 1886, when he visited his brother Orick. A report of his visit to Chatham printed in the *Chatham Monitor* states that he was a portrait painter in his younger days and that "…several evidences of his skill now adorn the walls of Chatham homes." The *Monitor* states the Nickerson was one of only three of those who sailed on the *William Penn* still living.

Clearly none of the men who sailed to California in 1849 with high hopes of making their fortune by mining gold succeeded, but the experience undoubtedly changed their lives forever.

Toward the end of his life, David Crowell, who outlived all the others, was asked by a visitor if he had enjoyed his long years on the sea, "Yes," he replied, "but when she's on her beams' end and dips her yards under, it's then you think of home."

Captain Crowell died May 9, 1920, just seven months before his 100th birthday.

Attributed to Ensign Nickerson, this painting is believed to be a self portrait. *Courtesy Chatham, Massachusetts Historical Society.*

1862-1912

A Quiet Backwater Begins to Stir

By Debra Lawless

In 1862 the Town of Chatham passed its 150th birthday without fanfare. That summer something other than celebration preyed on the minds of those 2,710 townsfolk old enough to worry: the Civil War. President Abraham Lincoln had been inaugurated in March 1861, and the first shots of the war rang out just under six weeks later. In August, a 22-year-old clerk was the first to enlist from Chatham, and the following July voters at town meeting agreed on a bounty of $200 to each army volunteer. Eventually about 270 men of this seafaring town served in the army or navy.[1]

The Civil War marked a turning point. Although the Union prevailed, sixteen of Chatham's men were dead;[2] equally sad, some of the brutally wounded were roaming the streets, reminding all of the horror of the recent war down south.[3] Fishing declined and so did the town's population as young men sought their fortunes elsewhere. By 1912, the year of the town's bicentennial, the population had dwindled to 1,564.

During the waning days of the 19th century Chatham remained a quiet backwater where many of those who couldn't fish or sail the high seas turned to the cultivation of cranberries, or to some other agricultural pursuit. New businesses opened in the Old Village and on Main Street: Marcus W. Howard's 1873 dry goods store; Josiah M. Rogers's store for stoves, hardware and house furnishings; Hattie E. Gill's 1879 millinery and ladies' boots store; the 1886 Boston Store for dry goods; Kimble R. Howes's bakery of 1884; Samuel Atwood's 1889 market on Main Street and E.M. Nickerson's bowling alley and billiard hall.[4] Interest also stirred in establishing

Five-pointed brass stars mark the graves of Civil War soldiers and sailors in Chatham's Union Cemetery. *Photo by Debra Lawless.*

Chatham ignores its 150th birthday. About 270 men serve in the Civil War. Collins Howes, J. H. Tripp, and Asa Nye open an outfitters' store on Harding's Beach, along with a wharf on the bay side. Post offices open in South Chatham and Chatham Port.

businesses for the new tourist trade, and at least six hotels and more boarding houses opened during this period.

West Chatham, which served as a connector to South Chatham, was primarily an area of cranberry cultivation and farming. Unlike the nearby cities off-Cape, Chatham did not attract immigrants as there were no factories and this was not the land of opportunity.[5]

Always Focused on the Sea

Yet a living was still to be made by those who watched the sea, such as the keepers of the lights in Chatham, which boasted twin lights. Other lights were established at Monomoy Point and Stage Harbor. This fourth light, on Harding's Beach, went into service on July 15, 1880, shining a white light visible for twelve nautical miles.[6] Men in the U.S. Lifesaving Service plucked sailors from the dangerous shoals and reefs that cast many a ship into the waves as it rounded the Cape's elbow. Four stations of the Humane Societies Houses of Refuge were established along Chatham's beaches beginning in 1872.

In March 1902, the barge *Wadena* was wrecked off Monomoy. The barge had been stranded for several days when William Henry Mack, the 29-year-old owner from Cleveland, Ohio, arrived. He was aboard the *Wadena* when a spring storm wrecked it. The U.S. Lifesaving Crew on Monomoy tried to save Mack and his four-man crew. Seven lifesavers and five from the barge, including Mack, drowned in Shovelful Shoal, with Seth L. Ellis the sole survivor of the wreck. In October 1903 a monument with the story of the wreck was dedicated by Mack's "loving mother and sister." Like the town's Civil War monument, the Mack Monument is in the shape of an obelisk. Not until the Cape Cod Canal opened in 1914 would the peril along Chatham's famously dangerous coast lessen.

The Mack Monument was erected in 1903 after the barge *Wadena* wrecked off Monomoy in 1902. Lost were owner William Henry Mack, the *Wadena's* crew of four and seven Lifesaving Service rescuers. The obelisk-shaped monument is in a grassy area by Chatham Light. *Photo by Debra Lawless.*

By the late 19th century, Monomoy was, to all practical purposes, an island; the school that had run there for three months of the year had been closed, sold in 1862, and floated to the mainland. By 1888 children attended school in seven schoolhouses in five areas of town.[7]

The town regularized its own affairs to some extent in 1877, when it expended $5,000 to build a 45-by-65-foot building in which to conduct town business. This building would burn down

The town discusses bringing the railroad to Chatham.

L. D. Buck starts a grocery store in West Chatham.

1863

1865

in 1919, sadly taking with it many of Chatham's historical records. Fortunately, the Harvard-trained attorney William C. Smith had long before begun work on his four-volume *A History of Chatham, Massachusetts*, the first volume of which he published in 1909. Still, Smith was hampered in his

The Town Hall was built in 1877 at a cost of $5,000. Town business was conducted on the first floor while dances were held upstairs. A smoldering cigarette left after a dance was blamed for the 1919 fire that destroyed the building and many historic documents. *Photo courtesy of Chatham, Massachusetts Historical Society.*

research by another fire at the beginning of this period, in September 1861. The parsonage of the Congregational Church burned one evening while the Reverend Edward B. French and his wife were attending a prayer meeting. This fire wiped out the records of the Congregational Church whose history was inextricably entwined with that of the town from the early days, when William Nickerson arrived.[8] Soon after this fire, French volunteered for the Civil War and became a chaplain in the army.[9]

A Trickle of Visitors See the Beauty

The latter half of the 19th century was, in a sense, a post-war era when the town woke up and slowly recreated itself in its modern image. Everything was in place – the awesome and beautiful waters on three sides, the many ponds, the enviable climate – but only a trickle of visitors from elsewhere had discovered the town's natural charms. The train, which finally connected Chatham to the rest of Cape Cod and Boston, in 1887, would promote tourism. Hotel Chatham, which opened in 1890, had its own train stop but alas the luxurious hotel's position off the beaten path, in Chatham Port, killed it by 1895.[10]

Yet by 1912, when the town celebrated its bicentennial, townspeople seemed to have some inkling of where the town was headed. During an August weekend of games, food and gaiety, those who stood up and addressed the crowds nodded more than once to the tourists and visitors among

A new Congregational Church is built on the corner of Main Street and Old Harbor Road, using material from the one in Union Cemetery.

A monument in Sears Park is dedicated to those who "fell in the late war."

1866

1867

them. The fifty years between 1862 and 1912 are, then, a kind of stepping stone between the slower, isolated world that had always been and the fast-paced, electrically-lighted, fossil-fuel powered world of the future.

CIVIL WAR IN CHATHAM

After an "almost sleepless night" Samuel Harding of the Massachusetts 58th Infantry Regiment wrote home to his wife Hannah to report that his cousin Lt. Franklin D. Hammond, age 32, "has ended his duty on earth." The previous Thursday, June 23, 1864, Hammond took a picketball – a lethal .45-caliber bullet – through his bowels before the Siege of Petersburg, Virginia. He lived for about 15 minutes in turmoil, then died. Embalmed by a Dr. Burr for $50, he was then dressed in a pair of drawers, a shirt, and a pair of stockings that Harding obtained from the Massachusetts Soldiers Relief Association. Hammond was shipped back home and buried in Seaside Cemetery.

The Soldiers Monument was erected to honor those whose lives were lost in the Civil War. Dedicated in July 1867, the obelisk in Sears Park was originally surrounded by an iron fence. *Photo courtesy of Chatham, Massachusetts Historical Society.*

Before the war Harding was a master carpenter and Hammond a mason. When he died, Hammond left his wife Basheba and three children ages 6 through 13.

Hammond's name is one of thirteen carved on the fifteen-foot Chatham Soldiers' Monument dedicated to "the memory of our soldiers who fell in the late war of the Rebellion."[11]

During a July evening in 1867, just about two years after the war ended, a crowd gathered in the center of town on a triangle of grass called Sears Park. They stood just below Joshua Nickerson's flat-topped Italianate house built four years previously. It was an evening of "favorable" weather, and the group sang, prayed, and listened to scripture readings as it gazed at the recently unveiled monument.[12]

The structure was an obelisk made of granite and Italian marble and capped with an urn spanning 10 inches. For many years a sturdy iron fence surrounded the monument.

The village school house is built on School Street.

A storm on November 14 breaks through North Beach.

1869

1870

Obelisks were the shape of choice for 19th century cemeteries and monuments commemorating the dead. Napoleon introduced Egypt to the world with his expeditions of 1798-99, and as many associated Egypt with the mortuary arts, Egyptian revival architecture was often used in mortuaries and cemeteries.[13] Yet the obelisk was a symbol of timelessness, and one that pointed to the sky, to heaven. So its association for the dead was also one of promise: We will not forget you. The Washington Monument was completed in 1884 and, closer to home, the Bunker Hill Monument in Charlestown was completed in 1843.

So common did the use of the obelisk become, in fact, that when Provincetown residents wanted to erect a monument to commemorate the Pilgrims' landing, they deliberately turned away from the obelisk shape and instead chose a 13th century Italian tower.[14]

James H. Jenks of West Dennis chiseled the names of thirteen of Chatham's fallen soldiers on the monument. Some today believe the names of at least four other Chatham residents who died as a result of the Civil War were erroneously left off the monument. Others are disturbed by the apparent misspelling of the battle of "Coal Harbor," which they want changed to the proper "Cold Harbor." But Coal Harbor was a common error of the day, begun by a New York newspaperman's misunderstanding after the June 1864 battle there.

Giddings Hyde Ballou
Crosses into the Spirit Land

It was very dry that spring of 1886, the spring before the portrait painter Giddings Hyde Ballou died. All over Chatham, when acquaintances met, the conversation turned to the lack of rain, and to the dryness of the streets where horses' hooves kicked the sand and the dust of the roads into the air.

And then, on May 11, a Saturday, "copious and abundant showers" made everything green.[15]

It was in the evening of Tuesday, June 8, just under two weeks before the longest day, as the light glimmered on and on into the evening, when Ballou "passed quietly into the spirit land" after "a long, lingering and wasting sickness."[16] Ballou had been born off-Cape in Stafford, Connecticut, in 1820 and raised in Roxbury, Massachusetts, where his father, a Universalist minister, ran a private school in his home. In 1840 he traveled to Cape Cod on a health cure for his bad lungs and in 1867 married into Chatham's extended Atwood family.[17]

But by 1886, despite Piso's Cure for Consumption which "Cures Where All Else Fails" and also "Tastes Good," Ballou's time had run out.[18]

Ballou died in the house his wife Azubah's first husband, a ship's captain, had built at 177 Cross Street. When James Snow Taylor married Azubah Collins Atwood in 1838 he may have dreamed of a large family. The impressive Federal-style house, with its central cupola that seemed to

Chatham Monitor first published, edited by Dr. Benjamin D. Gifford.

Atkins Eldredge opens a hotel, the Eldredge House, on Main Street.

Monomoy Life Saving Station is established; Josiah Hardy becomes fourth keeper of Chatham's twin lights.

1871

1872

Giddings Hyde Ballou, an itinerant portrait painter who married a Chatham widow, is remembered in a tintype photo of the sort that took away his livelihood recording likenesses. *Photo courtesy of Chatham, Massachusetts Historical Society.*

look out to sea, was made for such a dream. But Taylor and Azubah had but one daughter, whom they adopted. Taylor died in 1861, at age 45, a few months after the beginning of the Civil War. When his widow married Ballou she was beyond the age of child-bearing; all hopes of filling the bedrooms with laughing children were past.

Ballou's funeral was held in the afternoon three days after his death. His father Hosea – who was appointed the first president of Tufts College – and mother Clarissa, as well as his five younger sisters and brother Charles, had already crossed through the veil before him, so the Ballou side of the family was represented solely by his brother-in-law the Reverend Russell A. Ballou of Boston, who had been married to Giddings's late sister Harriet.[19]

Azubah, too, hailed from a large family of five girls and a boy. Some tension was, perhaps, buzzing among the Atwoods gathered around Ballou's coffin because just about a month previously Azubah's niece, Mrs. Patia A. Chase, brought suit against Azubah and attached her aunt's house to the tune of $5000 for "alleged slander and defamation of character." Chase was the daughter of Azubah's older sister Patience, who also used the nickname Patia. Yet a week after Chase brought suit it was announced in the *Chatham Monitor* that Azubah settled with Chase by paying costs. "Mrs. Ballou declared herself innocent of the charge, but preferred to pay the costs and avoid further controversy." What Azubah said, and why Patia deemed it so offensive, remains unclear.[20]

The Reverend Henry M. Couden of the Universalist Church conducted the service, assisted by the Reverend L.P. Atwood of the Congregational Church who read the scripture and closing prayer. The Reverend Couden was blind, and perhaps spoke extemporaneously or had memorized pertinent passages of the Bible. Couden, who came from Ohio, was maimed in the Civil War. "Total blindness in both eyes... compelled him to study and earn his living as a clergyman."[21] Perhaps Couden mastered Braille, which was developed in 1825 by a blind Frenchman, to conduct his Biblical studies.

But blindness was not Couden's only trial. Two years previously his wife Lydia Jane, a Dickinson from Amherst, had

Azubah Atwood Ballou married Giddings Hyde Ballou in 1867. She would outlive Giddings by 26 years, dying in 1912. *Photo courtesy of Chatham, Massachusetts Historical Society.*

Distance from twin lights to bank is 190 feet; four years later the distance is 38 feet.

West Chatham and North Chatham schools are built

1874

1875

died suddenly, leaving him with four small children. Couden was then just one year into his ministry in Chatham. Lydia's sister Julia and Couden's own sister traveled to Chatham after Lydia's funeral to help Couden raise the children.[22]

While the Atwoods were active Congregationalists, the Ballous were Universalists. Ballou's great uncle, in fact, was a founder of the Universalist sect in America.[23] The Universalist choir sang and the coffin bumped down the front steps with Capt. Hiram Harding, Erastus Nickerson, Kimble Ryder, and Capt. Elijah Crosby bearing the load at the four corners. Ryder, a fisherman, was the youngest of the pallbearers at 32. Harding and Crosby were both master mariners in their 60s, and Nickerson was a grocer.

The coffin, now on some kind of wooden hearse pulled by a horse, most likely traveled north up Cross Street, hooked a left on Main, and progressed down to Union Cemetery and the Atwood family plot. To older people, the front of the cemetery still looked bare, as the boxy white Congregational Church had been dismantled and trundled, piece-by-piece, to a low hill on the corner of Main Street and Old Harbor Road, where it became known later as "the little church on the hill." The move divided the congregation and by January 1867, when the new church was officially rededicated, the church counted thirty-three men and eighty-two women as members. Two months later two prominent men in town, Levi Atwood and N. Snow, were delegated to "visit and confer with members not attending public worship with this Church." It is not known if they were able to boost membership or not, as many of the disaffected had already joined the Methodists.[24]

The Reverend Henry Couden of Ohio was blinded in the Civil War and, being unfit for physical work, entered the ministry. He was prominent in Chatham's Universalist church after 1883. *Photo courtesy of Chatham, Massachusetts Historical Society.*

Ballou knew a great many people in town – you could say all of them – because in 1880, employed as a government census taker, he trudged from house to house, covering every house in thirty days, taking off only Sundays. He began on Tuesday, June 1, with a visit to the vast Howes family. If Franklin Howes, a 52-year-old master mariner, was at sea, Ballou probably interviewed his 42-year-old wife Mercy, a mother of eight, who had a 19-year-old servant named Nellie Bassett to help her.[25]

On and on Ballou walked and rode, day after day, house after house, duly noting the names and ages of the Atwoods, Bearses, Eldredges, Eldridges, Hardings, Hardys, Howes, Goodspeeds, Kendricks, Nickersons, Ryders, and Smiths – all the good old names of Chatham. Unlike

New Town Hall is built at a cost of $5,000. A third set of twin lights is built and opened farther from the bank than the previous set.

The house and farm of James Taylor in West Chatham is bought as the town poor farm. Oliver Eldredge runs a marine railway at what later becomes Kenney's Dock.

1877

1878

enumerators off-Cape in the urban areas, Ballou would have few foreign names to puzzle out and few exotic places of birth to note. Just about everyone in Chatham was a white person born in Massachusetts of parents also born in Massachusetts.

On June 7, Ballou visited Chatham's twin lights and enumerated the two families living there: Lightkeeper Josiah Hardy, 58, his wife Harriet, 56, and their son Samuel, 9, a schoolboy. Also living there were assistant lightkeeper Cyrenus Hamilton, 68, a widower, and his widowed daughter Eunice Smith, 43, who kept house for him.

Hardy had retired from the sea in 1871, and the following year became assistant keeper of the Chatham Lights. By the end of that year he was the keeper of the lights, a post he would hold until 1900. Due to a violent storm on November 15, 1870, that broke through the outer beach, the sea was inching closer and closer to the twin lights as erosion took its toll on the bank. A new pair of towers, set back from the bluff, was opened in September 1877, the same year the new town hall opened. In November, Hardy and his wife moved into the new keeper's residence, a substantial cottage with three fireplaces. At 1 P.M. on December 15, 1879, the south tower tumbled down the embankment.[26] When the north tower fell 15 months later, pirates' pieces-of-eight were found, creating a frenzy among townsfolk bent on finding more coins.[27]

These twin lights replaced earlier lights that fell into the sea after a period of coastal erosion. Lightkeeper Josiah Hardy and his family lived in the house between the lights. When the northern light was removed in 1923 it caused a hue and cry. *Photo courtesy of Chatham, Massachusetts Historical Society*

On the Saturday before the summer solstice and on the solstice itself, Ballou filled out five sheets, according to his records, visiting fifty-one families on the 21st alone. He took it easy the following week before heading out to Monomoy on Wednesday, June 30, where he finished his task by enumerating the family living in the Monomoy Point Lighthouse: Asa L. Jones, the 39-year-old keeper of the light and a wounded Civil War veteran suffering from chronic neuralgia

South tower of the twin lights falls into the sea on December 15.

Universalist Church is built on Main Street.
Stage Harbor Light established and first lighted on July 15.
Captain Levi D. Smith carries the last cargo of natural ice to Barbados.

1879

1880

and rheumatism;[28] his 29-year-old wife Clara; their 5-year-old son Maro; and, oddly, a 12-year-old "mulatto" named Joseph P. Chisholm from South Carolina, listed as their boarder.[29] On the census form the lighthouse was dwelling number 523 or the 596th and final household.

Ballou knew Monomoy well. During Monomoy's winter school terms of 1856 to 1861 Ballou taught teenage fishermen the three R's. When the Civil War began in April 1861, Ballou forsook his bed at Monomoy's Monomoit House, where the "window casings rattled, and the latchless door banged throughout the night."[32] He traveled off-Cape, possibly to Washington, D.C. where he reported on the war for the *Gospel Banner*, a Universalist weekly based in Augusta, Maine, from 1863 to 1864.[33] Following that he held government jobs in the Capitol. Eventually he returned to Chatham and to the bed of Azubah Atwood Taylor, whom he married on May 2, 1867, just before her 50th birthday. The couple may have lived for a time in Washington as Azubah's obituary says she attended receptions at the White House during the 1869 to 1877 terms of President Ulysses S. Grant.[34]

Azubah Collins Atwood Taylor Ballou was born on June 27, 1817, and named after her paternal grandmother. She lived on what was then called Atwood Street (today's Stage Harbor Road) surrounded by relatives. Her father, Joseph, was a grandson of the builder of the 1752 house that is now the Chatham Historical Society's Atwood House Museum at 347 Stage Harbor Road. Azubah herself grew up in an 1812 Federal style house at 223 Stage Harbor Road, just down Cross Street from the house to which she moved as a bride.[35]

If Ballou painted either his wife or his step-daughter, also named Azubah, these paintings are yet to be found. He did, however, paint the man who would later become his brother-in-law, Dr. Joseph Atwood, Chatham's "mechanical" dentist for 48 years.

Dr. Atwood still lived in the family home, now with his wife Alzira. Their daughter Nina was, at the time of Ballou's funeral, 11 years old.

Dr. Atwood invented a patent medicine called "Atwood's Pain Destroying Victor. Try It Once and You Will Always Use It," as a newspaper ad said.[36] The good dentist, in a testimonial, said that he took it for a cough from which he suffered every Chatham winter. Another patient, who suffered from "bleeding piles" for 18 years – "the name is withheld from motives of delicacy" – was also cured after bathing his delicate parts with a mixture of Victor and water.

In April 1849, Ballou painted Atwood not with a bottle of Victor but with two plaster jaws and a set of false teeth lying on the table in front of him. In his hand is a pair of dental pliers.

Two days after Ballou was buried, on Sunday, June 13, it was sprinkling, with a moderate shower in the afternoon and evening. It was so cool that "furs and overcoats are comfortable."[37] One wonders what Azubah, about to celebrate her 69th birthday, was thinking now, back alone in the big house with the summer about to start and herself widowed for the second time by husbands who both died coughing.[38] She did, in fact, have 26 years of widowhood ahead of her. Eventually she was known for her lilac bushes; the house her first husband built for his bride was known as "Azubah" until the 1950s, when it became a guest house called "Hiawatha."

On the morning of March 27, 1912, Azubah, perhaps "the oldest lady citizen in town," died, just before Chatham geared up to celebrate its bicentennial in high style.[39]

North tower of lighthouse falls into the sea on March 26

Town Meeting votes to require the constable to enforce the law relating to Sabbath-breaking in any form. On a motion to see if the town will grant licenses to sell intoxicating beverages, the vote is 65 no; 5 yes.

1881

1882

Go to Union Cemetery now on a peaceful summer morning and you'll find the whole town, all those Atwoods and Nickersons and Youngs, who loved each other and hated each other. Some died quietly in town, some died screaming with fever in exotic parts of the world. They're all lying here now, silent, their places marked with stones set among the yellow dandelions. Azubah Atwood Taylor Ballou lies in the Atwood plot with James Taylor on one side and Giddings Ballou on the other. Lichen climbs over the stones. All are at rest.

Giddings Hyde Ballou lies at rest on one side of his wife Azubah in the Atwood family section of Chatham's Union Cemetery. *Photo by Debra Lawless.*

First telephone comes to town.

Sylvester Small opens the Travelers' Home, now Cranberry Inn.

1883

1884

PORTRAIT PAINTERS AND PHOTOGRAPHERS

The itinerant portrait painter Giddings Hyde Ballou first ventured to Cape Cod in about 1840, when he was 20 years old. He returned in 1847, boarding with a local lawyer in Brewster. While there, Ballou began painting the shipmasters of Brewster and their families, charging $15 or $20 for a portrait.[40]

In Chatham in 1856, Ballou painted Joseph Atwood's wife Alzira. That same year he painted Joseph and Alzira's daughter Nina Modesta. In about 1850 he painted Atwood's sister Patia Howes. And eventually he painted Polly Atwood Sparrow, Ephraim Taylor, and Thankful Taylor. He also painted Elwina Clarence Smith, who died at the age of 6 of "fitts." This portrait of the little girl may well be posthumous, after a convention of the time. Ballou never signed his paintings, and through scholarly efforts many were identified over 150 years later by Ellen St. Sure, who directed the Ballou Project in 2003.

Ballou joined the ranks of the itinerant painters at precisely the moment when the profession was on the wane, challenged by roving photographers who charged less. Already in the 1840s photographers began to replace painted likenesses.[41] By the end of the 19th century, demand for the "product of the itinerant limner" was gone forever.[42] In June 1850, Ballou took out an ad in the *Barnstable Patriot* stating that he would be available to paint portraits at the widow Francis Hallet's in Yarmouth Port "for a short time." He also announced in November that he would execute portraits from Daguerreotypes rather than from live models.[43]

In December 1871, the photographer J.W. Ryder announced in the *Chatham Monitor* that he would be in town for a brief time. Ryder could be found at the "Old Stand Over R. Bearse's Clothing Store" for two weeks.

"This is the cheapest place to get pictures on Cape Cod," his ad advised. Four ferrotypes on cards were $1; a dozen tintypes were 25 cents – a far cry from $20 or more for a painted portrait.

And in 1886 the photographer Heath was located over E.T. Bearse's Jewelry Store on Main Street. Ferrotypes were now four for 75 cents. "View of residences made to order."

Tintypes were inexpensive instant photos recorded on sheet iron. Because they took only a few minutes to develop, they were a favorite technology of roving street photographers. And because ferrotypes and tintypes were the same thing, Ryder's ad must have been distinguishing prices based on their size. In 1863 a card was patented to display the metal images in photo albums.[44]

By 1887, photographer M.N. Shorey was pulling at the heart strings by describing a mother who failed to have her child's photo taken because she believed it was too expensive. Wasn't that mother sorry when her baby died! "Mother, don't let this be your sad experience, improve the present, the future is uncertain."[45]

The future might be uncertain but it was clear that photography, not portrait painting, would be the trend of days to come.

Dr. Gifford makes a motion at town meeting that druggists be appointed to sell intoxicating beverages for "medicinal, mechanical, and chemical purposes." The vote is 18 no, 22 yes.

1885

Dr. Benjamin Gifford and Chatham's Epidemics of 1888

As the "cold, blustering" winds of February howled outside, the nine sick, feverish Kendrick children huddled in their beds in the farm house in West Chatham.

The faces of the sick children – seven boys and two girls – were flushed, as though sunburned, with a pale area around their lips. Their skin felt rough as sandpaper and their tongues resembled strawberries. Some were hot, despite the chill in the air, with fevers of 101 degrees or higher.

Dr. Benjamin Gifford lived on Cross Street in this spacious white Greek Revival house. In outbuildings he ran his medical office and a pharmacy where he sold children's books, perfume, cigar cases and toiletries as well as drugs. *Photo by Debra Lawless.*

Scarlet fever was the diagnosis that Dr. Benjamin D. Gifford gave. Gifford, who had been appointed by the town board of health as its physician and agent after the epidemic began, rode in his four-wheeler between the isolated farm houses a couple of miles west of town hall. For his duties that year of 1888 the board of health would pay him $71.30, money that most probably felt was well spent.[46]

Scarlet fever, often called scarlatina in the 19th century, was caused by the bacteria *A Streptocuccus* and was spread through a cough or a sneeze or by sharing a drinking glass or fork. A hand that had come into contact with the bacteria carelessly dabbing an eye or a lip could also spread the disease. Children were the most susceptible.

As the winter wind blew, Captain John Kendrick, 45, a farmer who had recently given up life on the sea, and his wife Eunice, 44, tended the nine ailing children. Perhaps Eunice's young unmarried cousin, Rebecca Young, 27, who shifted among various branches of the Kendrick families working as a servant, also helped cool the children's fevers, feed and bathe them.[47] The patients ranged in age from John Jr., who had just turned 17 on February 2, to the baby, little Albert, who was 3. The Kendricks lived on what is today's Route 28, east of Barn Hill Road.[48]

Despite the distance between the farms, the disease fanned out of the Kendrick house and infected children in five other families. Altogether twenty-one children fell ill.

Gifford, who had been practicing medicine in Chatham since 1871, sometimes serving as the sole physician for the town, recognized the danger. He may have known that many years before, in the midst of the Civil War, an epidemic of scarlet fever rushed through Fredericksburg, Virginia, killing one hundred or more children in the late fall of 1861.

The Crystal Spring Laundry opens in what later becomes the Sail Loft, with Walter Eldredge as proprietor.

1885

In the *Chatham Monitor*,[49] Gifford spelled out guidelines as agent of the Board of Health. If scarlet fever was present in a household, Gifford must be notified. It was forbidden to enter a dwelling where the afflicted lay. Members of the family were forbidden to communicate with outside persons, except in a few instances. And finally, the same regulations applied in cases of diphtheria. As a precaution, Gifford closed the schools in West and North Chatham.[50]

"It is difficult for some to realize that a mild and easy case of scarlet fever or diphtheria is capable of communicating the disease in its worst and most fatal form," Gifford noted the following July.

It is ironic that on February 21, around the time the epidemic was incubating, an unsigned

Main Street near Dr. Benjamin Gifford's house. The doctor rode in his four-wheeler to visit the scarlet fever patients in the isolated farm houses a couple of miles west of the center of town. *Collection of Debra Lawless.*

article in the *Monitor* – very likely written by Gifford himself – proclaimed that "it would probably be difficult to find a town in Massachusetts where so few deaths of children occur in proportion to the inhabitants as in Chatham. The death of a child under 10... is quite [a] rare occurrence." In the nine-year period from 1879 to 1887 a total of nineteen children died – about two per year.

Today scarlet fever, once diagnosed, is treated with antibiotics. In the late 19th century nothing could be done but nurse the patient and pray for the best.

Sweating was among the "allopathic" medicine methods of the day that included bleeding, leeching, cupping, blistering, purging, puking, poulticing, plastering, and rubbing with toxic agents. The idea was to cast the disease from the body. A common purgative was calomel, a form of mercuric chloride that often caused more harm than the condition for which it was prescribed. By the second half of the 19th century, however, medicine was advancing on the heels of Frenchman Louis Pasteur's pioneering discoveries in microbiology. Doctors finally gave credence to the germ theory.

When he visited a contagious case Gifford donned a suit of clothes and overcoat that he kept in an old valise, swabbed over with carbolic acid, in the barn of the patient's home. He also "washed well with carbolic before leaving," his daughter Minnie Gifford Buck would recall in 1925.[51]

Despite all precautions, on March 3 one of the Kendrick's nine would die – Alonzo, the next to the youngest, at 6 "a bright little son."[52]

Mrs. Hattie Baxter opens the Baxter House on Old Wharf Road for paying guests opposite the Old Red Tavern; The last Salt Works closes at Eastward Point.

The Rhode Island House on Holway Street is opened as a boarding house. It later becomes Dill House.

1886

It was no doubt a dreary day when the eight convalescents observed their young brother removed from the house in a coffin. Little snow fell in Chatham during these short, late winter days, yet off-Cape the winter was marked by unusual snowfall. What was later known as the famous Blizzard of '88 dumped up to four feet of snow in Boston, downed telegraph lines and stopped trains. Here in Chatham the thirty-six-hour storm on March 11 and 12 would be nothing more than "an ordinary easterly gale." On March 13 the temperature hovered at 23 degrees.[53]

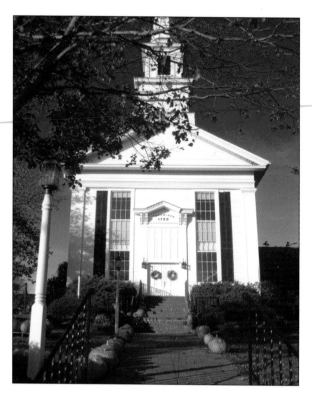

In 1872, Dr. Benjamin Gifford founded a Masonic Lodge that met in the vestry of the Congregational Church on Main Street. By 1890 the lodge boasted a regular membership of forty-seven. *Photo by Debra Lawless.*

Gifford, 46 in 1888, was used to Cape Cod's raw weather. A native of Provincetown, he was a son of Simeon, a trader, and Marinda, after whom Gifford would name his elder daughter. Gifford took his medical degree in 1866 at Albany Medical College and practiced medicine for five years in Fond du Lac, Wisconsin, and Gloucester, Massachusetts. By the time Gifford and his wife Mary Elizabeth moved to Chatham in 1871, they were the parents of two young daughters. Marinda, known as Minnie, was born in 1868 and Romenia was born two years later.

From the time of his arrival, Gifford had many irons in the fire. In October 1871 Gifford founded the *Monitor*, a weekly newspaper published every Tuesday evening. Although after two years he turned over the editorship to Levi Atwood, Gifford continued to toil at various aspects of the paper. All requests for subscriptions and orders for printing were to be left at Gifford's office.

Noting that the town had no Masonic presence, in 1872 he founded a lodge that met in the vestry of the Congregational Church on Main Street. By 1890 the lodge boasted a regular membership of forty-seven.

In 1882, Gifford bought a spacious white house on Cross Street, a block from Main Street. In outbuildings he ran his medical office and also a pharmacy where he sold children's books, perfume, cigar cases and toiletries as well as drugs. The 1828 Greek revival house would remain in the family until 1940, when his daughter Minnie blew herself up in a "freak gas explosion" in the old round cellar and died a few hours later from her injuries.

The Chatham Railway Company begins operations and the depot is built.
The Stage Harbor Packet to New Bedford ceases operations.

1887

For many years Gifford covered a territory with a radius of about ten miles, sending cases of extreme emergency to Boston on the train. (Until 1887 a patient had to travel by stage coach to Harwich to board the Boston train. Bringing a train spur to Chatham was one of Gifford's editorial crusades in the *Monitor*.) Dr. Gifford named his own horses for drugs: Cassia, Stellengia, Belladonna, Victoria. The cat in his drug dispensary was Physic.

During that bleak winter of '88 Gifford had no sooner isolated the scarlet fever in West and North Chatham when diphtheria broke out in South Chatham. The houses there were built closer together than those in West Chatham; Gifford again quarantined those households where the disease had struck.

Diphtheria is an acute infectious disease caused by the bacteria *Corynebacterium diphtheriae*. It is spread through coughs and sneezes and it, like scarlet fever, causes a sore throat. A tough, fiber-like gray-to-black covering can block the airways, suffocating its victim and giving the disease the gruesome nickname "the strangling angel of children." A tube was often inserted into the patient's throat to allow the patient to breathe.

As that winter gradually gave way to spring and a few snowbells stuck their heads above the ground,

In the late 19th century, houses were set far apart and travel was slow and dusty on roads of rutted sand. This house overlooks Oyster Pond. *Collection of Debra Lawless.*

Gifford ordered the houses of the diphtheria patients disinfected with carbolic acid and chloride of lime. After that the houses were fumigated with a sulfurous acid vapor. In some cases the houses were re-papered and re-painted inside, "these precautions not seeming unnecessary under the peculiar circumstances," Gifford wrote a few months later, in July, in the 1888 *Report of the Town Officers*.

Daffodils were blooming on April 24 when Benjamin F. Chase, one month short of his 4th birthday, died of diphtheria at the home of his parents Heman and Emma Chase. Chase was the second child to die in the epidemics of 1888.

Luxurious Hotel Chatham opens on what is now the fourth fairway of Eastward Ho! Country Club.
The old grist mill is in operation, with Zena Nickerson as proprietor.

1890

Both Gifford and his wife Mary promoted public health and so encouraged Minnie, after her 1886 graduation from Chatham High, to study dentistry. In 1889 Minnie graduated from Philadelphia Dental College (now part of Temple University), one of eight women in a class of 98.

Minnie began to practice dentistry as Gifford continued to treat cases ranging from obstetrics and appendectomies to accidents and shipwreck victims. For several years after 1893 Minnie practiced in Boston until illness struck the Gifford family. In about 1900 Mary died of pneumonia and about a year later Romenia died of consumption. At some point Minnie moved back to Chatham, probably to serve as caregiver to the invalids. When Gifford's mother Marinda could no longer live on her own in Provincetown, Gifford arranged for her to move into the Cross Street house under Minnie's care. For forty more years Minnie practiced dentistry in the house where her father had practiced medicine for so many years.

At age 64, Gifford remained a man of unusual vitality. He took a new wife, Alice Pike, who was thirty-two years his junior, exactly half his age. Gifford and Alice, who was born in Maine,

CLYDE LINE S.S."ONONDAGA" ASHORE ON CHATHAM BEACH, CAPE COD. SUNDAY MORNING, JAN. 13, 1907.

The S.S. *Onondaga* came ashore on a Chatham beach on January 13, 1907. This was one of the many mishaps and wrecks that occurred at Chatham and Monomoy before the Cape Cod Canal opened in 1914, making it unnecessary for ships to travel around the Cape's elbow. *Collection of Debra Lawless.*

At Town Meeting, fifty women who had previously registered are allowed to vote for the school committee for the first time.

Captain George Eldred reports four breaks in North Beach allowing water to flow into Stage Harbor. This might be stopped for $1,832.20. On June 27, 1891, voters appropriate $1,500 to protect Stage Harbor.

1891

tactfully established a new household up the street from where his mother and daughter lived. At just about that time Minnie, a day short of her 39th birthday, married a retired seafaring man named Benjamin Buck. Benjamin was about fourteen years Minnie's senior and got along well with Gifford, with whom he shared a passion for popular melodramatic plays. Two years later in 1909, Minnie bore her only daughter, Josephine.

By 1909, Gifford had scaled back his office hours. He would see patients before noon and after 3 P.M. only, giving over the middle of the day to lunch and perhaps a siesta. Or perhaps he continued his newspaper work, or his work for the Masons. His medical practice at this time was "especially devoted to diseases of the eye, including correction of poor sight, ear, nose and throat."[54] A couple of years later, after he retired, he was elected to the state House of Representatives.

On May 16, 1918, a year and a month after the United States entered the Great War, Gifford died of pneumonia at age 76. He did not live to witness the Spanish influenza epidemic that would strike the entire world that fall. Soon the widowed Alice Gifford would register with the Metropolitan Chapter of the Red Cross in answer to an emergency call for nurses.

A few years after his death Minnie Buck called her father "human, full of frailties but inherently a friend to man, to suffering mankind, full of sacrifices that no one can now fathom."

"MEET ME IN HEAVEN"

The perils of life in the second half of the 19th century were many. Sailors died at sea during storms and shipwrecks. People burned to death in unquenchable fires, and they committed suicide. Many others died in infancy, or in childbirth, or of terrible diseases.

Read a 19th century necrology and you're bound to spot a few causes of death that are unfamiliar. Here is an anthology of death as written by the town clerk in Chatham's *Town Annual Reports* of the late 1890s. Definitions follow.

Acute mania: A violent derangement of the mind, insanity.
Apoplexy: Gross hemorrhage. Paralysis due to stroke.
Bright's Disease: Any of several diseases causing degeneration of the kidneys.
Consumption: Tuberculosis, a wasting of the body.
Dropsy: Accumulation of water, edema.
Erysipelas: Streptococcal cellulitis of skin, St. Anthony's Fire. Redness of some part of the skin, accompanied with fever.
Exhaustion: Loss of strength through excessive voiding or lack of food, fatigue or disease.

The *Chatham Gazette* begins publication.
The 1790 schoolhouse is moved to West Chatham near the present Jordon Village. It becomes a paint shop and is struck by lighting and burned in 1930.

1892

Hardening of stomach: Induration caused by inflammation or accumulation of blood.

Softening of brain: Due to stroke, hemorrhage or inflammation.

Marasmus: Wasting away of body tissues, in infants and those under three. Probably caused by a protein deficiency.

Overdose of morphine. Morphine was a legal drug.

Paralytic insanity: May result from syphilis.

Puerperal fever: A fatal infection after childbirth.

Suppurative pylaphlibitis: Inflammation of the portal vein to the liver.

Uremia: Complex biochemical abnormality occurring in kidney failure.

In the 19th century before antibiotics, improvements in child birth and sanitary measures, many were the ways of death. Maria "Fannie" Brown, buried in Chatham's Seaside Cemetery, was hit by a train in 1879 at the age of 16. *Photo by Debra Lawless.*

Josephine Atkins and the Tragic Kingdom

It was a summer visitor, one Dr. White, who first spotted the orange flames licking the black pre-dawn sky. The roof of the barn was engulfed.

Dr. White, whose horse was one of three horses in the barn, dashed from his room into the yard to give the alarm. Within seconds, it seemed, the owner of the house, retired sea Captain James A. Kent, appeared in the yard with a couple of neighbors.

Imagine this: The smell of burning wood and hay and feathers and the terrified whinnying of the horses in the flaming barn. Horses are strange animals; they won't willingly leave a burning barn. If you don't toss a blanket over them they won't come out. And if you don't tether them at a safe distance before removing their blankets, they'll dash back into the fire. Together, working in only the light of the blaze, the men saved the three horses and several carriages from the barn. The fire was so intense however, that they were unable to pull out two hogs and a flock of poultry.

Charles Andrew Howes buys the Crystal Spring Laundry and opens a sail loft.

1893

Kent dashed across the yard to warn his wife, Almena, that the fire might reach the house. Earlier in the evening, the winds had been heavy. Although the winds had died down after midnight, you never knew what a fire might do. The captain re-emerged in the yard, heading back to the burning barn, and then appeared to trip. He lay on the ground without moving. The neighbors carried him into the house where he "died in about five minutes from heart failure, caused by the excitement." It was strange, in a way, that the captain died like that because just the previous Sunday he had marched with the Odd Fellows in church and seemed perfectly fine.

The remaining men continued to fight the fire and, when the blazing barn was reduced to a sickening smolder, they turned their attention to the house and the other buildings, running them over with water from a hose.

When dawn came, Almena's husband lay dead and the barn was burned to the ground. Later the men blamed the spontaneous blaze on combustion from the sweet-smelling new-mown hay that had been siloed in the barn just a few days earlier. It was August 24, 1896.

Fire. It was a constant threat. Every day a housewife used fire to light lamps and light stoves. Houses were heated by fires in the hearth, and sometimes burning cinders ignited the roof. Yet with the threat so pressing, there was no organized fire department. Chatham residents were well aware of the famous Chicago fire in October 1871, supposedly started when Mrs. O'Leary's cow kicked over a lantern. Samuel M. Nickerson, a native of Chatham, lost his "elegant residence and its contents" in the fire that destroyed four square miles of Chicago.

Yet as a commentator in the *Chatham Monitor* noted, "not even a bell is rung to warn us of our danger. We go to bed at night with no surety that our dwelling will be anything but a pile of ashes in the morning." The writer advocated for a "good second-hand engine."[55]

Despite the threat, Chatham would not organize a fire department until 1911, when it acquired an American LaFrance fire extinguisher wagon pulled by a single horse and carrying soda-acid extinguishers.[56] Before that residents relied on neighbors and a bucket brigade. To fight fire that way meant you had to wake up in time. It was a risky business.

James and Almena Kent became guardians of young Josephine Atkins after her mother Lizzie died and her father Joseph moved to Mexico. Kent would die of a heart attack while fighting a fire in his barn in 1896. *Photo courtesy of Chatham, Massachusetts Historical Society.*

Taking of scallops is limited to the period between November 1 and April 1.

1894

Lizzie Payne Atkins lost her own parents in a shipwreck when she was four. She would die of a brain tumor when her daughter Josephine was only two. *Photo courtesy of Chatham, Massachusetts Historical Society.*

The fire and the death of Captain Kent were two more strange and dramatic events in the life of 9-year-old Emma Josephine Kent Atkins, the motherless girl who was the Kent's ward. Josephine was no stranger to tragic death, and she would see more before the dawn of the new century.

Josephine was born in Chatham on the Fourth of July 1887.

Her parents were Elizabeth "Lizzie" Payne and Captain Joseph Atkins. Lizzie was, herself, a daughter of a sea captain, John Payne who, along with Lizzie's mother, was lost at sea in 1863 on the *Madelia* between the Philippines and San Francisco. The orphaned Lizzie, age 4, and her sister Emma, age 6, were then cared for by Captain and Mrs. Myrick Kent. In a weird twist, Myrick Kent was the father of Captain James Kent, whose wife Almena would eventually raise Lizzie's daughter.

Lizzie married young, at 18. Her new husband was an older man of 32, and, despite the loss of her family to a shipwreck, she was plucky enough to spend the first four years of her married life sailing on her husband's ship to Australia and other exotic places. By 1886, when she found herself pregnant, Lizzie was established in a fine house in North Chatham as she waited for her *accouchement*.

The Fourth of July was clear, dry and warm. Josephine's birth was accompanied by the sound of bells and the "snapping and cracking of muskets, pistols, torpedoes and fire-crackers" set off by the merry-makers beginning in the early morning. The day was hot, about 80 degrees inside the house where Lizzie lay in labor. At midday dories raced on Mill Pond, and in South Chatham a quahog chowder-and-ice cream fest was on. In the evening fireworks were set off in various spots around town. The night, when the newborn lay in her crib, was cool and "right for refreshing sleep."[57]

The mother and baby shared barely two years unclouded by the mother's illness, perhaps just long enough for Lizzie to nurse the infant Josephine and wean her. Just after Josephine's second birthday Lizzie began experiencing troubling symptoms: dazzling

Almena Kent would survive to raise the young Josephine. Kent died in 1924. *Photo courtesy of Chatham, Massachusetts Historical Society.*

Shore Road is constructed and named The Boulevard.
Hotel Chatham closes.

It is voted to locate the lock-up in Chatham Town Hall.

1895

headaches, double vision, a dragging leg. The diagnosis: Brain tumor. Looking for the best medical care, she traveled to Boston and lay in a hospital bed for three months "fighting against that dread monster death."[58]

That autumn a fleet of white ships sailing to Boston passed Chatham. Although they could be observed by anyone standing near the shore, a "good glass" aided viewing, and many crowded up into the Main Street observatory run by William Nickerson in a tower atop his home.[59]

On Thanksgiving Day 1889, a storm from the southeast blew in and was so severe that services could not be held at Chatham's Congregational Church. The next morning Lizzie died. She was just 30. Her body was brought back to Chatham on Saturday, and a grim trip that must have been for Captain Atkins – who himself had been unwell – her sister, and her brother-in-law. The group arrived at the Chatham train station at noon.

On Sunday, December 1, with the weather "cool and crisp," a crowd attended Lizzie's funeral in her home on Old Harbor Road. The coffin was draped in a broadcloth-covered casket of ashes of rose with a robe of delicate blue. The Reverend Couden of the Universalist Church, a widower and no stranger to tragedy, conducted the service. "The wild geese are now playing lively marches on their way to the sunny South, turning their backs on the northern winter," the *Chatham Monitor* reported a few days after the funeral. Snow was soon on the way, with Chatham's children attempting to go sledding.[60]

"The little one, too young to know its loss, we trust may be spared to be [the Captain's] comfort in future time," another newspaper account rhapsodized. Joseph Atkins was appointed guardian to his young daughter the following month as Lizzie's estate was probated.

Soon thereafter Captain Atkins – seeking fortune, fleeing sorrow – left for a three-year sojourn in Mexico where he was in care of floating equipment at the construction of the Tampico Jetties. He placed Josephine in the charge of the Kents.

"How am I going to get through the world without Lizzie?" he asked in a November 1892 letter to Almena Kent. "I don't live I only exist."[61]

With Captain Atkins living abroad and her mother dead, Josephine's young years differed from those of many of her schoolmates. Yet to celebrate her 6th birthday it was Almena, no doubt, who had a pretty invitation printed with a pale green waffle border:

> *Miss E. Josephine K. Atkins*
>
> *requests the pleasure of your company*
>
> *to a Birthday Party*
>
> *on*
>
> *Tuesday Afternoon, July fourth,*
>
> *from two to five o'clock*
>
> *1893.*[62]

Eldredge Public Library is opened by Marcellus Eldredge on July 4.
Edna May Hardy serves as librarian from 1911 to 1954.

1896

The following year, Captain Atkins wed Sarah Nickerson. Yet somehow Sarah didn't become a new mother to Josephine. And in 1896 Captain Kent died abruptly in his yard in the light of the burning barn, leaving young Josephine with Almena, who was now 53 years old.

Always there is something special about one born on the Fourth of July. Wouldn't it be easy, especially for one very young, to confuse the general celebration with a celebration for one's own birth?

The Eldredge Public Library was a gift of the philanthropic, beer-brewing brothers Marcellus and H. Fisher Eldredge. The building, which was dedicated on July 4, 1896, looks much the same today as it did over 100 years ago. *Photo by Debra Lawless.*

On Josephine's 9th birthday a town library was dedicated. The building was named the Eldredge Public Library after its chief benefactors, the brothers Marcellus and H. Fisher Eldredge, native sons who had made a fortune brewing beer in Portsmouth, New Hampshire. While Marcellus put up the money to build the library, Fisher donated two thousand books.

The Eldredge brothers came from solid Chatham stock. Their mother was Mary Harding, and their father Heman Eldredge. Marcellus was born in 1838 and Fisher, his only sibling, thirteen years later, in 1851. The family still summered in Chatham and devoted the rest of the year to Portsmouth where Heman and his sons had been brewing ale, porter and lager beer since the 1850s. Marcellus built a summer home on Watch Hill Way and Fisher had a summer home by the twin lights. Both men had their fingers in many local business concerns such as Hotel Chatham and bringing the railroad to Chatham.

The morning of July 4, 1896, began with the usual patriotic parade. After lunch a procession of school children wearing roses, perhaps with Josephine among them, followed a marching band from Marcellus's house to the new library across from the Methodist Church on Main Street. While many stood on the lawn, the speakers addressed the crowd from the library's wide front steps, below a canopy of flags and bunting.

The Committee to investigate repairs to the Mitchell River Bridge reports as follows: $800 repair the bridge with wood; $1,000 to build an earthwork bridge; $5,300 to build an iron bridge; $4,100 to build a trestle bridge.

1896

"In my boyhood, no collection of books was accessible," the lawyer J.W. Hawes, then a resident of New York, reminisced. Dr. Benjamin Gifford, too, addressed the group. "Long after every individual who is now here is dead and almost forgotten – a century hence – this noble edifice will stand the centre of learning and education."

After the speeches, the crowds toured the library. Gifford called the $30,000 Romanesque library, built in red West Barnstable brick, "an ornament to the town."[63] Today the original part of the library, which resembles a manor house with its oak wainscoting, stained glass windows and prominent fireplace and mantel, doesn't look substantially different from the way it did in 1900 photos.

Josephine Atkins donated many pieces of china, furniture and paintings collected by her guardian James Kent and other sea captains engaged in the mid-to-late 19th century China Trade. This is the Atkins-Kent room at the Chatham Historical Society. *Photo by Debra Lawless.*

Marcellus Eldredge would not live long enough to derive great satisfaction from his largess to his hometown. In March 1898 he died at age 59 in Boston's Hotel Touraine on "the breezy corner" of Boylston and Tremont. Six hours later his wife Mary died in a nearby hospital where she had been operated on for cancer. Imagine the poignancy of the big burly brewer with his thick walrus moustache succumbing before his delicate wife. Eldredge had been "neglectful of his own health, and, by exposure during the stormy weather... contracted a severe cold which turned from pneumonia." Fisher Eldredge took charge of the remains of both his brother and sister-in-law.[64] "The bodies lay side by side in the suite in the Hotel Touraine all day yesterday, and friends of the dead man called to look for the last time upon his face," says a news clipping. They are buried in Forest Hills Cemetery in Boston.

In 1870, not yet 20, Fisher had built a three-story barn at the back of the family house on Main Street. On the second floor was a hall called the "Temple of Reason" where spiritualists held meetings and tried to communicate with the dead.[65] That sect met for nearly ten years, perhaps giving Fisher some insight into how to communicate with the departed after death. Unfortunately Fisher left no record of conversations he may have conducted with his late brother and sister-in-law or anyone else.

At Town Meeting, $500 is voted to repair the Mitchell River Bridge.

1897

In any event the Eldridge Public Library was well-endowed and continued to expand its collection of circulating books. Josephine meanwhile worked on her penmanship, filling workbooks of the Spencerian System of Penmanship: F: Felix fears Find fame and P: Peter's pony Persis' prizes.[66]

As the final leaves shook off the trees in the fall of 1897 Myrick Kent, Almena's father-in-law, died. Embalmed, "the features presented a natural appearance, having been embalmed by Undertaker J.H. Taylor," a news clipping proclaimed. John H. Taylor served as the town's undertaker, embalmer, and funeral director. "Night bell promptly answered," read his ad. In 1889, Taylor had expanded the business of his general store to include undertaking after learning the techniques of "arterial embalming." Benjamin Cahoon, who since 1863 had been selling oils and paints on Depot Street, had also added a sideline in undertaking in 1879.[67]

Whatever turmoil might have been occurring, Josephine carried on, visiting Boston with Almena in December 1897. In February 1898, Josephine began soliciting autographs of her friends in a red leather three-by-six album. For nearly two years Josephine collected autographs until the album read like a Who's Who of a particular generation of Chatham students: Blanch M. Edwards, Miss Amy Gill, Katie Snow, Rhoda Nickerson, Luella C. Bearse, Grace F. Hardy "your loving teacher," Grace Eldridge, Maria Edwards, Marion A. Nickerson, Arthur Payne Crosby, Jennie C. Eldredge, Lulu M. Griffin, Jennie M. O'Neil, Pearl E. Blount, Edith Eldredge, Susie M. Small, Agnes Bailey, Guesta Hyde, and finally Lillie Osborn who waxed poetic on July 25, 1900: "Dear Josephine: Remember me when far away and only half awake/ Remember me on your wedding day and send a slice of cake. Ever your loving friend, Lillie Osborn."[68]

Preserved among Josephine's papers on a scrap of paper at the Chatham Historical Society is a penciled poem Josephine's friend Alice M. Rogers wrote about her. "I like her very well. Her name is Josephine, She is pretty fat; So she is not lean."

Josephine was a talented pianist, and at Christmas 1899, at the age of 12, she played the wedding march at her friend Ethel Eldredge's wedding.

A few months later, another horrifying event occurred in Josephine's young life. On the morning of Wednesday, April 25, four months into the new century, Captain Atkins left the home he shared with his wife Sarah and went to work about half a mile distant in the yard at "the old homestead," the place where he was born. When he didn't return for dinner, Sarah and her relatives went to look for him. The 55-year-old captain was lying under the trees, with two bullet holes in his head and a revolver "firmly clinched in his right hand." He had been dead for about six hours, and his working tools had not been taken from the wagon. Later it would be said that the cause of death was a "temporary aberration of the mind" as "domestic relations were of the pleasantest character." On the other hand, perhaps after his years of excitement abroad, he was tired of his quiet life in Chatham "perfecting a patent dumping scow."[69]

Police work at the time was perhaps not all it could have been – a police chief was not appointed until 1922 – as no one seemed to question how or why a man who had just shot himself through the head might fire off a second bullet. Did anyone consider foul play?

A macabre incident of twenty-four years previous raises more questions than it explains about this bizarre death. In May 1876 in Port Chalmers, New Zealand, a tornado suddenly sprang up. Atkins was standing with a friend when suddenly the friend's house was swept away into the swirling river with his wife and infant clinging to the roof. "The distraught father pleaded with Captain Atkins, whom he knew was an excellent shot, to put the two out of their misery. He thrust a revolver into the captain's hands... He felled his friend's loved ones with a single shot."[70] So while in 1876 Atkins killed two people with one bullet, in 1900 it apparently took him two bullets at close range to kill one.

A month after the captain's death Almena Kent was officially appointed as Josephine's guardian. During the years after that, Josephine and Almena traveled frequently to Boston, staying with friends in Boston and Brookline, sometimes for the holidays. In 1904 Josephine attended a prep school for young ladies on Marlboro Street.[71]

In 1909 Almena and Josephine traveled to Quebec City. Almena later reported on the trip to the ladies at the Methodist church. The pair departed Boston's North Station on September 27, 1909, on an 11 A.M. train. They passed that night at Crawford Notch in New Hampshire's White Mountains, where it was raining hard. The following day, the rain increased. After the train they caught a ferry where a "nice-looking gentleman" took Josephine's suitcase. Josephine, who had lost her mother and her father and her male guardian, was so nervous about her suitcase that she would not let the man out of her sight. Eventually the man was pointed out to the pair as "one of the prominent men of the city," Almena reported.[72]

In Quebec, they checked into the Chateau Frontenac, the luxurious castle-like hotel overlooking the St. Lawrence River, and, as the weather improved, they toured the city. Moving on to Montreal they visited the churches. They traveled home through Vermont, admiring the colorful foliage, and arrived back in Boston in the evening.

Josephine Atkins never married, and never sent her friend a piece of her wedding cake. In 1912 she served on the committee that arranged the concert and ball that was held on the evening of the second day of the bicentennial celebration, August 2.[73] It is interesting to note that special attention was devoted to veterans of the Civil War, 12 of whom were invited to the August 1 dinner.[74] After the death of Almena Kent in July 1924, shortly after her 37th birthday, Atkins sailed on in the long, thin house on Main Street where the road turns toward Chatham Light. During the 1920s she shared the limelight on the Fourth of July with Calvin Coolidge, the only president born on the Fourth of July. In 1927, accompanied by her friend Emma Crosby, she traveled cross-country and up the Pacific Coast for five weeks. A year later she moved for a time to Brookline to earn a doctor of divinity degree at Boston University. When she returned to Chatham, she sometimes preached in the Methodist Church. She gave piano lessons in her home and she organized the furniture, rose medallion china, and other 19th century artifacts that her father and Captain Kent collected on their trips to the Far East. She gave these things to the Atwood House Museum where they are now on display in the Atkins-Kent Room.

Josephine died in 1974 at the age of 87.

CHATHAM RAILROAD

If the Cape girls want to dance
Till morn puts out the taper,
Let every Cape man show
That he is ready for a caper.

Chatham has always been a town that knows how to throw a party. When the Old Colony Railroad officially began the Chatham run on Monday, November 22, 1887, townsfolk threw a dance at Town Hall, just a stone's throw from the new station built in the Railroad Gothic style. The evening train brought in all who wanted to attend, and took them home free of charge at 2 a.m. Bee's Orchestra provided the music, and the entire town looked like it was done up for the Fourth of July, with flags flying. "Everybody and his team seemed to be out of doors."[75]

All day that day – "a carnival occasion" – the train carried passengers free between Harwich and Chatham. In the afternoon people jammed into the train on an average of five to a seat, with "persons either sitting, standing, leaning in all uncouth positions." The *Chatham Monitor* estimated that 700 people were crammed into the six cars, "from the cowcatcher to the rear platform" for the twenty minute ride along 7.07 miles of track.

The Chatham Train Station, in railroad Gothic style, was a landmark after the train spur came to Chatham in 1887. Today the Depot Road building is a railroad museum. *Photo by Debra Lawless.*

Chatham was no longer a remote outpost. Trains had been running to Sandwich since 1848 and to Hyannis since 1854. In 1873 the train reached Provincetown, and that left only the towns of Chatham and Mashpee off the line. By the end of the 19ᵗʰ century, as tourism was set to begin on the Cape, being left off the line meant economic death. Before the train spur, anyone wishing to travel by train from Chatham had first to begin his or her voyage with a stage coach ride to Harwich. (An alternate route to Boston was via a packet from Brewster.) While these trips were an inconvenience for all, for those injured or critically ill seeking medical care in Boston, they were torture. Since its inaugural issue in October 1871 the *Chatham Monitor* had taken it as a crusade to bring the train to Chatham. Now the day had come.

"Probably the quickest time ever made by human beings between Chatham and Boston was last Wednesday when the train, with the Railroad Commissioners and Old Colony officials, went from Chatham to Boston in 2½ hours," the *Monitor* noted. "This was not remarkably quick for railroad time, but it was unusually fast time from Chatham to Boston."

Like anything else, the railroad had a down side. In the dry season, as the train chugged along its tracks, sparks often flew off into the grass and started fires. One day, in early June 1903, a fire broke out after the Boston train passed through South Chatham. A general alarm was given and volunteers and railroad men rallied to fight the rapidly spreading blaze. At 5 P.M. the South Chatham schoolhouse burned down as did the house of Joseph A. Nickerson.[76]

And in August 1912 the train brought many summer visitors and dignitaries who wanted to help Chatham celebrate its 200ᵗʰ birthday bash in high style.

The wheels of trains often sent sparks into the Cape's dry summer grass, igniting fires. One wildfire in June 1903 burned down the South Chatham schoolhouse which was later rebuilt. Today the landmark building is an ice cream store. *Photo by Debra Lawless.*

At the town's bicentennial celebration in 1912, the past met the future in horses, cars and electric lights. Aging veterans of the Civil War, now in their seventies, were honored with a special table at dinner. *Photo courtesy Chatham, Massachusetts Historical Society.*

1912-1962

World Wars Transform Chatham

By Tim Weller

A few clouds, a little muggy, a fog bank hanging just off Nauset Beach – Sunday, July 21, 1918, looked to be just another sleepy, mid-summer morning as the sun tried to burn through the haze.

Lt. (jg) E. E. Williams stirred from his bunk, rose, shaved, and prepared for morning chow at the sprawling air base on Nickerson's Neck. He always looked forward to Sunday breakfast, which typically consisted of fried corned-beef hash, griddle cakes, syrup, bread, butter, and all the coffee you could drink.[1]

The Chatham Naval Air Station was an immense facility, spread out over thirty-six acres. It had sprung up in a little more than a year as the United States entered the First World War. More than 250 men were stationed there – but only 180 could be accommodated at the base's barracks. The rest were scattered throughout town. [2]

Bounded by Bassing Harbor and Pleasant Bay, with Crows Pond at its rear, the base housed seaplanes and dirigibles in an array of hangars and boathouses, most facing out across the channel to Strong Island.

It's "runways" consisted of the flat waters right off the beach, which allowed planes to take off in any direction.

Make no mistake – this base was cutting edge.

A Navy B-class blimp soars over the Naval Air Station in the summer of 1919. *Photo courtesy of Chatham, Massachusetts Historical Society.*

Chatham Bars Inn opens. The "Brick Block" is built at the corner of Main Street and Chatham Bars Avenue. The Hotel Chatham is torn down.

The Orpheum Theater opens, hosting first-run films, town meetings, and high school graduations until 1985.

1914

1915

The base's primary mission was to protect U.S. shipping from threats posed by a potent new enemy weapon: the German U-boat. But pilots from NAS-C – as the base was called in military jargon – had not seen any action.

Of course pilots heard stories about lurking enemy subs. Just one month earlier, news reached the base that a passenger liner rescued fifty survivors of a torpedoed ship just off the coast of New Jersey. [3]

Chatham went on high alert. All leave and liberty was cancelled and planes were readied for extensive aerial searches. "The increased number of patrols continued for several days with exhausted flight crews performing beyond expectations," wrote Joseph D. Buckley in *Wings over Cape Cod*. But the planes never spotted anything.

One of the base's early commanders, unfortunately not identified. Lt. (jg) E.E. Williams could have reported directly to this man. *Photo courtesy of Chatham, Massachusetts Historical Society.*

Situation Normal: Boring, Routine Patrols

On a typical day planes would take off in pairs and patrol two zones. The Northern Patrol covered an area from Chatham up to Cape Ann and then west about 25 miles. The Southern Patrol reached from Chatham to Sankaty Head on Nantucket and then west to the Georges Bank. [4]

These seaplanes were woefully primitive by today's standards – some actually carried homing pigeons for emergency communications.

The R-9 so common at the base was actually a training plane considered fragile and flimsy by their crews.

Two pilots flew this biplane, which could reach speeds of 82 mph. It was armed with a machine gun and could carry two bombs – although most crews loaded just one to keep the weight down. Cruising range was four hours. [5]

In June, four new planes – Curtiss HL-1L flying boats – arrived in crates at the Chatham train station on Depot Road. Orders were to truck them to the base, assemble them and get them operational as soon as possible.

A crew of three piloted these flying boats: a pilot, copilot, and gunner/bombardier/signalman/observer. Powered by a 12-cylinder engine, it could fly at top speeds of 88 mph.

Naval Air Station Chatham opens on Nickerson's Neck. Chatham Yacht Club is founded.

1918

The NC-4 stops in Chatham as part of the first transatlantic flight.
Town Hall burns down, leaving only jail cells standing.

1919

As Lieutenant Williams finished his breakfast, one could assume he was apprehensive and on edge. As the base's executive officer, he would be dealing with whatever headaches came his way.

He had one major concern that Sunday: The only planes at the base were the newly arrived flying boats not yet ready for service. All the other planes were either under repair, flying routine patrols, or out searching for an overdue blimp.

Let's hope it's a quiet day, he must have thought as he began his rounds.

All Hell Breaks Loose

On that lazy summer Sunday morning in 1918 the ocean-going tug *Perth Amboy*, the pride of the Lehigh Coal and Navigation Co., made the turn around Provincetown bound for Vineyard Sound and on into New York City and Elizabeth, New Jersey.

The *Perth* was towing four barges as she steamed leisurely south, in sight of the Cape's outer beaches.

At 10:30 a.m., everything changed.

A German U-boat, the U-156, surfaced in the fog bank just to the east of the *Perth Amboy* and opened fire. All hell broke loose.[19]

One shell hit the wheelhouse. A raging fire broke out. Captain J.P. Tapley ordered the crews of the *Perth Amboy* and the barges to abandon ship.

The drama played out in front of a growing crowd on Nauset Beach, writes Joseph D. Buckley in *Wings over Cape Cod.* "The unfamiliar sound of gunfire attracted the attention of a large number of locals and summer visitors who witnessed the one-sided engagement from the beach."

Several shells landed on the beach. "Whether accidently or intentionally is not known, but they were the only enemy shells to land on United States soil in World War I, and the first to do so since the War of 1812," Buckley wrote.

Nineteen minutes later, at about 10:50 A.M. Lt. Williams's worst fears were realized: reports of the shelling trickled into the air station's radio room. The shelling was taking place just a few miles to the north, off Pochet.

Williams knew he had to respond, but with what? The only aircraft at the base were three flying boats – one was being repaired and the other two had just arrived on the base.

He had no choice. Williams ordered the planes armed and launched.

The first plane to actually get airborne and fly to the scene was HS-IL 1695, piloted by Ensign Eric A. Lingard, with Edwin M. Shields as co-pilot, and Chief Special Mechanic E.H. Howard at the bombsight in the bow cockpit.

Howard lined up the target directly amidships and Lingard made his first bombing run at a height of 800 feet. But when Howard pulled the bomb release, nothing happened.

Lingard circled back for a second run, this time coming in on the U-boat's stern at 400 feet. Howard again pulled the release, and again, nothing. Exasperated, he climbed out of his seat, and holding a strut on the lower wing, released the bomb with his other hand. The bomb dropped a few feet off the sub's stern – but failed to explode!

Chatham's population is 1,737, with 250 men fishing for a living.

1920

Only ten working farms remain in the town.

1921

Eastward Ho! Golf Club opens. The main section of the clubhouse is the old home of Ensign Nickerson, built around 1805.

Town establishes a police force with four officers.

1920

An HS-2L at the air base. Planes like this attacked the U-156.
Photo courtesy of Chatham, Massachusetts Historical Society.

A second plane arrived on the scene and dropped this bomb 100 feet off the starboard side. Another dud!

The submarine had had enough. She dove and stayed down.

More planes arrived and dropped at least two more bombs – one on an oil slick and one on what was thought to be a periscope. Both did not explode.[20]

The U-156 had escaped.

How the Wars Changed Chatham

In ways both large and small, America's two world wars transformed Chatham.

Service personnel swarmed into town. Residents endured rationing of all kinds. The threat of enemy attack was palpable – German submarines lurked off Chatham's coastline. Rumors about saboteurs who might creep ashore to blend in with innocent townspeople spread rapidly. Up and down the coast, residents used blackout curtains; the tops of their car headlights were blackened.

In the Great War, seventy-eight residents out of a total population of 1,667 saw uniformed duty. By the time hostilities ended, seven sons of Chatham had been killed: Edward S. Bearse,

Chatham Historical Society founded. North lighthouse tower moved to Eastham.

Coast Guardsman Richard Ryder intercepts dories filled with bootlegged liquor.

Chatham Beach and Tennis Club opens.

1923

1924

1925

Chester O.T. Eldredge, Emory F. Griffin, Herbert L. Macomber, Edwin F. Nickerson, Josiah D. Nickerson and Thomas J. Rogers.[6]

The town's leading families did their duty: fifteen Eldredges, six Rogers, five Nickersons, and five Cahoons all wore their country's uniform.

World War II impacted Chatham even more directly. A full 14 percent of the town's population – some three hundred men and women – enlisted to serve. Private 1st Class Robert S. Brown was killed during the Japanese attack at Pearl Harbor, the first Cape Cod serviceman killed in enemy action.

Chatham architect Edward C. "Ned" Collins was 11 when war broke out.

"The war didn't terrify us as boys, but it was very meaningful. It was all around us," Collins said. "At night you'd see flashes out there past North Beach and we assumed that ships were being torpedoed or sunk – or that our boats and planes were sinking German subs. This didn't happen every night, but it happened a hell of a lot more than you'd think.

"The beaches were covered with debris: crates, pallets, boxes, life preservers. There was plenty of evidence that incredible damage was being done very close by."[7]

Service personnel from around the country were everywhere.

"Chatham was very different in the war years," said retired commercial fisherman and selectman David Ryder. "All the local men had gone off to fight, and there were lots of new young men in town serving all over the place. It was good for the local ladies!"[8]

"There was a lot of military in town," recalled George Goodspeed, Jr., a young boy at the time.[9] By the summer of 1941 the Wayside Inn provided a room for off-duty servicemen to write, read and relax. An old building used by the Chatham Bars Inn to house chauffeurs on Chatham Bars Avenue was converted into a USO club. The Chatham branch of the American Red Cross made surgical dressings at a guest house on Oyster Pond owned by Mr. and Mrs. Henry S. Howes. Mrs. Francis G. Shaw opened a Victory Market on March 2, 1942, on Main Street, which sold everything from discarded clothing to kitchen utensils to eel spears.[10]

The town regularly held blackout drills. The Army Air Force installed a top-secret radar base on Great Hill.

"It wasn't a big secret because you could see it from the road," Goodspeed said. "They had this bullet-shaped cone that they would scan the sky with all the time. The guardhouse to that base was down by Old Queen Anne Road at the railroad crossing (where Stepping Stones Road is today). On each side of the guardhouse was a machine gun nest, so obviously they meant business."

The Navy WAVES also had a detachment in town. The women were based at the Rose Acres Inn on Cross Street. Each morning the women would march to the Hawthorne Inn on Shore Road for breakfast. Most of the women worked at the Marconi radio station, a well-known landmark along Ryder's Cove which was doing top-secret work intercepting radio traffic from German U-boats.

The Main Street School opens with grades kindergarten to grade 12.

1926

Atwood House Museum opens to the public.

1927

Wrote Robert D.B. Carlisle in *Weathering A Century Of Change*, "The town of Chatham had never faced such a demanding time before. Rolling with the punch, residents both male and female took on duties they could never have imagined. Rationing forced them to live Spartan lives…"[11]

"Even as early as the summer of 1939, you could feel the town getting ready," said Barbara Townson Weller. "They were getting ready for invasion." [12]

"Chatham Was So Full of Pride"

In the summer of 1939 Barbara Townson was a 16-year-old summer kid from Rochester, New York. Her parents owned property at what is now 162 Shore Road, which consisted of a main house, a windmill, a guest house and a garage.

She remembers spending that summer in the garage painting old furniture with her best friend, June Tyner, who lived next door. They hoped to sell the furniture at "a huge garden party" up the street at what was called the Crocker Estate. The party was called "Friends of France," and Townson remembers it featured pony and carriage rides. "It was the class act of the summer," she said.

When the family arrived for the summer in 1940, Townson could see dramatic changes. The Hawthorne Inn, the "great gray lady" as she called it, had been taken over by sailors and marines who worked at the Marconi station.

The Hawthorne just happened to be one house away from the Townson homestead – and for Barbara, her older sister Tony, and their friend June Tyner, this had real possibilities!

"For three pretty good-looking teenage girls, this was a bonanza," Townson said.

But the best laid plans…

"The problem was the severity of the blackouts on Shore Road. We had blackout shades on every single window. As I remember, some of them were even tacked up so they were absolutely taut.

"The house was so dark you needed a seeing-eye dog. You couldn't read or anything. And here we were hallucinating about picking these guys up at the Hawthorne and having bonfires on the beach. Well forget that! You couldn't light anything.

"Of course that summer we were all learning to smoke, and we all had Zippo lighters. But the [air raid] wardens patrolling the beach were so strict you couldn't even light a match on the beach at dark."

She recalls the wardens patrolling the beaches and streets in World War I style helmets. "They tended to be older men," she said. "The young guys had gone off to enlist.

"That summer Chatham was so full of pride because it knew it was in danger."[13]

A Mechanic Helps Make History

In 1917 George Goodspeed Sr. was a 19-year-old kid from West Chatham struggling to make a go of it. An eighth-grade dropout, George worked for George Bearse down at Bearse's

---

Wilfred J. Berube begins clearing land for Chatham Airport, with an able assist from George Goodspeed.

1929

Artist Alice Stallknecht paints *Christ Preaching to the Multitude*, featuring living Chatham residents.

1931

Chatham Town Band is formed.

1931

Garage (now Chatham Ford). His specialty was repairing a newfangled contraption known as the automobile.

He was more than pretty good at it and it wasn't long before he developed a reputation as being Chatham's "engine guy."

"If that man had a chance to go to college nobody could have stopped him," said his son, George Jr. "His intelligence was unbelievable, even though he had no formal education or training."

Goodspeed avoided the draft "because he was the responsible person of the family and the sole breadwinner," his son said.[14]

For George Sr., the war years passed by unremarkably. But he was fascinated by what was going on inside the gates of the Naval Air Station. He had seen the blimps float over town and heard the roar of the seaplanes taking off.

He dreamed about flying.

Naval aviators began turning their attention to other pursuits as World War I wound down. What challenge could engage their skills and adrenaline?

The brass in Washington, D.C., soon had their answer: A transatlantic flight.

George Goodspeed played a key role in the first transatlantic crossing by the NC-4. *Photo courtesy of Chatham Town Band.*

Five years earlier, in 1913, the *London Daily Mail* newspaper offered a £10,000 first prize – a staggering amount for the times – to the first aviator to fly between North America and Great Britain or Ireland in either direction.

Primitive aviation technology and the war prevented any serious attempts. But by 1917 Congress appropriated money to build four huge flying boats capable of escorting U.S. convoys to Europe, thus crippling German U-boat attacks.

It was a huge advancement in aviation.

The Navy gave the contract to the Curtiss Aeroplane and Motor Co. of Buffalo, New York, but the war ended just as the company completed two prototypes – NC-1 and NC-2 – which stood for "Navy-Curtiss." The Navy also decided to build two additional planes, NC-3 and NC-4.[15]

The press quickly dubbed them "Nancy boats" or "Nancys."

The planes were massive, with a wingspan of 126 feet. Each plane was 68 feet long and 24 feet high. Four, 400-pound Liberty engines powered the boats. Even with a full crew of six, the NC could reach speeds of about 95 mph.

By April 1918, the Navy high command decided to go for the *Daily Mail's* prize – their overall strategy was to seek out high-profile peacetime challenges to keep the men sharp. Although the Navy couldn't collect the prize money, the resulting publicity could be a windfall for the service.

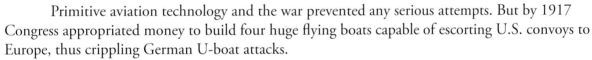

Elizabeth Fuller, Marian McClay, and Fritz Hovey found Stage Harbor Yacht Club.

Spaulding Dunbar begins building boats in a former sail loft building on Bridge Street.

1932

1933

On May 8, 1919 the quest began. Three Nancy boats – the NC-1, NC-3 and NC-4 – took off from Rockaway, New Jersey, bound for Halifax, Nova Scotia. The NC-2, earlier damaged by fire, was held in reserve for spare parts.

Several hours into the flight, the NC-4 developed problems in two of its four engines and Lieutenant Commander Albert Read ordered his pilot, Lieutenant Elmer Stone, to land in the ocean about eighty miles east of Chatham.

For the next fourteen hours, Read, using his two good engines and well-honed navigation skills, plotted a course to the NAS-C, arriving there at dawn on May 9. Read was no stranger to Chatham – as a child he grew up on the Mill Pond and his father was a preacher who preached at the local Baptist church.[16]

Mechanics at the base teamed up with the plane's own mechanic and engineer as they worked frantically to repair the damaged engines. But they were outmatched.

So the call went out to George Goodspeed – that era's version of the NPR "Car Talk" Tappet brothers, Tom and Ray Magliozzi. Come quickly.

"I heard stories that my dad worked round-the-clock on those engines," said his son George. "They somehow overhauled everything and got the plane going again in four days. It was amazing."

You can probably guess the rest of the story: On May 14, 1919, the NC-4 took off from Pleasant Bay and rejoined the two other Nancys which had already arrived in Halifax. On May 16 all three departed for the Azores, 1,200 miles away. The NC-1 became lost in the fog and had to make a water landing, where heavy seas wreaked havoc. The NC-3 suffered the same fate.

The NC-4 flew on, reaching the Azores to refuel. Then it was on to Portugal, Spain, and finally, on May 31, to Plymouth, England.

The NC-4 had set the record.

"It was a proud achievement, and my dad played a big role in it," said George Goodspeed, Jr.

The front page of the *New York Times* trumpeted the transatlantic crossing. *Photo courtesy of Chatham, Massachusetts Historical Society*

Rail service to Chatham ends.

1936

Mary Winslow begins operating the Monomoy Theatre.

1938

Town population swells to 2,138.

1940

AN ACTIVE LIFE

George Goodspeed Sr. also served in the Coast Guard Auxiliary, served as fire chief, and was an air raid warden during the war. He and Wilfred Berube flew the first air mail off Cape Cod, lugging mail from Chatham and Hyannis and Boston to New York. [17] He also helped Berube clear land for what would later become Chatham Airport.

America's Youngest Heroes

Edward C. "Ned" Collins II was 12 in the summer of 1942. And, even though the war raged just offshore, life was good!

On this particular summer Wednesday in July Ned and his cousin Grant Howes set out for another morning of harmless mischief. By the end of the day, and after a truly great adventure, they would end up as "War's Youngest War Heroes." [18]

Ned and "Granty" were spending the summer with their grandmother, Fannie Lewis Shattuck, at her rambling estate on Bridge Street. "Gammy" grew a Victory Garden across the road, at the edge of woods, marsh, and upland. Typically the boys would venture into the woods only as far as the garden, swiping a few carrots for their trip back.

But on this day they decided to be more daring.

"We screwed up a little courage and decided to go beyond the garden," Collins recalled. "This was like a jungle to us, but we had a BB gun, so I suppose that made us a little braver."

The boys found a narrow path that headed south and east in the direction of Morris Island.

Their mission? "Well I'm not proud of this, but we were shooting cat birds because they're pretty dumb," he said. "Our gun wasn't highly powered by any means and the BBs pretty much bounced off the birds, but that was our fun."

Ned Collins and the *Time* magazine cover. *Photo by Tim Weller.*

The boys kept walking and kept shooting until something caught their attention. "All of a sudden we looked to the right and there was all this dead material. Cranberry plants, all kinds of stuff, placed there. It was strange. So we brushed it aside and we saw a knoll that was just about completely covered in red pines. When we got to the crest of the knoll, we noticed fish netting that started way up in the trees and hung down. The needles from the high limbs had fallen on the netting but otherwise you couldn't tell that the netting was there."

Federal government takes over Acme Laundry to do laundry for prisoners and military personnel at Camp Edwards.

1941 to 1945

The boys pushed aside the netting and peered in.

Behind the netting was a clearing, maybe twelve feet by twelve feet. A small table was inside and on top of the table was a box of some sort, covered with canvass. Dangling down from the box was a set of headphones.

"Being little boys during the war we figured these are spies! This is a clandestine radio operation. We were highly suspicious!

"So what did we do? We did what all 12-year-olds do – go home for lunch."

Coast Guard Helps "Youngest Heroes"

For Ned Collins and his cousin, lunch was awkwardly quiet on that summer Wednesday in 1942.

"This was our secret and we weren't going to tell them," Collins said, referring to his other cousins – mostly girls – who sat around the lunch table. "They thought we were sick or something, but of course we weren't. We ate everything in sight and left."[21]

The boys walked east on Bridge Street, turned right onto Morris Island Road and continued all the way to Coast Guard headquarters on Morris Island.

"In the Navy and Coast Guard, Wednesdays are called 'Rope yarn Sundays,'" Collins said. "It's kind of an afternoon off where you're supposed write letters home.

"When we arrived, these guys were spread out all over the lawn writing their sweethearts or their mothers. We approached the first guy we saw and told him we had discovered a spy's nest. He smiled and said, 'That's great, guys! Tell you what, why don't you go over and tell that guy sitting over there?'

"We got the same answer from him, and were sent to a third guy. But this guy had a lightning bolt on his uniform, which we knew meant that he was involved in communications and probably worked in the radio room.

"We told him our story and he said, 'You're kidding! Show me where!'

"So he jumps up and off we went. We walked and walked and finally got onto the path that led to our spy's nest.

"When we arrived, the Coast Guardsman walked under the netting, shook his head, and uttered, 'Oh, my God.'

"The first thing he did was look for an antenna, and there it was, wrapped around a pine tree right near the table. He bent down, pulled the canvass off the radio and turned it on.

"Just then, in through the netting comes this husky young man with a bayonet in his hand – we figured he had seen only the two of us kids and maybe he was maybe going to do us in.

"Well, the Coast Guardsman turns and hits the spy's upper arm so hard that he dropped the bayonet. He then grabbed it, put it in the spy's back and said, 'You're my prisoner.'

"Go Coast Guard!

"So picture this, a Coast Guardsman, a Nazi prisoner, and two little boys walking down Bridge Street. It's a Norman Rockwell cover!

Air Raid Report Center is established and staffed by 300 civil defense workers; Francis Shaw opens a Victory Market to raise money for wartime causes.

Coast Guard Spars begin operating highly secret LORAN station.

1942

1943

"We march down to the lighthouse, ring the doorbell, and take the prisoner inside. Then someone says, 'That's it boys, nice work! You go home now.' And that was that."

Understandably, young Ned sat down and wrote a letter to his father laying out his great adventure. His father, Charles P. Collins, a lawyer working in Philadelphia, was riveted and told the story to a Time-Life employee whom he met on his commuter train.

A few weeks later, *Time* magazine published a short story about "America's youngest heroes."

However the next week, the magazine retracted the story, saying that the boys made it up.

Well that didn't wash with proud Mr. Collins. "The next time my father met the Time-Life man, he threatened to sue him," Collins said.

The next week the boys were back in the magazine, heroes again.

The Aftermath

Collins never learned the identity of the "spy" but heard years later that he was an American Nazi sympathizer. The man was released from custody after the war and returned to Germany.

Collins said the location of the hideout high up on a knoll would have allowed the spy – if he had a good pair of binoculars – so see the shipping lanes off Chatham.

A close-up of the *Time* magazine cover.
Photo by Tim Weller.

Collins also said he learned later that the Coast Guard radio room on Morris Island had been picking up strange signals but couldn't locate the source.

"The spy's nest was right under their noses. They knew something was out there because they kept hearing something. They just couldn't figure out what it was," Collins said.

Later during that eventful summer, he was out rowing on the Mill Pond one day, when his grandmother called to him to row ashore.

A man was there who wanted to talk with Ned. The man leaned against a tree swing as he began talking when a gun fell out of his pocket. The man picked up the gun and promptly left. Collins doesn't know who the man was but suspects it had something to do with the spy.

"All that summer, Granny and I slept with a knife under our pillows," Collins said. "Just in case our spy's buddies decided to come after us."

Hurricane destroys Kenny's boat yard and shed, and shanties along Stage Harbor, and blows down the Universalist Church tower.

Chatham population is 2,195 residents, living in 1,315 houses.

1944

1945

As reported in *Time* magazine:

Blond, bright-eyed Edward Collins, 12, lives in Rye, N.Y., and spends his summers romping around his grandmother's Cape Cod cottage. One morning he and Cousin Grant Howes set out to explore the bayberry thickets, to find a new short cut to the beach. Instead they found something that set their pulses racing: a hidden, camouflaged tent filled with radio equipment.

They ran to a Coast Guard base, panted out their story. Coastguardsmen followed them to the tent. This time it was guarded by a husky teen-aged German-talking youth, who charged at "Neddie" Collins with a bayonet, ran smack into a Coast Guard fist. As Neddie and his pal watched wide-eyed. Guardsmen hauled away spy and radio – a two-way, short-wave station complete with hidden aerial.

The Coast Guard kept mum about the spy's origin. But it did concede that Neddie and Grant broke up a radio station which for months had sent messages to sea-roving Nazi submarines. In Rye, proud citizens are out to get Government heroes' medals for the boys.

Dodging Bullets As They Fished The High Seas

Retired commercial fisherman David Ryder. *Photo by Tim Weller.*

The war years were mostly kind to Chatham's commercial fishing fleet. Most of the men were considered essential to the war effort and local economy, so they weren't drafted. The big trawlers out of Provincetown and New Bedford were converted into mine sweepers, leaving all the fish to the little guys who fished "inshore."

"It was very good," recalled David Ryder, who by 1941 had been fishing commercially for four years.[22*] "There were some restrictions on us, but not too many. As I remember it, we could not go out before daylight and your boat had to be painted white or a light color so it didn't attract a lot of attention. Some of the larger boats had radios put in so they could call and report in if they saw any sign of a German sub."

"It was really a profitable period for all of us. The fish just seemed to jump on our hooks."

What Ryder remembers most during those years was the secrecy. Events he witnessed or heard about were kept quiet – but he never knew by whom.

Voters approve plan to spend $20,000 to complete the wharf and fish packing house at Aunt Lydia's Cove.

Four electric street lights are installed on Crowell Road. Chatham Light is electrified.

1946

1948

"One time when we were out there fishing, one of the boats got strafed," Ryder said. 'It was an American plane flown by one unhappy pilot, I suppose. One of the bullets went right through the top of the dog house. But this never made the papers; it was hushed up very quickly." [**Editor's note:** The Army Air Force established a bombing and strafing range on Monomoy Island during the war. Most likely the plane was taking target practice but decided to have a little fun with the fishing fleet.]

Another time Ryder was out in his back yard on Barcliff Avenue when he heard a high-pitched sound coming from the sky.

'I was out in the yard and I heard the scream of a plane coming down," Ryder said. "I jumped in my car and took off. I could see where the plane had cut the top of the trees off; it was right in the woods behind Slim's garage (at the corner of Stony Hill and Orleans Road). I started to walk into the woods and I met the pilot coming out. I don't know if it was a Navy plane or what. It was just kept quiet. Back then there were a lot of secrets."

Fear seeped through town. With so many military personnel stationed here, everyone seemed on high alert.

Ryder learned this the hard way when he decided to visit Coast Guard headquarters on Morris Island – by way of his fishing boat.

Ryder's father, Richard, was a career Coast Guardsman who served at lifesaving stations up and down the East Coast. At one point Richard and his family – including young David – did a tour of duty at the Morris Island station. Young David grew up exploring the island and knew the woods by heart.

So he thought nothing of paying a visit to his old stomping grounds.

"Well one day we decided we were we were going out fishing the next morning, and we decided to steam down off the island and pay the station a visit. It was dark when we anchored

Ryder anchored off Morris Island before he "invaded." *Photo courtesy of Chatham, Massachusetts Historical Society.*

Wilfred J. Berube deeds land to town for construction of a 2,500-foot runway.

Willard and Frances Nickerson open Nickerson's Fish Market at the Chatham Fish Pier.

1949

1950

and rowed ashore. Well we worked our way up the hill, and just as we got to the top we heard the command: 'Stop! Who goes there?'

"They had heard the boat coming down the harbor and got suspicious when we cut the engine.

"Believe you me, the commanding officer called me into his office. 'Don't you ever come down here without calling us first!' He was yelling!

"I started calling that 'The Invasion of Morris Island!'"

"It Was a Wonderful, Wonderful Meal"

For Chatham residents, food – or lack of it – was a huge focus in both world wars.

"Everyone had a Victory Garden," recalled George Goodspeed, Jr., who was a youngster living on Seaview Street during World War II. "Ours was about a quarter acre and my folks had me working in it all the time. We grew just about everything."[23]

The idea behind the gardens was to indirectly aid the war effort by reducing the pressure on the public food supply.

Mrs. Francis G. Shaw and service personnel. *Photo courtesy of Chatham, Massachusetts Historical Society.*

But more importantly, these gardens empowered civilians and boosted public morale –growers felt they were helping the war effort in a tangible way.

And Chatham took it one step further.

"One of the town's classic organizers thought up another program the first winter of fighting," wrote Robert D. B. Carlisle in *Weathering a Century of Change.* "(It) was designed to raise money for war-related causes. Mrs. Francis G. Shaw had scoured for a way, in (Chatham author) Joseph Lincoln's words, to 'coax even a little extra money from the purses of her fellow townspeople…without those coaxed being exactly aware of the coaxing.'

"Her solution: A Victory Market. Opened on March 2, 1942 on Main Street, it showcased what Mrs. Shaw called a 'glorified rummage sale.' She had put out a call for 'discards' and in no time at all was deluged with everything from clothing, kitchen utensils, and andirons, to music boxes, eel

Mrs. Jacob Cox donates the town's railway station to the town.

1951

Harbor Coves, the town's first residential development, is built on the former farm of H. Fisher Eldredge. 90 lots are available.

1953

spears, plaster statuettes and rat traps. When Joe Lincoln wrote his paean about the market in '44, it had brought in $5,842.10 (or more than $62,000 in today's dollars). Of that, $2,250 went to Cape Cod Hospital while $2,685.05 was funneled into the ambulance fund of the Massachusetts Women's Defense Corps. Concluded Joe Lincoln, 'The Chatham Victory Market…deserves appreciation, encouragement and applause … [and] imitation.'"

But it was food – especially the lack of meat – that residents craved.

"Sure, there was plenty of fish," said commercial fisherman David Ryder. "And the shell fishing gave you some variety.

"But we didn't have as much meat as we would have liked, that's for sure," Ryder said. "I'd go out hunting for rabbits, chicks, and ducks, and that helped out some. The problem was you couldn't get any (shotgun) shells….but I had some and I knew how to get more!"

Barbara Townson Weller can't vouch for the story, but she said the only reason her father, Douglas C. Townson, joined Eastward Ho! Country Club was because he heard rumors that members could get a steak dinner. "I don't know if that's true or not," she said. "But we heard the story often enough to think it probably was."[24]

Families used "ration books" to purchase items is short supply like butter, but it was meat everyone craved.

"My parents would send me down to Atwood's (grocery store), and Gladys Atwood would see me coming in and say, 'Now Bah-brah, we got no meat for your family today. What else do you need?'"

Ned Collins recalls an outing to Monomoy that started badly but turned into an unexpected feast.[25]

"Well one day we sailed our catboat down to the tip of Monomoy," he said. He and his cousin, Grant Howes, wanted to collect some souvenirs from the Army Air Force target range on the island. Our mission was to pick up bomb casings – they used smoke bombs – and 50-caliber machine gun shells. Boy did we love those casings!

"So one day we're out there, and the tide came in instead of going out, and our boat drifted all the way around the tip and out to sea.

"During that time, there were three Coast Guard stations out there: the one on Morris Island, one halfway down Monomoy, and one at the tip. So we walked down to the station at the tip and tried to explain our stupidity – we probably cried a little, I can't remember. But they reassured us and went out and got our boat back.

"Then, best of all, they kept us over for dinner! Oh it was something! We got corn on the cob, real butter, all the things that we couldn't otherwise get. It was a wonderful, wonderful meal!"

For George Goodspeed, the ever-so-rare family treat was Spam [**Editor's note**: Spam, in this case, is not unwanted e-mail, but rather a precooked meat product made by Hormel Foods Corp. Spam consists of chopped pork shoulder, ham, salt, water, potato starch, and sodium nitrate. It is covered with aspic, a gelatinous glaze.]

"Spam was a real treat," Goodspeed said. "My mother added cloves and made a brown sugar sauce. Ahh! It was special."

Holy Redeemer Church is dedicated, the first Roman Catholic Church in Chatham since 1915.

The Christopher Ryder Restaurant opens.

Chatham population reaches 3,000.

1954

1955

Robert Scott Brown

Scotty Brown was ahead of his time.

He was a bodybuilder before pumping iron was in vogue.

He refused to participate in some sports at Chatham High School because he was afraid his strength might injure other students. He was popular, with a great sense of humor.

And on the morning of Dec. 7, 1941, at Hickam Field, Hawaii, Robert Scott Brown, 26, became Chatham's – and Cape Cod's – first casualty of World War II.

Private Brown was, according to a 2001 story in the *Cape Cod Chronicle*, "conspicuous in his bravery, assisting in the repair of an airplane during the [Japanese] attack."

"Later, a severe attack of bombing and strafing was centered on the hangars. Private Brown was killed in this attack."

On Sunday, April 26, 1942, 300 town residents turned out for Brown's memorial service at the First United Methodist Church.

His name lives on as one of the three men for whom the Brown James Buck VFW post on George Ryder Road is named.

Chatham lost three other native sons in the war: Roland James, Lewis Reynolds, and Robert Buck.

But tragically, Scotty Brown was the first.

Robert Scott Brown in Hawaii. *Photo courtesy of Chatham, Massachusetts Historical Society.*

The Coast Guard's Finest Hours

Residents of Chatham awoke on the morning of Feb. 18, 1952, to a howling nor'easter, driving snow, and below-freezing temperatures. Not a good way to start the week.

"I remember it well," recalled George Goodspeed, whose father was fire chief. "It was town meeting day, and some of us wondered if we could get enough people for a quorum."[26]

Across town at the Chatham Lifeboat Station, business was brisk, but not in a good way.

By mid-morning on that Monday, radio operators learned that a World War II-era T2 tanker, the *SS Fort Mercer*, had broken in half forty miles east of Chatham. Closer to home, boats from the

The Godfrey Windmill is donated to the town and moved to Chase Park.

The Depot Road Elementary School opens.

1956

local fishing fleet broke their moorings and washed up on beaches up and down the harbor. The owners flooded the station with calls asking for assistance.

Commanding Officer Daniel Cluff, a southerner from Chincoteague, Virginia, knew he had to act. But his men were wary. Cluff was new to the Cape, and the extreme conditions off Chatham Bar were new to him. Few men trusted his judgment.[27]

Bernie Webber heard Cluff order Chief Donald Bangs to gather a crew and set out in a 36-foot motor lifeboat to find the *Fort Mercer*. Webber thought to himself: "My God, do they really think a lifeboat and its crew could actually make it that far out to sea in this storm and find the broken ship amid the blinding snow and raging seas with only a compass to guide them? If the crew of the lifeboat didn't freeze to death first, how would they be able to get the men off the storm-tossed sections of the broken tanker."[28]

As if Cluff could read Webber's thoughts, the chief turned and ordered him to gather a crew and use another motor lifeboat, the CG36500, to start pulling fishing boats off the harbor's beaches. Webber must have wondered if he was being punished.

And perhaps he was. By mid-afternoon, Webber and his crew had completed their assignment. They moored the lifeboat in Aunt Lydia's Cove and rowed ashore, looking forward to warming up back at the station.

Cluff met them at the beach. Another T2 tanker, the *SS Pendleton*, had broken apart off Provincetown and was drifting south. It might run aground on North Beach between Orleans and Chatham.

Cluff ordered Webber and his crew to take the station's Dodge wagon and drive to Orleans to see if they could spot the crippled tanker and render aid if the ship came ashore.

"Oh you could see it all right," recalled commercial fisherman David Ryder. "We could see the lights from it as it floated down the outer Cape. It kept blowing its whistle."[29]

• • • • •

At 5:40 that morning, Captain John Fitzgerald had the *Pendleton* standing off Boston and the tip of Provincetown, riding out the storm.

Suddenly a large wave hit the tanker. As it rolled from the impact, a second wave struck near amidships. Seaman Fred Brown said the resulting noise was "like the tearing of a large piece of tin. It's a noise that sends shivers up and down the spine and jangles every nerve."[30]*

The tearing noise startled Carol Kilgore awake. He dressed quickly and ran up on deck. "When I got there I couldn't believe my eyes," he said. "The bow was gone."

Eight men, including Captain Fitzgerald who was at the helm, were trapped on the bow. Thirty-three men on the stern watched the bow slowly drift away.

Chief Engineer Raymond Sybert took command of the stern. The bulkheads were holding, they had power and Sybert could steer with an emergency rudder control system.

The crew listened to reports about the *Fort Mercer* on a portable radio, but they weren't sure if anyone knew what was happening to them. Sybert decided not to run the tanker's stern aground on the outer Cape but keep it offshore in moderate seas.

U.S. Army Corps of Engineers builds a dike connecting Stage and Morris Islands to the mainland, while closing in Stage Harbor from the ocean.

1957

Webber met up with members of the Nauset Lifeboat Station in Orleans and drove to the top of a hill near Mayo's Duck Farm.

They were stunned at the sight before them. There offshore was "a ship, rather a half of a ship, black and sinister, galloping along up and down in huge waves," Webber said. The stern was heading towards Chatham.

Webber and his crew turned around to head for Chatham to spread the alarm.

Webber arrived back at about 5:30 P.M. It was almost dark.

"I sensed Cluff's course of action," Webber remembered. "My suspicion was confirmed when I heard him say, 'Webber, y'all pick yourself a crew. Y'all got to take the *36500* out over the bar and assist that thar ship, y'hear?'

"It took me a moment to digest his words. A sinking feeling came over me."[31]

As Webber assembled his crew – engineer Andrew J. Fitzgerald, seaman Richard Livesey, and seaman Irving Maske – he learned that Donald Bangs's crew had found the *Pendleton's* bow. But he was about to get whipsawed. Bangs was ordered to divert to the stern, then ordered back to the bow when another ship close by reported a man on deck.

If the men on the stern held out any hope, Bernie Webber somehow, some way had to find them.

Irving Maske, foreground, and Bernard Webber arrived back at the Chatham Fish Pier exhausted. Webber said later he began to tremble and sob when he realized what they had accomplished. *Photo courtesy of Kelsey Kennard Photo Gallery and www.capecodphotos.com*

Webber lost track of time. He just headed into the waves, hoping to steer near the Pollack Rip Lightship, which would tell him where he was. Suddenly "it appeared that a blackness much darker than I had been peering into existed ahead of us… I knew we had found the *Pendleton*."

Meanwhile Chief Sybert had ordered the *Pendleton's* engines engaged so that they would miss Chatham Bar. But he shut everything down after hearing a radio report that a motor lifeboat was on its way.

"We waited all day for rescue," said seaman Frank Fateaux. "We hoped for the best but our spirits were pretty low until we saw a glorious sight! It was the light of a single light bobbing up and down in the rolling sea…we were spellbound."[33]

• • • • •

Circling aircraft dropped red flares to illuminate the scene, creating an eerie sight. One of the crewmen on the stern dropped a Jacobs's ladder off the starboard side and some of the men started down.

"I moved the CG36500 in close to the hull of the *Pendleton*, timing my maneuver so as to be alongside at the right moment to let a man jump for our boat," Webber

President John F. Kennedy signs bill creating the Cape Cod National Seashore.

1961

said. "My crew were now forward on the CG36500, hanging on for dear life, waiting to catch the *Pendleton* crewmen as they came aboard."

Webber repeated the maneuver again and again. Finally only three remained, including ordinary seaman George "Tiny" Myers, the ship's 350-pound cook. One by one they jumped. Tiny missed.

"He was swallowed up by the sea and we lost sight of him," Webber said. They finally spotted him, hanging onto the side of a propeller blade.

"I eased ahead with the lifeboat," Webber said. "Suddenly, I felt our stern rise up and knew that a big sea was coming from behind."

He threw the lifeboat into reverse but "it was too late. The lifeboat was pushed ahead out of control and too sluggish to respond to any effort I made to steer clear," he continued. "I was backing the lifeboat full speed when we hit the *Pendleton,* smashing into Tiny Myers."

Amazingly Webber had rescued thirty-two of the thirty-three sailors on the *Pendleton's* stern. Counting the crew there were thirty-six men jammed onto a 36-foot lifeboat.

Somehow, Webber miraculously guided the CG36500 safely back into Chatham Harbor.

"When we got close to the fish pier, I looked up and was overwhelmed by the crowd standing there – men, women, even children of Chatham had turned out on this stormy night to greet and aid the survivors," Webber said.

"I stood at the stern of this little lifeboat, her name only CG36500, and realized she had carried us out into the unknown on a mission of mercy," he said. "Watching the *Pendleton* crew being assisted ashore by the Chatham folk, I began to tremble and sob. With my crewman Irving Maske beside me, I unashamedly cried in the near solitude and gave thanks to God for guiding us through the unknown."[34]

The Coast Guard awarded Webber, Maske, Fitzgerald, and Livesey the Gold Lifesaving Medal – comparable to the Congressional Medal of Honor – for their selfless heroism.

After the Sinking

The bow of the *Pendleton* the morning after the rescue. *Photo courtesy U.S. Coast Guard website.*

The eight men on the *Pendleton's* bow did not survive.

Mountainous seas swept them from the ship as rescuers watched helplessly, unable to get close to the vessel.

The *Pendleton's* stern drifted south before grounding just off Monomoy Island. By early evening on Feb. 18, the bow grounded on Pollack Rip Shoal.

Town celebrates 250th anniversary.

Construction begins on a new high school on Crowell Road.

Chatham Conservation Foundation is formed.

1962

For David Ryder the rescue seems like yesterday. "I remember it quite well because we were so concerned with those Coast Guard boys who went out," he said.

"A few days later we steamed down to the stern and went aboard. But there was not much for the taking."[35]

Prohibition: Dark Years After The War

During Prohibition Cape Cod was a perfect setting for rum runners. With miles of coastline and remote beaches it was a bootleggers' paradise.

Prohibition became the law of the land with ratification of the 18th Amendment on Jan. 16, 1919. But during the Great Depression, prohibition became increasingly unpopular. Forces advocating repeal, led by conservative Democrats and Catholics, argued that repeal would generate much needed tax revenue and weaken organized crime.

Yet on the Cape rum running was a fact of life.

"Liquor was going to the wealthy people, most of them summer people, no question about that," said David Ryder, retired commercial fisherman.[37]

Ryder's father, Richard, who was a Coast Guard officer at the time, spent most of his time chasing down rum runners. "Father was tenacious," Ryder said. "His job was to stop it from coming in."

But come in it did, often on the boats of local fishermen. "That's true," Ryder admitted. "Several men – including one in particular who I don't want to name – worked with the rum runners to bring in the loads.

"In fact a friend of mine, Captain Alvin Wright, came across a crew landing liquor in South Chatham and one of the guys pulled a gun on him. Well, Alvin got the heck out of there!"

Even lighthouse keepers got into the action.

Stanley M. Gunderson was keeper at Stage Harbor Lighthouse in the early '30s. According to an account in NElights.com, a group that promotes lighthouses in the Northeast, Gunderson "made extra income for himself by storing and bootlegging liquor, which he kept under the floorboards in the walkway that connected the lighthouse tower with the keeper's house."

The account goes on to report that one day a lighthouse inspector arrived for a surprise inspection, noticed the loose floorboards, but only told the keeper to repair them immediately!

The Dawn of Development

Although tourists and summer visitors had visited Chatham since the late 19th century, the years after the war saw the start of what would be a tsunami of residential development – and all that came with it.

"At the end of the war, I would guess that about 75 percent of the families living around here had no money," said George Goodspeed, who works as a real estate agent. "And it was probably true just about everywhere.

"But when people started coming back from the service and could find work and start settling down and raising a family, that's when things started to happen."[38]

Robert D. B. Carlisle recounts one failed developer who tried in the late 1920s.

"With his sights on North Chatham's Whiddah Road section, he erected a stone entrance gate and opened up roads," Carlisle wrote in *Weathering A Century of Change*. "Then came the crash and that project went into mothballs."

But by the 1950s summer cottage rentals started to take off. In 1953 the biggest subdivision to date materialized: Harbor Coves at the eastern end of Nickerson's Neck.

"Cleveland, Ohio, builder A. B. Smythe drew up a plan to build there on 90 lots," Carlisle wrote. "The homes would surround Fisher Eldredge's turn-of-the-century farmhouse on the rise overlooking Crows Pond. Smythe offered inside sites one-half to three-quarters of an acre in size; waterfront properties were bigger – one acre or one and a half."

The work was finished by 1956, "just in time to welcome a freshet of people looking for second homes" Carlisle said.

But the father of all Chatham subdivisions was just on the horizon: Riverbay Estates.

Harold J. Moye made Riverbay happen.

"I think more than anything he just decided to take a big, big chance," Goodspeed said. Moye, a successful car dealer in Quincy and Newton, owned a summer home in Chatham.

He soon moved to Chatham to open Harold J. Moye & Associates, and started looking at a 300-acre tract bordered by Old Queen Anne Road, Old Comers, and Training Field roads.

Soon he struck a deal with the land's owner, Gershom D. Hall. "He just had a knack for that sort of thing," Goodspeed said.

Riverbay Estates opened on May 29, 1962. For select one-acre sites overlooking the Monomoy River, or Muddy Creek to the locals, the price range was $10,500 to $11,000. Half-acre sites elsewhere cost $3,500, or perhaps a little higher.

Today there are 378 house sites in the community with only a few buildable lots remaining.

"It was so different in the war years," Goodspeed said.[39]

But slowly, the wars began receding from memory.

1962-2012

A Time of Change

By Eric Hartell

The 1960s arrived with the strengthening post-war economy. There was a certain autumnal slumber to Main Street after the busy summers of tourists and second home owners. There were days in February when only a few stores might be open: Puritan Clothing, the Cape Cod Five Cents Savings Bank, the Mayflower, the Wayside Inn, the Epicure, and Nickerson Liquors, Bearse's Store, and the A&P by the lights at Crowell Road. But in the summer, it was a different story.

The rhythms of summer haven't changed much over the years. As soon as colleges began winding down in May, students would arrive looking for work, along with the fun and games of vacation. There would be jobs for them in the shops, hotels, restaurants, with landscapers, and along the waterfront where the fishing industry has plenty of use for strong backs.

The population in 1960 clocked in at 3,273 and had doubled to 6,625 in 2000; in summer the town swells to some 20,000 or more.

Seasonal growth begins in June when some homeowners return from Florida and other warm weather alternatives, and when schools let out. A crescendo of in-migration hits in time for the July 4th weekend, which is perhaps the largest of the year, although in the 1990s began to be rivaled by First Night on December 31 each year.

The summer swoops through July and August and begins winding down towards Labor Day. Then in September and October the tour buses arrive with lots of visitors the shopkeepers depend on to keep things going into the autumn while the weather is still cooperative.

This keeps up until the first really cool days of November when there is a bit of a drop off; then the town is busy again for Thanksgiving as homeowners and visitors arrive to enjoy the holiday in warm New England style. Another drop off in early December is followed by an annual rush for the year-end holidays and also for First Night on New Year's Eve.

All of this is followed by the doldrums of winter.

"What do you do there in the winter?" we're always asked. The response, of course, is always polite. Family life is pretty much the same no matter where we live, and family life in Chatham is really no different than family life in any other location.

While digging a cellar for the Misses Lienau, Joe Dubis discovers a grave of two Native Americans. They were wrapped in eelgrass, lying on their sides, knees bent and hands together.

Stone Horse Lightship off Monomoy is decommissioned; The new high school opens.

1962

1963

Except those who call Chatham home have the long beaches to stroll on nice days – and there are plenty of them in the winter. Or there are wooded trails to explore. There's a great deal of wintertime theater and musical events, art exhibitions, and craft expositions. For a real change of pace, there are trips to Boston or Providence or farther afield, all without much danger of traffic tie-ups at the bridges.

Then there is the highly regarded winter vacation week in February, particularly for those who work hard in the summer when the population in town seems so enormous. Many townspeople have second homes, or at least vacation destinations, in places like Florida (for warmth) or northern New England (for winter sports).

A Surge of Growth

As the national economy strengthened, the pressure on Chatham increased. More and more people wanted to live here – or at least vacation here with the thought of later retirement. Existing summer homes – many without heat or insulation – were upgraded to provide for year-round use. New jobs opened in the building trades. But steps were taken as more homes were built and open land began to disappear at a pace that alarmed a number of townspeople.

Chatham began to explore its future. Residents began studying the potential affects of overdevelopment on the town's infrastructure, its water supply, its tax structure, its schools, and its ability to serve a burgeoning population. These concerns were championed by people like Alice Hiscock, perhaps the "mother of Chatham conservation," and Robert McNeece, the quiet selectman who always seemed able to look ahead and anticipate. Realtors E. Melson Webster and Hudson Eldridge, among others, saw that overdevelopment would endanger the quality of life in town, and they stepped forward to promote caution as the years proceeded.

Eventually study turned to action and town meetings approved articles approving formations of a Planning Board, a Zoning Board of Appeals, a Conservation Commission and other measures to help the town plan and control an orderly future. These agencies and their policies were perpetually under scrutiny. The constant tweaking tries to take into account changing living and building patterns and strives to keep these in close concert with the natural realities of living by the seacoast. Chatham's protective by-law is the envy of many Massachusetts cities and towns that haven't taken adequate precautions or didn't until the horse was out of the barn.

Changing Coastline

Nothing seems particularly new about the ever-changing shoreline that cradles Chatham on three of its sides. There is constantly shifting sand, coastal erosion, gain and loss to implacable tidal vagaries. No one is exempt, no area truly stable.

Chatham Bars Inn, for example, was built at a point opposite where the Chatham Harbor entrance was at the turn of the 20th century. After that time, the benign-looking barrier island of

500 children are enrolled in swimming classes at Oyster Pond.

October 24: The fishing vessel *Glenn and Maria* washes ashore on North Beach. The hull was later burned.

Town Architectural Board is formed.

1964

1965

1965

North Beach moved southward relentlessly at an almost measurable distance each year. It became so fragile in 1987 that a winter storm had its way with the beach, smashing through and creating a new harbor entrance. The result was deadly for several homes across the way, at Holway Street and elsewhere, washing away their underpinnings and dumping them into the harbor.

Local alarm was immediate.

As homeowners in the affected area sought solutions to keep their homes from a similar fate, the town sought guidance from experts. Oceanographer Graham Geise from Woods Hole studied the situation and found a cycle of erosion and build-up, erosion and build-up that dated back as far as he could find records: the 18th century.

Indeed there was nothing new about what had happened except that now a considerable amount of expensively developed real estate was at risk where previously little or none had existed. Homeowners eventually were granted permission to install rocky revetments where their lands met the capricious harbor waters. In recent years, at certain tides, a passing boater can sometimes see evidence of erosion behind these revetments, brown water indicating the presence of sandy soil coming from beneath the boulders.

In 2007 there was another break, this time across from Minister's Point in North Chatham, an event that caused similar homeowner alarm and is still being defended against. The break cut off a number of North Beach summer camps and carried away others.

Not all the town's coastal erosion occurs in the Chatham Harbor area. Wind and waves take their toll on lands facing Nantucket Sound as well. Some homes on the water in West and South Chatham are losing valuable protective land in front of them.

Conservation Efforts

As awareness of Chatham's fragility heightened in the early 1960s, the vision of Selectman Robert A. McNeece evidenced itself in the founding of the Chatham Conservation Foundation Inc.

He enlisted the aid of John Manson, founder of Manson Motors (now Chatham Ford), and retired General Lucius Clay. Clay was a deputy to General (and later President) Dwight D. Eisenhower during World War II. He was postwar military administrator of the American Zone and created the Berlin Airlift. The two men created a privately held nonprofit corporation, called the Chatham Conservation Foundation, to answer the concerns of those residents who were hesitant to donate land to a political entity. Chartered in 1962, it was the first private land trust on Cape Cod and, again, a model for surrounding towns, many of which have followed suit.

Robert McNeece.
Courtesy Chatham, Massachusetts Historical Society

In its formative stages there were seventeen life members who pledged ten acres of land. Today the foundation has some 1,000

Chatham Shopper News begins publishing.

Local fishermen for the Chatham Seafood Cooperative broker their catches, with a warehouse and retail outlet at Crowell and Tipcart Roads; it filed for bankruptcy in 1983. Weir fishermen broke off from this group and established their own cooperative, Chatham Weirs, which is still operating.

1965

1966

The founding officers of the Chatham Conservation Foundation receiving the certificate of incorporation from Governor John Volpe in 1962. L-R: State Rep. Hastings Keith, Peter Grey, John Manson, Gov. Volpe and Frank Love. *Courtesy Chatham, Massachusetts Historical Society.*

members and owns some 160 parcels totaling more than 524 acres in town. In addition, the organization holds deeded conservation restrictions on twenty-four parcels totaling nearly fifty-five acres. Some of these areas are in key areas along the Oyster River, Sears Point and some beach front along Shore Road.

The foundation also has acquired and maintains walking trails along Frost Fish Creek, Honeysuckle Lane, and Barclay's Pond. The group has partnered with the Town Land Bank since 1998 and together they work to identify properties that might be available for conservation designation. In 2003 the foundation assisted the neighboring Harwich Conservation Trust purchase some forty-three acres along Muddy Creek.

Selectmen continued to explore the future, appointing a number of committees to assist in fact-gathering. The Natural Resources Advisory Committee blazed the way for some by-law changes and policy revisions.

Growing Concerns

Along with the increasing number of residences and expanding business growth came the realization that government was becoming more and more complex. As growth and modernization continued, so too did local services and the town's government and infrastructure.

Because of demographics (Chatham at one point claimed 39 percent of its population was retired, the highest percentage on Cape at the time), a Council on Aging was formed to see to the specific needs of the elderly. It moved from one small office space to another in various locations and now is permanently sited on Stony Hill Road in North Chatham.

There is housing for the elderly in The Anchorage on Crowell Road, built with a great deal of state funding.

During the 1960s when there was legitimate concern about drug use and other youth-related issues, Monomoy Community Services was formed largely through the efforts of Dr. E. Robert Harned. It has permanent quarters today on Depot Road.

Monomoy Community Services is founded.

Chatham Shopper News evolves into the *Chatham News*, later called the *Lower Cape Cod Chronicle*.

1968

1968

Also certain delivery systems – town water principally among them – were becoming antiquated and needed updating, if not replacement. The state ordered the old disposal area off Sam Ryder Road closed, along with every other dump in the state.

These sorts of problems, along with the rigid new financial strictures of Proposition 2½ – enacted in 1982 – became somewhat overpowering for the volunteer board of selectmen, which sometimes was just 2½ men as longtime Selectman David Ryder, a commercial fisherman, opted for the part-time position which enabled him to fish during that season. The board expanded to five in 1987.

Voters ultimately approved a change establishing the position of town administrator, a person to take care of the daily minutia of town affairs, leaving the selectmen to set policy and to hire and fire.

After a studied search, James Lindstrom was the first selected for this post in 1986. He was followed by Thomas Groux and then by Town Manager William Hinchey. By the time the 1990s rolled in, the job had expanded to invest even more responsibility with the manager, including recruiting assistants, hiring and firing.

Working with the selectmen and other town boards, Hinchey reshaped services, combined providers of these services, and established new coordinating positions within the local government. Capital planning became systematized to anticipate maintenance and future needs and thus protect taxpayer investment in buildings and equipment.

Hinchey's departure from Chatham town government occurred in 2011 when selectmen voted 3-2 not to renew his contract, a decision which upset a segment of the community that felt he had done a superior job for the town. What followed was a recall attempt – the first in Chatham's history – that failed to get the required number of votes to force a new election. Selectmen then hired Jill Goldsmith as town manager after a long job search, and she took office in the summer of 2011.

Large projects accomplished during the last years of the 20th century included purchase of the Chatham Water Company, replacement of antiquated mains, and expansion of the entire delivery system. The disposal area was capped and the entire facility was redesigned to become a

Marker at the entrance of Volunteer Park. *Photo by Eric Hartell.*

The playground by Veterans Field. *Photo by Eric Hartell.*

Edward Harrington is elected selectman, serving until 1978.

Creative Arts Center on Crowell Road is founded.

Chatham Housing Authority established. The Chatham Drug Action committee put in place, chaired by Dr. E. Robert Harned.

1968

1969

1969

transfer station where trash is collected for delivery to a plant in Rochester. There it is burned and turned into electrical power that is fed into the New England power grid. The old disposal area also was turned into an almost all-inclusive recycling center.

In 1989, a modern children's playground was built next to Veterans Field off Depot Road. Volunteer Park, a spacious combination of playing fields off Sam Ryder Road was constructed in a wooded area. The old Main Street School, which at one point was the town's only school building but had been empty for years, was converted into a community center in 2006.

The long-crowded Chatham Police Department moved to brand new quarters off George Ryder Road in 2011 on property that once was home to Airport Lumber back in the 1960s and 1970s. This public works project included another building that houses several town agencies that have outgrown their space downtown in the Town Office Building. A study is already underway to modernize the old fire headquarters downtown. The town continues to move ahead.

Fishing and Shellfishing

The most traditional of all Chatham's industries, dating back to the 17th century, fishing came under fire during the latter part of the 20th century.

Natural trends, as well as increased worldwide demand for fish and greatly improved fishing efficiency brought some North Atlantic fish stocks down to the point where the federal government stepped in and began regulating the fisheries.

The number of families which depended on fishing for their livelihoods declined. Regulations kept changing and frustration set in. The Cape Cod Hook Fisherman's Association was formed in 1991 to try to deal with the ever-changing regulations. It is based in West Chatham and is an important function of continued commercial fishing interests.

Shellfish remains a vital crop, providing for several hundred families in town who fish commercially and for thousands with family permits. In the 1970s, then Shellfish Constable Katherine (Kassie) Abreu – the first female in Massachusetts to hold such a position – engineered legislation in Boston enabling Chatham to have its own revolving fund for shellfish propagation. It derives its income from shellfish permit fees. Spat (shellfish spawn) is purchased, nursed until it can be introduced into the wild, and then is seeded in beds that have been overfished and closed.

This aquaculture procedure, along with natural propagation, keeps Chatham's industry vital – at least insofar as producing quahogs and clams. The mussel crops that once were so prolific have been decimated by the town's burgeoning gray seal population which seems to prize them as much as humans do.

The seals, which once had a town bounty (50 cents, payable at town hall in the early 1960s) on their noses, have grown into a population of several thousand since being protected by federal law some thirty years ago. They like Chatham waters because they are home to plenty of fish on which they feed. This, of course, puts them into direct competition with fishermen, which is why there was a bounty on them those many years ago.

Chatham Chorale is formed by Marjorie Bennett Morley and Dr. E. Robert Harned.

Victor Horst gives seventy acres of Strong Island to conservation.

Formation of Natural Resources Advisory Committee approved at town meeting.

1970

1971

1972

The seals also attract tourists and great white sharks which are known to consider the seals a delicacy. The tourists like to see the seals, which sometimes cavort for them and are always interesting to watch. They don't like to see the sharks, which represent a substantial perceived hazard for swimming and other water sports. The town continues to wrestle with the problem of swimming safety, particularly in the area of Lighthouse Beach.

The town has improved its town landings to accommodate residents, summer visitors and daily transients during the peak fishing and boating seasons. There are several thousand boat moorings permitted in Chatham waters, and the number of boaters attracts a lot of traffic. Particular attention has been paid to Ryders Cove landing and Stage Harbor Road.

Ernie Eldredge and Shareen Davis
"It's a whole different world of fishing now"

Ernie Eldredge and Shareen Davis are making a living as a fishing family, despite restrictive regulations, quotas and diminishing fish stocks. Ernie is a trap fisherman. He uses fixed gear – also known as weirs – to take his catch. He's been doing this all his adult life, and even before, while he was in school.

"I remember my graduation party (from Chatham High School) at the Beach and Tennis Club. I left that party and came directly to the dock to go out to the traps that morning," he recalls. "I guess I must have started going out to the traps when I was 11 or 12." His father was Lester "Boney" Eldredge, a well-known trap fisherman who taught his son the trade. Ernie has been at it since 1969.

Ernie Eldredge and Shareen Davis at their pier on Stage Harbor. *Photo by Eric Hartell.*

The season begins in March, when biting winds blow. Great hickory poles are set from the open boat into the frigid waters off Hardings Beach or on the Common Flats west of Monomoy or along the Nantucket Sound beaches in Harwich, Dennis, and Yarmouth. The nets are strung and the fish are harvested until the end of June when the season winds down, and the nets and poles are retrieved until next year. The poles are laid in piles along the Stage Harbor cut-through, and the nets are mended. Every three to five years the state reviews the permitting process and keeps tabs on the trappers. Some of the trap permits date back to the 1800s, and some as recently as 1982.

Shareen Davis and Ernie have been a team for many years. She is from the family of Kenneth Cobb "Cobby" Eldredge. "We're the Stage Harbor Nickersons, not the North Chatham Nickersons,"

Congregate Housing opens at Captain's Landing.

1972

Old Harbor Life Saving Station is moved by the National Park Service from North Beach and eventually reaches Race Point Beach in Provincetown. The station is renovated in 2011.

1973

she explains. Both Ernie (8th generation) and Shareen (13th generation) were born in Chatham. Ernie says he has some Wampanoag blood somewhere in the family.

Shareen and Ernie also manage a dockside facility on the shores of Stage Harbor. The dock itself has been in continuous use since 1782, and they have some documents that indicate it might date back as far as 1711. At one time it was a landing for steamboats plying the waters of Nantucket Sound. Today the dock provides fish landing facilities, refueling capabilities, sells ice, and provides access for trucks to pick up landed catches.

The couple is feeling the pinch of fishing restrictions, both in their own catches and in those landed at their dock. In the late 1960s there were four trap companies operating from docks in Stage Harbor. During the 1990s there were as many as 13 men making a living there. By 2011 though, only two or three families were making a living by trap fishing.

During the 1980s as many as a half-million pounds of mackerel was taken in a given season. In 2011 the total was five hundred pounds. Fisheries reports in late 2011 said that inshore water temperatures in southeastern New England had risen to the point where mackerel no longer swims here.

In an attempt to counter the trend of what is called "factory" fishing and the onset of increased competition from predators such as seals, the Eldredges and other fishermen have started up an enterprise called the Cape Cod Community Supported Fishery. This is a seafood cooperative, whereby the public can pre-buy certain seafood delivered to a public site for distribution at a designated time. The trend is catching on and is energetically promoted by Shareen and other women associated with the fishing industry.

Shareen's other career is as a photographer, and her work has been widely published on the Cape. She collaborates with Ginny Nickerson at the Nickerson Gallery on Main Street. She uses her photography as a tool in promoting the Community Supported Fishery and trap fishing in general. She and Ernie have presented programs on the industry at the Cape Cod Maritime Museum in Hyannis, where their daughter, Shannon, is educational director, and at the Cape Cod Museum of Natural History in Brewster. They've also put on educational programs inside the salty confines of their Stage Harbor dock.

They continue to carry the ball for what they term "artisanal fisheries." They maintain that certain species such as squid, scup, butterfish, black sea bass, fluke and bluefish can be harvested sustainably. Livings can be eked out by innovating and carefully using the product, they say, along with continued public education.

Summer Workers

The nature of the summer labor force has changed over the past twenty or so years. As summer crowds prompted more shops and inns to expand, local student help no longer was sufficient. In the 1980s seasonal workers began arriving from Jamaica, and their presence in town is now year-round. A memorable July 4th parade some years ago featured a stake-body truck with workers from Jamaica standing in the back on a very hot day – all dressed in winter clothing to show

Monomoy Community Services is established.

Cape Cod Chronicle begins publication; it evolved from the *Lower Cape Cod Chronicle*.

1973

1974

they were not used to Chatham's "temperate" climate! The show of great good humor was a hit with those attending the parade, and they cheered their new neighbors.

In the last years of the 20th century, young seasonal workers began arriving from Eastern Europe each summer, and they too have been welcomed. Many of them work in shops and restaurants, others with landscaping companies.

Changing Schools

Chatham's schools have evolved markedly in the past fifty years. The K-12 population has dropped off a bit over the years, and the high school became a school-choice facility in the 1990s that permitted students from neighboring towns to be schooled here. Three times since the 1960s, a merger with Harwich schools was proposed as a cost-saving measure for both towns, but was rejected twice. Then in 2011 the towns, both facing severe financial constraints, agreed to combine their school facilities.

That process was in high gear as Chatham's tricentennial commenced. The plan is for a new regional high school in Harwich, conversion of Chatham High School to a middle school for both towns, and retained use of each town's elementary schools.

In the early 1970s, Chatham joined with twelve other mid- and lower Cape towns to form the Cape Cod Regional Technical High School district. That very successful facility opened in 1975 and claims enrollment of about 800 students in grades 9-12 from throughout the district.

Draw for Well-known Names

Chatham is the hometown of Todd Eldredge, the 1996 World Figure Skating Champion and six-time national champion.

Over the years the town's beauty and life style have attracted many from the worlds of arts and government. The late jazz trumpeter Bobby Hackett (1915-1976) lived in West Chatham for a number of years, and is buried in Seaside Cemetery. The late stage and television actress Shirley Booth lived on Bay Lane for many years. Actress Julie Harris has a home in West Chatham. Singer Harry Connick, Jr.'s home overlooks Oyster Pond. Retired Supreme Court Justice Sandra Day O'Connor is a homeowner. Former U.S. Senator Paul Tsongas (1941-1997) kept a home on Shore Road, and his widow, U.S. Representative Nikki Tsongas, is a frequent visitor.

Many Cultural Outlets

Chatham has always been blessed with a vibrant cultural life. The Chatham Drama Guild, dating back to the 1930s, still provides entertainment for the community and opportunities for those who want to participate.

In the summer Ohio University theater students and arrive in town to stage their annual series of productions at the Monomoy Theatre, bolstered with a number of local actors and

As a result of revaluation, the total value of real estate and personal property in town jumps from $56 million in 1973 to $258 million in 1974.

1974

Council on Aging is established.

1974

volunteers. John and Elizabeth Baker developed Mary Winslow's Monomoy Theatre into the inviting theatrical venue on Main Street in 1958. Christopher and Charlotte Lane presided over this local institution for many years. Now it is a labor of love for Alan and Jan Rust, who also maintain a home in South Chatham.

The Chatham Chorale, now a regional musical force with one-hundred auditioned singers, was founded in 1970 by Marjorie Bennett Morley and Dr. E. Robert Harned. The group has toured in this country and abroad to great acclaim.

The Creative Arts Center on Crowell Road was founded in 1969 and has organized the juried Chatham Festival of the Arts in Chase Park each summer since the early 1970s. The Chatham Artists Guild formed in the 1990s and represents several dozen local painters.

WFCC-FM radio was founded in Chatham in 1987 and operated there for several years. It's the only classical music station in the area, and now is part of the Cape Cod Broadcasting group in Hyannis.

The *Cape Cod Chronicle* was founded in 1965 as the *Chatham Shopper News*. It has evolved from a twice-a-month, book-sized, free distribution publication to a paid circulation weekly carrying primarily news of interest to Chatham and Harwich residents. It flourishes today under the leadership of Henry C. Hyora, whose father was a commercial fisherman here.

The Eldredge Public Library, most capably run by librarian Irene Gillies and assisted by an enthusiastic staff and a devoted coterie of Library Friends, has become a model of modern public service, offering books, genealogical records, films, Internet enhancements, and programs for children.

The Chatham Historical Society is justifiably proud of its museum and meeting hall in the Atwood House on Stage Harbor Road. This organization has been accumulating family records and historical documents since 1923. Their resources, special programs and exhibits are a rich enhancement of community life.

The Nickerson Family Association has its own meeting house and museum at the head of Ryders Cove where William Nickerson first built his homestead when he founded the town.

Nearby is the new Chatham Marconi Maritime Center, a restoration of the radio center once used for communications traffic with Atlantic shipping. It opened to the public in 2010.

Public Events

Public ceremonies have always been a part of Chatham's schedule each year. The July 4th parade takes on a life all its own and thousands of spectators line the long route from the corner of Shore Road and Main Street, down Main Street and past the rotary. Dozens of Chatham's seemingly endless battalion of volunteers work all year to make this special event possible.

In 1991, a group led by Marie Williams, which included Marge Long, Larry Hamilton, Lettie Sullivan, and many others, put together Chatham's First Night, a rollicking New Year's Eve festival for the whole family that has grown each year. There's a hilarious costumed road "race,"

Cape Cod Regional Technical High School District is formed.

Chatham Historical Commission is formed.

Town Hall is expanded.

1975

1976

1978

a town photograph taken at the Chatham Light, a noise parade for children, ice sculptures, food stands, and hourly entertainment acts in churches and schools. It is a true crowd-pleaser that draws thousands of people – both residents and visitors – to the downtown area each December 31.

Every summer the Cape Cod Baseball League – a premier showcase for college players – cranks up, and the Chatham Anglers are a big part of it. Thousands attend the games that are played from Orleans to Wareham. And not all those sitting in the stands are residents and visitors. Some are major league scouts (usually with speed guns to clock the pitchers), and they have discovered a number of players who have gone on to professional status after their college careers. The Anglers are the pet project of the Chatham Athletic Association, which sells gear and passes the hat during games to help meet the costs of fielding the team.

Perhaps the most venerated of all of Chatham's institutions is the Chatham Town Band, which miraculously has survived since before World War II, anchored by Eldredges, Nickersons, Goodspeeds, and all their friends. They march in the July 4th parade and give concerts every Friday night of the summer in Kate Gould Park on Main Street. If you listen to a concert, you may imagine you hear the rich baritone voice of the man who led them for many glorious years, the man for whom the charming Victorian bandstand is named – Whit Tileston. His angel certainly still hovers there.

Development and Developers

Chatham's popularity as a vacation and retirement destination goes without saying. In fact, a few years ago, the National Trust for Historic Preservation bestowed on the town the title Destination of Distinction. Even with the economic stuttering of the OPEC oil embargo of the mid-1970s, the value of Chatham real estate continued to escalate, almost dizzyingly, until the beginning of the 21st century.

In 1973 the town's total assessed valuation rested at a modest level, just under $56 million for all real estate and personal property. This number produced a tax rate of $49.50 per $1,000 assessed. Then came Proposition 2½ in 1982, and after the revaluation fallout, the property valuation rose to more than $250 million, thus reducing the tax rate to only $12.50. The enormous change in taxed values forced some long-time homeowners into sale of their properties. They couldn't afford the taxes based upon adjusted values. It was a time of change.

The values continued to grow with the burgeoning American economy. In 1981 the assessed valuation was just under $300 million. Somewhere between 1987 and 1988 it reached a significant milestone: $1 billion. The spiral continued upward for a while reaching a combined valuation in 2007 of nearly $6.5 billion. Since that time the total has dipped slightly, but even in 2010, after several years of tough economic structuring, it remained at more than $6.3 billion. As a consequence, Chatham continues to have one of the lowest tax rates in the Commonwealth of Massachusetts.

A good measure of this escalation in value was due to inflation during the period. Prices rose everywhere, but the demand for Chatham real estate was unrelenting. A significant component

February 6: A sever winter storm, with winds reaching 100 mph and 20-foot seas, breaches North Beach in four places, with ten camps suffering serious damage and eight more with water damage. A break one-third mile wide severs Monomoy from Morris Island.

Eldredge Public Library hires its first professional librarian: Irene Gillies.

1978

1979

of increased valuation was new construction, additions to buildings, and rehabilitation of older buildings. More people were retiring earlier and creating destinations for this purpose. Still others, still working, were able to move their entrepreneurial activities out of urban environs and come here. While some, pursuits, such as fishing, lost jobs, the building trades produced new ones.

Bill Marsh

Bill Marsh
Photo by Eric Hartell.

A major player in this growth has been Bill Marsh and his company, Eastward Homes. As of 2011 they built some 1,000 homes in Chatham, Harwich, and elsewhere on the Cape since the early 1970s. Marsh and his financial chief, Donald Poyant, say it is a $20 to $25 million a year business. Eastward Homes has employed as many as thirty-two people during peak years of operation, sometimes producing sixty homes a year, or more than one a week. And although Marsh has been in business for more than forty years, he's eager to continue.

Marsh and his family came to Chatham from North Adams in the Berkshires in 1971. His father had been a building contractor there, but that area was experiencing an economic downturn and he moved the family to the Cape to seek work. Marsh worked for his father for a while, recalling he was paid the going rate of $3.75 an hour.

He then set out on his own and soon had a mentor and strong guiding hand in the person of Harold J. Moye, developer of Riverbay Estates in Chatham and other projects elsewhere on the Cape. Moye showed Marsh, then only in his early 20s, how to acquire property and develop it. He stood up for Marsh in the banking community. His overriding advice to the young man: "Work hard and pay your bills." Marsh never forgot Moye's kindnesses to him.

As Marsh's enterprises grew, so too did the economy. Off-Cape banks in depressed areas were seeking new avenues of investment, Marsh recalls, and many of them targeted the Cape and particularly the home-building industry. Eastward Homes became a beneficiary of this trend. But in 1974-75, economic troubles surfaced again and March suffered through foreclosures before getting back on his feet again in 1976-77.

After that ordeal a consultant suggested that Marsh find a financial person to take that particular load off his shoulders. He began the search that ended with Poyant joining the company. Since then, the company has been financially stable, and Marsh gives the credit to Poyant. He had been the town's financial director and is generally known to have been architect of the town's solid financial footing. Marsh says Poyant is more that chief financial officer for Eastward Homes. "He's more like a chief operating officer."

Marsh lives in a home overlooking Stage Harbor and has a racing/cruising sloop he can be found in on the best sailing days of summer.

Attorney William G. Litchfield is elected to Board of Selectmen. At age 25, he is the youngest person ever to be elected to Chatham's board. He serves on the board through 1987.

Friends of Trees is formed.

1980

1980

David Oppenheim

Another lightning rod for business in Chatham is David Oppenheim, whose interests and successes include home building and land development, but are certainly more diversified, too.

Like so many others of his generation on Cape Cod, he came here as a young man, a student looking for summer work. He says he began his career by selling hot dogs on the beaches of Yarmouth during his college summers. He studied briefly at the Cornell University hotel school and then shifted to a business major at Clark University.

In Chatham, Oppenheim most visibly is owner/operator of the Chatham Wayside Inn, which has been in its present location on Main Street in one form or another since about 1860. He and Boston venture capitalist Grant Wilson (who lives on the Oyster River) acquired it in 1993. Oppenheim since has acquired sole ownership.

The inn has undergone extensive modernization and expansion under his stewardship. It has fifty-six rooms and a dining room seating 275. He also owns the Bradford Motel on Cross Street and has modernized that facility as well. The inns together employ some 130 people in the peak summer season. Of these, fifty are year-rounders either full or part-time. Ten have been with Oppenheim for fifteen years or more.

David Oppenheim
Photo by Eric Hartell.

His first enterprise in town was the acquisition in 1986 of the Chatham Yacht Basin from then-owner Skip Hall. At this facility on the Oyster River in West Chatham, a great deal of updating has been done to create a marina with sixty-six slips and thirty moorings. Oppenheim says the yard took care of about 150 customers in 2011.

But he was always interested in building and even tried carpentry for a while as a young man. During his years in Chatham, he figures he's built about 175 homes and has been responsible for another twenty-five modernization projects such as the two inns, the so-called Epicure Building on Main Street, the condominiums at the former Christian's restaurant, and the conversion of the former Town House Inn on Library Lane into a private residence. He developed the old Dolphin Inn property on lower Main Street, converting the inn's main building into a residence. He is pleased the LaRose property that he owned in West Chatham across from Barn Hill Road turned out well is now headquarters of the Cape Cod Commercial Hook Fisherman's Association.

In 2011 Oppenheim said that between 1980 and 1997 the number of overnight accommodations for visitors to town had doubled and he saw no need for future increases. "There was no demand for the Town House Inn, and the Dolphin had to be knocked down," he said.

A main concern for Chatham's economic future, he said, is parking. "We're just going to have to learn to share what parking we have today," he said.

Proposition 2½ is enacted, lowering Chatham's tax rate while increasing property valuations.

1982

Over the years Oppenheim has joined Chatham's community of volunteers. He served on the Finance Committee, Underground Utilities Study Committee, Historic Business District Review Committee, and the Police Annex Review Committee.

He and his wife, Gail, have been benefactors of various philanthropic causes locally, among them the Fontaine Medical Center in East Harwich.

The Preservation Movement Grows

As residential and commercial development proceeded apace during the end of the 20th century, some residents became alarmed. These people began tracking events they felt were jeopardizing the town's historical and cultural riches. They volunteered to serve on the key committees where they felt appropriate protections could be put in place.

Two clear leaders of this movement have been Norm Pacun and Gloria Freeman, whose efforts eventually brought about some toughening of zoning rules and practices and heightened community awareness of these issues.

Pacun, a career attorney from greater New York, admits to always having been a history buff. After he moved to town permanently in 1987, he was taken in tow by the late local historian Claire Baisley. Soon he found himself serving on the Chatham Historical Commission. He served for eleven years, nine as its chairman. He was instrumental in the inclusion of 500 to 600 homes in town being surveyed for listings with the State Historical Commission. These listings serve to slow down a process of demolishing old homes in favor of new construction.

This led, in 1992-93, to enactment of a local demolition delay by-law. Previously, an owner wishing to demolish an older home had to wait six months. This was expanded to a full year and then, in 2008, the Chatham Historical Commission voted to extend the demolition delay to eighteen months for any home over 75 years old. Pacun feels this measure has put a damper on the loss of historic buildings in town.

"But we still lose perhaps seven out of ten old homes," he says, in that they often are added onto with modern wings that are out of keeping with a traditional neighborhood appearance.

A significant accomplishment of preservationists, he says, has been the creation of a National Register Historic District in the Old Village near the lighthouse. This has provided another buffer between the traditional appearance of this neighborhood and those who would change it.

As of late 2011, Pacun says his greatest satisfaction would come if his long campaign to preserve the wooden structure of the Mitchell River Bridge is successful. "It is the only wooden drawbridge left in the United States," he says, and certainly worth preserving. The Massachusetts Department of Transportation has said the bridge must be repaired or replaced. With what materials and who will pick up the $11 million tab have been matters of controversy. In 2011 the bridge was deemed eligible for the National Register of Historic Places.

Gloria Freeman, a familiar figure at town meetings, is a strong ally of Pacun. A career educator from Baltimore, Freeman was head of the Johns Hopkins University School of Continuing Education. She also worked closely with the Joseph P. Kennedy Foundation. The worlds of politics

Friends of Stage Harbor Waterways, now Friends of Chatham Waterways, is formed.

1983

and government liaison were not unknown to her when she moved to town in 1994. But she thought retirement would be different.

"We moved here because of Chatham's special character, its long shoreline, historic character, its beaches and marshes. I had no idea I'd be involved in politics here," she recalls. But soon after she settled into her retirement home on a quiet North Chatham street, the property across the street was subdivided and soil was brought in great quantities, she says, to make a hill which would afford a water view for the new home to be built there.

She started going to Planning Board meetings to find out what she could about development laws and practices. She thought she could make a difference so she volunteered for and served on that board. She also served on the Historic Business District Commission, the Historical Commission, the Community Preservation Act Committee, and worked on the town's Comprehensive Plan with the Long Range Planning Committee. She finally gave up committee work, believing she could be more effective working outside the strictures of committee protocols.

Freeman was instrumental in getting the town to replace the new but rusty guard rails along Stage Harbor Road by the Oyster Pond. The current wooden guardrails are smaller and more in keeping with that beautiful area. She also has to her credit the preservation of the two old homes– one the residence of the late Holly Thayer and the other originally the home of Levi Atwood but later the home of the late Edward and Marcia Norman, overlooking the Oyster Pond on Stage Harbor Road. Both were slated for demolition when Freeman spearheaded a major effort that ultimately convinced their new owner to preserve the landmark homes rather than build new ones on the site. Both were beautifully restored with most of their traditional appearance retained. She also worked to insure that the old Sou'wester restaurant building in West Chatham was retained. It now is home to a Dunkin' Donuts.

Another successful venture was her championing of the Chatham Village Market at the intersection of Queen Anne Road and Main Street. The market was targeted for closure and replacement by a CVS store. Due to a vast effort in which Freeman collected thousands of signatures, the market was relocated to a new building next door to its original location, with the CVS occupying the former market building. Freeman says she was very honored by the store's owners asking her to cut the ribbon at the grand opening in 2011.

She also worked on the formula business establishment zoning by-law now in place. This law requires a chain store (or formula business) to go to the Planning Board for site plan review and to the Zoning Board of Appeals for approval. The purpose of this regulation is to protect locally-owned businesses and to help maintain the town's character by assuring that a building is in keeping with local architecture. Evidence of the beneficial effect of this by-law is the attractive building that now houses the Chatham Village Market and the new CVS Store.

She hopes in the future the zoning by-law will be revised to be in better concert with the town's Comprehensive Plan, and that there be stronger protection of historical assets. And, she wishes more people would go to public meetings and speak up for better preservation.

"Small changes do add up," she says.

State Department of Environmental Quality Engineering closes all of Oyster Pond to shellfishing due to high levels of fecal coliform bacteria.

Friends of Pleasant Bay is formed.

1983

1984

David Doherty, Jack Farrell
Rollercoaster Real Estate

Chatham is known around the world for its quality of life and value in real estate. That, according to David Doherty, head of E. Melson Webster Inc., the eponymous real estate agency founded by his late father-in-law.

Doherty says there are fewer than one thousand lots left on which new housing can be built. So the up-and-down real estate market in coming years will be largely one of re-development, where existing homes will be altered, expanded, or replaced by new buildings.

Doherty remembers when real estate mortgages in the early 1980s were commanding interest rates of 18 percent or higher, but that didn't deter people from coming to town and investing in a summer home and then eventually retiring here.

The quality of life and real estate values are due in large part to the layers of regulations that have been hammered out by town boards and committees over the years.

Jack Farrell, long-time attorney and now an associate of Doherty's at the Webster firm, says Chatham has always been ahead of the curve on these protective by-laws. Chatham had a septic code eight years before Massachusetts issued its regulations. The town's sign code also is rigorous, Farrell says, and the new town-wide sewer project is a benchmark for other communities across the Commonwealth.

David Doherty
Photo by Eric Hartell

These are factors that make Chatham so attractive, they say. And, the fact that the town is so out-of-the-way and not intruded upon by the Mid-Cape highway enhances real estate values.

Of no little consequence to the town's appearance and desirability is the constant presence of the Chatham Conservation Foundation, the private entity formed fifty-one years ago to acquire lands, both by gifts and purchases, to prevent it from being developed. Doherty has served as the Foundation's president.

The nature of the real estate sales industry in town has changed significantly in the years Doherty has been in Chatham. In the mid-1970s, when he began, there were perhaps five or six realty offices. Recently, there have been as many as 130 brokers and sales representatives vying for Chatham's listings.

The Multiple Listing Service was inaugurated across Cape Cod in the late 1970s and early 1980s. That revolutionized the industry but was minor compared to today's internet conveniences. Today, would-be Chatham property owners can shop online from around the world, Doherty says. Many of the town's real estate offices now have national corporate roots, further widening the market.

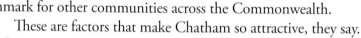

William Nickerson Memorial Park opens just off the Chatham Rotary.

1995

Margo Fenn becomes Chatham's first town planner.

1986

Jim Lindstrom is selected as town's first "executive secretary," with duties of an administrator.

1986

The first so-called summer homes, were built to be just that – summer homes, Doherty explains. They weren't insulated or constructed for year-round habitation. Today's regulations no longer allow for that type of construction.

Many homes in Chatham are not used throughout the summer and a great many more are not used year-round. "There are thousands of rental units available in Chatham," Doherty says, most for one- or two-week periods.

John Whelan
"Where everybody knows your name"

Certainly one of Chatham's most recognizable "townies" is John Whelan, affable financial services retiree, sports buff, organizer, volunteer, and perpetual booster of Chatham and its people.

His forbearers were the Shepard family who came to town in the early years of the 20th century to help build Chatham Bars Inn. John's grandfather, John Shepard, was from the Worcester area and was successful bidder on the heating and plumbing work when the inn was built in time to open for the 1914 season. He went on to work on successive landmark projects: the Chatham Links golf course, Eastward Ho! Country Club, and the Main Street School (now the Chatham Community Center). His brother, John's Uncle Charlie, ran the plumbing and heating business into the early 1980s.

John's mother, Ellen Shepard, was a teacher in Franklin when she met Leonard Whelan, a Tufts Dental School student who played the saxophone in bands each summer to pay his tuition. After they were married he hung out his shingle in Chatham.

Sometimes, like many other professional people who decided to live here, Leonard had to accept quahogs for services rendered. Although no one in the family starved, he did decide to go back to central Massachusetts. The family was always drawn to Chatham, however, and moved back in 1956. John began his schooling here, and when he went away to the Loomis School in eastern Connecticut, there were four Chatham residents teaching there – Alexander "Sandy" Flash, David Haller, Frank House, and Spencer Grey were on the faculty.

John Whelan
Photo by Eric Hartell.

As a youngster he went to Everett "Gunny" Eldredge's Camp Malabar in West Chatham in the summer. Later he spent his summers as a seasonal letter carrier at the Chatham Post Office, which helped fuel his love of the people in town.

From Loomis, John tried the pre-dental program at Tufts but really didn't care for it. He tried one term at the University of Pennsylvania and then landed at Babson University in Boston for investment studies followed by graduate school in business. There was a stint in the U.S. Army where, he says, he pretty much "ran the quarter-mile." At Fort Jackson and at Fort Sill, Oklahoma, in those

The eastern third of Oyster Pond is declared off-limits to shellfishing due to below-standard water quality.

1986

A winter storm breaks through the fragile North Beach barrier, creating a new entrance to Chatham Harbor. Several homes are washed away. Another storm in September strips away at least thirty feet more.

1987

days, the base commanders were fiercely competitive with the athletic prowess of their troop and John was quite swift on his feet, so . . . that's how he spent much of his brief Army career.

When he returned to Chatham, John and Martha Murphy were married and had two children. Merritt is now married and has three children all residing in Pennsylvania. Son Chris works for ESPN in Connecticut. He's married and has two children. Martha, daughter of the late Dr. Charles Murphy, died many years ago. Her brother, Tony, is a mainstay at Stage Harbor Marine.

John at first was going to become a financial analyst in the automotive field, but he's just too much of a people person. So he became a securities broker, helping people with their investments. He was based in Boston for his first two years, but by 1968 he was back in Chatham, working first for Bache & Co., then Merrill Lynch, then Shearson, before settling with Paine Webber from 1988 to 2003. At that point he joined the Trust Management department at Cape Cod Five and enjoyed that position for four years before retiring. He and wife Nancy live on a side street near the lighthouse in the Old Village.

John really doesn't sit around much. He has served on the Finance Committee, Cultural Council, Community Preservation Committee, Erosion Advisory Committee, Cable TV Advisory Committee, and Historical Commission. He's even tried his hand at children's literature and writes a humorous, warm column for the *Cape Cod Chronicle.*

An early and abiding love is the Chatham Platform Tennis Association. No one today has had more to do with the formation and perpetuity of this very active and popular group founded in the early 1970s. He's served the club in almost every capacity, including president and – oh yes – one of its foremost players! He's still playing.

But his greatest passion is the Town of Chatham itself and its people. He says we all should give continuous thanks to all the people over the years who gave so much to keep the town as beautiful as it is. And the best part of all is the people who live here. "They are absolutely spectacular people," he says.

Dougie Bohman
Waiting for a Bridge

Douglas Ann Bohman is known by all as Dougie. She's a physiotherapist by trade, a pretty good golfer and a very competent public official. She was the town's first female chairman of selectmen.

She and her late husband, Ray, came to town from Gardner in 1966 after a few summer rentals in the Dennisport area. Local real estate agent Dick Rochette showed them a house on Bay Lane, just down the road from Main Street, where they would make their home for about forty years. Ray wrote transportation articles for *Logistics* magazine and newsletters for the trade.

Not long after they moved here, Dougie was in the old Bearse's Store on Main Street and met Lucy Buckley, the affable owner of a physiotherapy business in the West Chatham building now occupied by Chatham Pottery. The two hit it off and Dougie began to work for Lucy, first on a part-

WFCC-FM classical music radio station begins broadcasting.

1987

Board of Selectmen expands to five members.

1987

About thirty revetments are installed in two sections: Claflin Landing to Holway Street and Andrew Harding's Lane to the Chatham Beach and Tennis Club.

1988

time basis and then full time. Eventually, the shop moved to Route 137 in East Harwich by the fire station.

Meanwhile Dougie and Ray were raising their family of three sons. The oldest, David, now lives in Drum, Pennsylvania, and is a news reporter and anchor for a local television station. Jack is a principal in a local real estate firm and is married to Sally Munson, owner of Chatham's Munson Gallery. Jack in an earlier career, was the golf pro at Eastward Ho! Country Club, where Dougie still chases the ball around at least once a week. The youngest of Dougie's sons, Andrew, also is in real estate and has worked at Pate's Restaurant "forever."

Public service began tugging at Dougie's sleeve many years ago. Attorney Bill Riley suggested that she'd be ideally suited as a Finance Committee member. Thus began a 12-year stint on that board, all in the years before the town had a finance director to keep tabs on the minutia of local funding.

Douglas Ann Bohman and her bridge.
Photo by Eric Hartell.

She remembers one time when then Highway Surveyor Gibby Borthwick came before the committee in hopes of getting funds for a new department truck. "Gibby had been welding the truck together for far too long," Dougie recalls. In her final years on the FinCom she co-chaired three years with Ben Goodspeed and three years with Harvey Huetter.

William Litchfield first suggested that Dougie run for selectman. She was doing full-time physiotherapy work then and didn't campaign well, she says. Norman Howes won that election, but three years later in the early 1990s, she did win a seat. "I was the last selectman candidate to run without putting campaign signs on the lawns," she says. Thus began a fifteen-year stint as a town selectman. She wasn't the first female selectman – Josephine Ives has that honor – but was indeed the first lady chairman of selectmen and served in that capacity for five years.

"You know it's the greatest feeling when you know you're helping the town," she says. Her favorite memories include "walking the bounds." That is an age-old custom dating back to colonial times in Massachusetts whereby town officials literally walk the town lines with abutting officials – in this case Harwich – to make sure nothing's been moved or markers damaged. Apparently it's quite easy to become ensnared in underbrush and otherwise impeded.

A Taste of Chatham premiers as a fundraiser for Monomoy Community Services.

1988

A children's playground is built next to Veteran's Field on Depot Road.

1989

The town changes its waste management from a dump to a transfer and recycling station.

1989

Despite long hours of hard work there were moments of fun. She recalls the visit to Chatham a few years ago of the *HMS Chatham* and the visit to town of the British vessel's officers and men.

Real high points of her tenure on the board include acquisition of the Marconi wireless station property in Chathamport and South Chatham and the eventual acquisition of the Chatham Bars Inn golf course, which she describes as "the Central Park of Chatham."

It wasn't hard to think of a gift for Dougie when she retired from her many years as Finance Committee member and selectman. She often had told the story of how her two grandfathers had been concurrent mayors of two municipalities in Ontario. When a bridge was built between the cities, Dougie's brother, Jack, was appointed ribbon-cutter at the opening ceremony, and the bridge thereafter as known as "Jack's Bridge." She had always been envious of this honor. Today the Mitchell River Bridge on Bridge Street is adorned with a sign reading "Dougie's Bridge."

It isn't a real retirement for Dougie. Today she's a member of the golf commission that administers the Chatham Seaside Links, which she worked so hard to acquire.

Tim Pennypacker
"Seems like I've always been here"

Tim Pennypacker has seen a lot of Chatham and known many of its people. He's from what he considers to be "one of the oldest wash-ashore families" hereabouts and, like many others, was a summer visitor but came early in life to live here year-round. He's been a summer laborer, a cop, a selectman, a process server, and always a caring, benevolent friend and neighbor.

And does he have stories.

Tim's grandfather, Henry Pennypacker, was headmaster of Boston Latin School and later dean of admissions at Harvard College. He came to Chatham around 1892 and rented the large Victorian home next to the Lighthouse parking lot. He bought the place in 1898 and it became the family home. Henry was a friend of Supreme Court Justice Louis Brandeis who was settling here with his family.

Tim's father, Captain Thomas R. Pennypacker, had a career in the U.S. Navy, and the family lived in Dover, outside Boston, when Tim was born. Not long after that, the family moved to Chatham.

Tim Pennypacker.
Photo by Eric Hartell.

As a boy here, he befriended many people. His father was about fifty years older than young Tim. This enabled him to meet many older people. He used to disappear and go over to "Good Walter" Eldredge's for breakfast; sometimes it was cold mussels or some such delectable local bounty.

Due to silting, Aunt Lydia's Cove must be dredged to a depth of eight feet.	Chatham Hook Fisherman's Association is formed (now Cape Cod Commercial Fish Hook Association).	Hurricane Bob and "Halloween Nor'Easter" hit Chatham.
1989	1991	1991

He recalls fondly some of his classmates during his school years here: Wayne Love, Danny Meservey, Judy Llewellyn. He then went to Bordentown Military Academy in New Jersey and Trinity College in Texas. Summers he could be found working at the fish pier or caddying at the Chatham Bars Inn golf course (now Seaside Links).

He wrote to Police Chief David Nickerson applying for a position there and began as a summer patrolman working on the town's first harbor patrol boat with John Summers. In those days the boat was rented.

In August 1966, Tim was hired full-time with the police department, working as a regular patrolman. After ten years, "Dave let me go," he recalls, "because I ran for selectman."

He was elected, replacing David Ryder, who retired, and was sworn into office on May 15, 1975. He served with Warren Sampson, owner of Chatham Hardware, and with Edward T. Harrington, who replaced Everett Small. During subsequent terms, he served with Robert Franz, Thorne W. (Bill) Campbell, and William Litchfield. He was on the board that hired James Lindstrom as the first town administrator. Lindstrom then was succeeded by managers Thomas Groux, William Hinchey and Jill Goldsmith.

Tim served a couple of terms before leaving the board and joining the Barnstable County Sheriff's Department as a process server, a position he still holds. He has four children and is married to Paige.

The town's complexion has changed in the years he's been here. In years past, he loved the simplicity of life here, and particularly the interdependence of the people who lived here. There was real camaraderie. People knew where those in trouble were and came to their assistance very quietly.

He remembers the efforts of four men in particular. Charles W. Brown III, Robert Our, and Frank Thompson, all of Harwich, and William Weinz, owner of Airport Lumber in Chatham, would get together as needed, sometimes prompted by Margaret Guild, Betty Tripp, or Fran Belliveau of the Visiting Nurses Association. They would identify needs, people in trouble, and do something about it very quietly.

Often it was Tim who would be asked to deliver a box of food or some other supportive contribution, unobtrusively and anonymously. It might be a bicycle or some other present at Christmas. No one ever knew where they came from.

Tim says Chatham has attracted lots of wonderful people over the years. He remembers the efforts of Natural Resources Advisory Committee, which laid the groundwork – along with the Chatham Conservation Foundation – for so many of the important land acquisitions. "Can you believe we bought the Golden Triangle (Old Queen Anne, Training Field, and Old Comer's Roads) for $195,000?" he says.

Meanwhile Tim has a small house off Eliphamets Lane, left to him by an old friend. He loves it, the town, and its people.

First Night Chatham debuts on December 31.
1991

An expanded and renovated Eldredge Public Library re-opens. The EPL is listed on the National Register of Historic Places.
1992

After 48 summers of conducting the Chatham Band, leader Whitney "Whit" Tileston dies.
1994

Joe Nickerson
Courtesy Chatham, Massachusetts Historical Society.

Joseph A. Nickerson Jr.
A True Renaissance Man

This tenth-generation descendant of Chatham founder William Nickerson probably studied more Chatham history than anyone else. He joined the Chatham Town Band when he was 13 years old. He built homes and furniture. He spent hours on Monomoy charting the wildlife he loved and bringing home some of its bounty.

He was a volunteer fireman. He took photos and organized slide shows on the history of Chatham and its people. He was an avid gardener. He adored slapstick comedies at the movies and was behind some notable Halloween pranks. He was a competent sketch artist. He had an extensive collection of Sandwich and Flint glass, one of the largest in the country. He was quite handy around the kitchen stove, as well, often cooking for his large family. And, of course, he could tell wonderful stories.

He knew just about everyone in town.

Joseph Atkins Nickerson, Jr., was born here June 28, 1918, attended local schools, and served in the U.S. Navy during World War II. He learned the building trade as a carpenter's mate stationed primarily on Guam in the South Pacific. When he returned, he worked for several local builders before setting up his own business on Stony Hill Road in North Chatham in the early 1950s. He built his own home across the street and often developed plans at the kitchen table for the homes he would build for others in coming years.

He and Louise Wentworth married in 1942. She was a waitress at the Melrose Inn in Harwich when they met. Together they had seven children: Jan, Kenney, Steven, Donna, Robert, Wendy, and Peter. All but Wendy live in or near Chatham. They remember their father with great warmth. Today, there are 13 grandchildren and two great-grandchildren.

It was early in their family life when Louise prevailed upon Joe to give up his golfing membership at Eastward Ho! Country Club and help her out with the large family. A favorite family activity for him was to go to Ken Haven's meat market, buy some delicacy, bring it home and cook it.

Joe's musical career was one of his earliest interests. There was always singing and dancing in his parents' home. By age 13, he had mastered the clarinet to the point of being ready to join the Chatham Town Band.

According to family legend, he could have joined earlier but his mother wouldn't hear of it. After all, when band rehearsals were over, members were known occasionally to go to a local watering hole, and that, she thought, simply wasn't appropriate for a youngster.

The Town Band experience also landed him a seat in the local dance bands – the Knick

Tom Groux succeeds Jim Lindstrom as town manager.

Chatham native Todd Eldredge is the 1996 World Figure Skating Champion.

Chatham Conservation Foundation partners with the Town Land Bank.

1994

1996

1998

Knacks before the war and afterwards The Dreamers. They played at school dances and other local social events. Over the years, The Dreamers stayed close and performed as recently as a few First Night Chatham dates in the early years of this century.

He was a talented athlete and played for the town's team, the precursor of the NCAA-sponsored Cape Cod Baseball League of today. The town team was comprised of local talent only.

He hurled a perfect game on one summer's day when he was 19. He once met Babe Ruth, and it is said the Red Sox "took a look" at him at one point before he went into the Navy. There's a family story about one gigantic hit attributed to Joe, a smash that left the confines of Veterans Field and landed on the roof of the fire station.

Central to Joe's active mind was history – local history, and maritime history. The latent interest was brought to the surface by Louise, who began tracing the genealogy of sea captains in her family. He began helping Louise but then branched out on his own. He talked with people in town, heard their family stories, and came to discover the wealth of documentation in the attics of Chatham people.

Sometimes in his work as a builder he would find old newspapers stuck beneath floor boards in old homes used as insulation. On occasion he was known to perform some household repair or improvement for a resident in return for some old papers or books that might lie within that house. He was a stickler for historical accuracy, and sometimes was known to take to task fellow historians whose reports didn't concur with his findings.

Joe also was a driving force in the large and ever-growing Nickerson Family Association, the now-national, even international, network of descendants that is based at the headwaters of Ryders Cove, where William Nickerson's homestead was located.

It was inevitable that Joe's all-consuming searching would lead him to the Chatham Historical Society, which was founded in 1923. He became an active member, an officer, its president, and was involved in maintaining the buildings and grounds of the society's Atwood House Museum on Stage Harbor Road.

It was largely for audiences at the Atwood House that he meticulously prepared historical slide shows and commentaries. If he was asked to revisit a particular topic for yet another audience – sometimes at the Chatham Retired Men's Association – he would always change the slides around a bit, add one here and subtract another there, out of respect for his audiences. It always interested him how curious people were about some of the strictly local figures of speech he would throw into his commentaries. People not accustomed to local usage would listen with interest when he'd say two objects were "side by each" or that he'd returned from Monomoy with a "mess of clams." He would add a few "aa-yuhs" as well.

After his beloved Louise died in the mid-1980s, Joe spent even more hours in pursuit of history in all its forms. He continued to work with his hands, making tables, jewelry boxes, chairs, duck bookends, spice racks, or whatever suited his fancy.

Later he met Geraldine and soon after they married. She remembers being attracted to him by his rich voice. "I was always impressed by his skill as a driver of vehicles," she smilingly recalls.

New Junior-Senior High School is completed. Grade schoolers move from Main Street School to Depot Road Elementary School.	Town acquires MCI property in South Chatham and Chathamport.	Bill Hinchey succeeds retiring town manager Tom Groux.
1998	1999	1999

So they began to travel a bit.

"Can you believe with all his love of history, he'd never been to Nantucket or Martha's Vineyard?" she says.

One Christmas his children presented them with a trip to Nantucket. Sadly when they arrived, they discovered the Nantucket Whaling Museum – a certain target of their island exploration – was closed for the season! But they also visited Martha's Vineyard on another trip. After that they went much farther abroad, cruising the Baltic Sea to Scandinavia, Germany, and Russia, and, on another cruise, Panama and Costa Rica.

They also researched and compiled *Chatham Sea Captains in the Age of Sail*, an account of twenty-five men who traveled the world in the 18th, 19th, and 20th centuries. This attractive, co-authored work was published in 2008.

Joe died in 2007 at age 89. His life was full and he made every moment count. His work for the historical society and for Chatham history in general can never be duplicated. The town is richer for having had him as a native son.

Coleman Yeaw

"Will you marry me and retire to Chatham?"

That's how Colie (Coleman) Yeaw proposed to wife Nancy back in the early 1960s. It all happened the way he proposed, but it took some time.

Colie and Nancy Yeaw. *Photo by Eric Hartell.*

The Yeaws had been summer visitors to Chatham since the turn of the century. Colie's grandmother was a Shattuck and had a place on Bridge Street dating back to the 1890s. Colie's parents rented for several years and then built a lovely summer home – "Windward" – that was completed in 1911 and has been in the family ever since. It's the one with the huge porch just around the corner from the lighthouse on the north side of Bridge Street.

It also has a flagpole from which flies, from time to time, one of the largest American flags in town. It was flying proudly a few days in July 2011, to commemorate Windward's 100th anniversary. A giant party celebrated all the good times experienced there over the years. Five generations have spent time there, and today 10 generational owners share the place.

Colie was born in December 1933 and spent some part of every summer but one in Chatham. He missed a summer at Windward when he was serving in Germany with the U.S. Army in 1956. But other than that he's been here.

Population is 6,625 year-round residents, swelling to 20,000 in the summer.

Chatham Historical Society expands Atwood House Museum.

Main Street School is converted into Chatham Community Center.

2000

2005

2006

He loves the place and the people who live here, many of whom are cousins. He says he keeps running into people who turn out to be relatives, however distant. An aunt, Helen Yeaw, was the person who bought the land on which the Chatham Beach and Tennis Club is located. She in turn sold the land to the club's founders.

Colie graduated from Williams College and, after Army service, spent thirty-six years working for Union Carbide in various capacities and several different locations. Colie and Nancy moved to Chatham from Old Greenwich, Connecticut to become year-round residents in 1992. Their two sons, Coleman and Scott, live close enough with their families so that they are regular visitors.

The Yeaws bought a home on Mill Pond Lane that had been a Chatham Bars Inn cottage at one time. Later it was owned by the Meincke family, beginning in 1935, and then by the Miller family from 1972 on. The home is a landmark in town for its boathouse right on Little Mill Pond.

Almost immediately after they moved here, the Yeaws became involved in town affairs. Colie began as a member of the Conservation Commission, later serving as its chairman. Then he joined the Land Bank Committee. He helped to promote the Community Preservation Act and became its first chairman when it was founded in the early 2000s.

He was going to "retire," he recalls. Then Town Moderator William Litchfield suggested he'd be good material for the Finance Committee. He's now in his third term and served as chairman for several years. Nancy has been active in town with the Historical Commission, the Historical Society's Atwood House Museum, the Underground Utilities Study Committee, as well as the Women's Club and Garden Club.

The best part of Chatham for the Yeaws is the people. He has had lifelong friends here. When Colie was growing up in the summers, his pals included Matt Plum, the late Ted King, Joe Manson, Fred and Charlie Leighton, Mary Olmsted, Barbara Chase, Julie Hibben, Barbara Larsen, and many others who still have ties to the town.

"Of course the town is gorgeous," he says. "And the water. Sailing was always important to me. There was always a catboat around to enjoy."

Barbara Matteson

For nearly forty years Barbara Matteson has been in a catbird seat to watch Chatham. As a loan officer for Cape Cod Five Cents Savings Bank, she has seen a lot of the town's recent history, its ups and downs.

She hails from Wilson, North Carolina, but has been in Chatham since 1972. Before starting her career in banking, she worked mornings for Frank Kennedy as a chambermaid at the Dolphin Court Motel.

At the same time she spent afternoons working at the original Northport Bakery when it was run by its founder, Bruce Woodland. She also had a stint as a cocktail waitress in the old Mill Hill Club in South Yarmouth.

A second break in North Beach occurs across from Ministers Point, washing away several summer camps. **2007**

Chatham historian Joseph A. Nickerson dies at age 89. **2007**

Chatham Marconi Maritime Center opens. **2010**

Voters approve Harwich-Chatham school merger. **2010**

She began at the bank in 1974 as a teller and has been there ever since. She went through a natural progression, first to head teller and then branch manager, in Centerville and then Chatham. As a manager she began taking mortgage loan applications and learning that end of the banking business. Since 1997 she's worked exclusively in the bank's mortgage department. She is very well known in the community because of her knowledge, her accessibility, and her community service.

Barbara doesn't know how many mortgages she's written for the bank, but there have been many of them. The economic upswing in 2003-04, she says, "nearly inundated us." Then it was a matter of first mortgages and refinancing of existing ones.

After that 2009 was also very busy, with a great number of refinancing agreements to help people stem the tides of recession.

She works very closely with customers seeking refinancing to alleviate consumer debt. She counsels them quite thoroughly and says she'll help them out once but not repeatedly. "People must learn to manage their debt," she says, "and home ownership should be the goal, not continuing debt."

"High-end real estate in Chatham has always been recession-proof," she says. "But the people who live here often are not so well protected."

She joins those community members who hope Chatham's Main Street area can remain small and diversified and not home to regional and national commercial entities.

When she's not putting together financing for townspeople, Barbara may be at a Rotary Club function or playing platform tennis. She was also treasurer of the Chatham Chamber of Commerce for twelve years.

Board of Selectmen votes 3-2 not to renew the contract of Town Manager Bill Hinchey.

Chatham Police Department and some town offices move to new quarters on property once home to Airport Lumber.

2010

2011

AFTERWORD

For one hundred fifty years Chatham's residents allowed the anniversary of the town's founding in June 1712 to pass without comment. Then in 1912, residents woke to their own history and celebrated the town's 200th anniversary with a great hoopla in August. Fifty years later in 1962, the town once again saluted its past. Many men grew beards to honor early settlers and the four-month celebration ended with a harvest dance in October.

Now in 2012, townspeople are once again honoring this proud town in a nine-month celebration that includes concerts, a banquet, a period ball, and a living history parade on July 4. The gala year ends on December 31 with First Night Chatham and a look toward the town's fourth century.

Author Biographies

Dana Eldridge is a twelfth-generation Cape Codder. His association with his beloved land encompasses a lifetime in and around the beaches and the salt water that permeate Cape Cod. He is the author of three memoirs: *Once Upon Cape Cod* (1997), *Cape Cod Lucky: In Another Time* (2000), and *A Cape Cod Kinship* (2008). He writes a bi-weekly column for the *Cape Codder* on the natural world of this lovely peninsula.

Mary Ann Gray earned master's degrees in Nursing Education at Wayne State University and in Library Science at Rutgers University. She also earned a certificate in Museum Studies at Tufts University. For the past thirteen years she has been responsible for creating and maintaining the archives of the Chatham Historical Society. Before moving to Chatham, she was a professor of nursing and director of bibliographic instruction at the County College of Morris. She served on the Editorial Board of *Orthopedic Nursing Journal*, and wrote a regular column on pharmacology for nurses.

Spencer Grey has been a resident of Chatham throughout his life. From 1955 to 1975 he taught English in Connecticut while summering in Chatham. From 1975 to 1996 he owned and operated The Sail Loft, a clothing store in Chatham, Cotuit, and Duxbury. Since retiring in 1996, he has been associated with the Chatham Historical Society, serving as president for eight years, chairman for three years, and now as a member of the Board of Overseers. With the late Robert D.B. Carlisle he helped produce two books published by the Society: *Weathering a Century of Change* (2000), and *Beyond the Bar* (2007).

Eric Hartell edited and published the *Cape Cod Chronicle* for eighteen years, developing it from a twice-a-month free publication to a paid circulation weekly. He then became vice president for news at WFCC radio when it opened in West Chatham in 1989. He also served as executive editor of Cape Cod Newspapers which published a dozen weeklies from Bourne to Wellfleet. Later he returned to Main Street, Chatham to manage the former Epicure store. He and his wife, Lynne, live in Riverbay Estates.

Debra Lawless is the author of three books published with The History Press: *Chatham in the Jazz Age* (2009), *Chatham in the Age of Aquarius* (2010), and *Provincetown: A History of Artists and Renegades in a Fishing Village* (2011). A second book on Provincetown's history is due in the spring of 2013. She has worked for many newspapers in Rhode Island and Massachusetts and currently freelances for *Cape Cod Magazine* and the *Cape Cod Chronicle*. A native of Providence, Rhode Island, Lawless lives in Chatham. She has degrees from Stanford and Boston Universities and also holds a certificate in Boston University's Genealogical Research Program.

Lynn C. Van Dine lives in a historically cited house in Chatham with her husband and business partner, Tim Weller. They co-own and operate Professional Writers & Editors, LLC. She is the author of the literary biography *The Search for Peter Hunt* (The Local History Company, 2003), and her work has appeared in publications including *Yankee* magazine, *Cape Cod Life*, *Cape Cod Home*, *Home Remodeling* magazine, *USA Today*, *The Detroit News*, and the *Detroit Free Press*. She has also written for art magazines, museum catalogs, and corporate publications. Lynn is communications coordinator for St. Christopher's Church in Chatham. She is the mother of two grown sons, Donovan and Alan "Dock" Howard.

Tim Weller co-owns Professional Writers & Editors in Chatham with his wife, Lynn Van Dine. He spent thirty-five years as a reporter and editor at newspapers around the country, including *The Detroit News* and *USA Today*. He left newspapering in 2004 and moved full-time to the Cape to open the business. He and his wife provide writing and editing services for a variety of clients on and off the Cape. Tim edited fellow collaborator Dana Eldridge's most recent book, *A Cape Cod Kinship*, in 2008.

Acknowledgments

We give special thanks to Amy Andreasson, assistant director/reference, Eldredge Public Library in Chatham, for her always cheerful and efficient help; and Mary Ann Gray, archivist at the Chatham Historical Society, for guiding us through the society's byzantine files and records.

Debra Lawless: My husband, John Lawless; Stuart G. Stearns, for sparking my interest in genealogy and local history; and my six co-authors for great inspiration.

Lynn C. Van Dine: Janet Whittemore, Isaac Bea Young House, Chatham; Massachusetts Historical Society; Sarah Peake, Massachusetts state representative, Fourth Barnstable District, and her office intern Jocelyn Cary, for assistance in researching the State House Library; Valley Forge National Historic Park, Valley Forge, Pennsylvania; Leslie Ray Sears III of the Sears Family Association; William G. Litchfield, Esquire, for important content assistance; and our writing team – Dana, Spencer, Mary Ann, Debra, Eric, and, especially, my/our editor Tim.

Tim Weller: William Litchfield, attorney and Town of Chatham moderator, for showing me the way; Spencer Grey, past president of the Chatham Historical Society, for guiding me and taking care of all the publishing details; Gerald Moore, landscaper, for suggesting dozens of people to interview; Cynthia Moore, photographer and writer, for her insights; George Goodspeed, realtor, for sharing memories of his father; Edward "Ned" Collins, architect, one of the best storytellers around; David Ryder, retired fisherman, former selectman, forever young at heart; Barbara Townson Weller, my mother, for helping to preserve a slice of family history; and my fellow writers: Lynn, Debra, Eric, Spencer, Mary Ann and Dana, for your patience and understanding. Special thanks to Debra and Lynn for stepping in at the last minute with outstanding editing help!

Spencer Grey: The late Rob Carlisle for providing the impetus for the book; Mary Ann Gray for her forbearance while I invaded her archives; Tim Weller for guiding us through the agony of creation and for skillfully editing the book; and especially the six fellow contributors for cheerfully producing under pressure.

Endnotes

Chapter 1

1　Henry C. Kittredge, *Cape Cod*, p.28. While "all Cape Indians belonged nominally to the Wampanoags," small regional tribes were organized under their own sachems. The Monomoyicks dominated Monomoit.

2　Nathaniel Philbrick, *Mayflower: A Story of Courage, Community, and War*, p.39.

3　*Ibid.*, p.43.

4　Giles Hopkins, who died in 1688-90, his sister Constance Hopkins Snow, who died in 1677 and Joseph Rogers, who died in 1678, were all living in the Town of Eastham (incorporated 1651) at the time of their deaths.

5　Kittredge, 89.

6　*Ibid.*

7　James W. Hawes, an attorney living in New York, returned to his hometown of Chatham in 1912, at the time of the town's bicentennial, to deliver a lengthy speech on the town's history to 1860. James W. Hawes, *History & Genealogy Historical Address, August 1, 1912, on the Occasion of the Celebration of the 200ᵗʰ Anniversary of the Incorporation of Chatham*, Library of Cape Cod, No. 78, Yarmouthport, Mass.: C.W. Swift, Publisher and Printer, 1912; Internet Archive (http://www.archive.org/stream/historicaladdress : accessed 25 September 2011).

8　This memorial stone, found at the end of A Leonard Way, off Training Field Road, was erected in 1915 in a Ryder family cemetery where victims of the virulent smallpox epidemic of 1766 are buried.

9　W. Sears Nickerson, *The Bay As I See It*, p.6.

10　The Nickersons embarked from their homeland toward the end of the period known as The Great Migration, 1620-1640. During this period about 20,000 English men, women and children settled in New England.

11　Two ships traveled together from Yarmouth, England: the *Rose* and the *John and Dorothy*. It is not known who traveled on which ship.

12　Delores Bird Carpenter, *Early Encounters*, p.196.

13　*The Nickerson Family Association* (http://www.nickersonassoc.org/willNickerson.shtml: accessed 25 September 2011).

14　Nickerson, *The Bay As I See It*, pp.6-7.

15　Kittredge, *Cape Cod*, 12. At this time Monomoit was said to be "overgrown with walnut, oak, and cedar." When William Nickerson arrived "he found its hills still covered with forests of oak, and the swamps filled with gigantic cedars." This would all change when, through poor land management skills, the first pioneers deforested the Cape.

16　Philbrick, *Op.cit.*, p.311.

17　Nickerson, *The Bay As I See It*, p.206. "I suppose The Old Sagamore [Mattaquason] and the old pioneer sleep their last sleep on the knoll overlooking the homestead of the first settler and the campsite of the old Indian. A stone marks the grave of the white man, but this hill was a Monomoyick burying ground long before the first white man ever landed on our shores." This sentiment is quaint but probably fanciful.

18　William Smith, *A History of Chatham Massachusetts*, 4ᵗʰ edition. Chatham, MA: Chatham Historical Society, 1992, pp.62-63.

19　Philbrick, *Op.cit.*, p.172

20　Smith, William C., *Op.cit.*, p.105.

21　*Ibid.*, pp.87-88.

22　*Ibid.*, p.89.

23　Smith describes Monomoit at the time of William Nickerson's death as "but little more than a Nickerson neighborhood," *ibid.*, p.92.

24　*Ibid.*, p.142.

25　*Ibid.*, p.148.

26　*Ibid.*, p.164.

27　*Ibid.*, p.165.

28   *Ibid.*, pp.178-9.

29   *Ibid.*

Squanto Article

1   *CapeCodOnline.com* (http://search.capecodonline.com: accessed 30 September 2011), "Are Chatham Remains Those of Squanto?" March 9, 2011

2   Elizabeth Reynard, *The Narrow Land: Folk Chronicles of Old Cape Cod* (Boston: Houghton Mifflin Company, 1934), p.74

3   Squanto may have been assassinated by the sachem Massasoit. "That Squanto, who had survived the infectious streets of London, should suddenly fall prey to disease on Cape Cod is highly unlikely." Philbrick, *Op.cit.*, p. 138

4   Carpenter, Delores Bird, *Early Encounters: Native Americans and Europeans in New England: From the Papers of W. Sears Nickerson* (East Lansing, Mich: Michigan State University Press, 1994), p.200

5   W. Sears Nickerson, *The Bay– As I See It* (So. Orleans, Mass.: Friends of Pleasant Bay, 1995), p.40

6   Philbrick, *Op.cit.,* p.138

Chapter 2

1   Smith, William C. *Op.cit.,* p.183.

2   Henry C. Kittredge, *Cape Cod: Its People and Their History*, p.81

3   *Ibid.*, p.82

4   Smith, William C. *Op.cit.,* p.182

5   Kittredge, p.82

6   *Dover New Hampshire 250ᵗʰ Anniversary Publication,* Oct. 28, 1883

7   Smith, William C., *Op.cit.,* p.187

8   *Ibid.*, p.278

9   *Ibid.*, p.294

10   *Ibid.*, p.250

11   *Ibid.*, pp.294-319

12   Gustavus Swift Paine, "Ungodly Carriages on Cape Cod," *The New England Quarterly,* Vol. 23 No. 2, June 1952, pp.181-198

13   Smith, William C., p.295

14   *Ibid.*, p.303

15   Carl Leonard Smith and Norma Smith, *Nova Scotia Immigrants to 1867*, p.283

16   Smith, William C., p.315

17   *Ibid.*, pp.289-290

18   Edwin Crowell, *A History of Barrington township and vicinity, Shelburne County, Nova Scotia, 1604-1870; with a biographical and genealogical appendix* (Reprint of original book published before 1923), pp.555-556.

19   Pauline Derick, Gertrude James and Barbara E. Goward, *The Nickerson Family: The Descendants of William Nickerson (1604-1689), First Settler of Chatham, Massachusetts,* p.150.

20   "Nova Scotia's Electric Scrapbook," (http://ns1763.ca/kingsco/plantermon.html: accessed 29 September 2011), information on Planters [colonists], 1760-1763

21   Crowell, *Op.cit.,* p.56

22   Smith, William C., *Op.cit.,* p.323

23   Smith and Smith, *Nova Scotia Immigrants to 1867*, p.96

24   Harold Horwood and Ed Butts, *Bandits and Privateers, Canada in the Age of Gunpowder* (Doubleday of Canada, 1988), pp.47-64

25   T. Morris Longstreth, *To Nova Scotia: The Sunrise Province of Canada* (New York: Appleton Century Company, 1930), p.51

26   *Ibid.*, p.60

27   Simon L. Deyo, *History of Barnstable County* (New York: H.W. Blake & Co. 1890), p.582

28   Smith, William C., *Op.cit.,* p.272

29   *Ibid.*, 236

30   George and Barbara Smith (Chatham, Massachusetts) to "Loving Brother and Sister" [Stephen and Mehitabel Smith], letter, 19 April 1766; held by the Chatham Historical Society, 347 Stage Harbor Road, Chatham, Mass., 2011

31   Smith, William C., *Op.cit.,* p.328

32   *Ibid.*

33   *Ibid.*, p.334

Chapter 3

1   Smith, William C., *Op.cit.*, p.358

2   *Ibid*, p.344

3   *Ibid*, p.345

4   *Historical Address Delivered by James W. Hawes, August 1, 1912, On the Occasion of the Celebration of the 200th Anniversary of the Incorporation of Chatham,* Pranava Books edition, p.10

5   Smith, William C., *Op.cit.*, pp.345, 346

6   *Ibid*, p.346

7   Hawes, *Op.cit.*, p.9

8   *Ibid*, p.10

9   Smith, William C., *Op.cit.*, p.351

10   *Ibid*, p.351

11   *Ibid*, p.351

12   *Ibid*, p.379

13   *Ibid*, p.375

14   *Ibid*, p.382

15   Reverend James Freeman, editor. *Collections of the Massachusetts Historical Society,* Volume VIII (first series). Boston, recording secretary for the Massachusetts Historical Society, *Description of Chatham. September, 1802.*

16   *Ibid*

17   Baisly Chronology

18   Freeman, *Op.cit.*

19   Smith, William C., *Op.cit.*, pp.380-381

20   *Ibid*, Smith, pp.381, 383

21   *Ibid*, Smith, p.383

22   *Ibid*, Smith, p.384

23   *Ibid*, Smith, p.357

24   *Ibid*, Smith, p.387

25   *Ibid*, Smith, p.345

26   *Ibid*, Smith, p.345

27   *Ibid*, Smith, p.352

28   Freeman, *Op.cit.*

29   Smith, William C., *Op.cit.*, p.350

30   *Ibid*, Smith, p.346

31   Battles cited from the papers of Joseph Young, Chatham Historical Society, and the records of the Daughter of the American Revolution.

32   Smith, William C., *Op.cit.*, p.351

33   *Ibid*, Smith, p.353

34   Valley Forge National Historical Park website

35   Smith, William C., *Op.cit.*, p.350

36 Virginia Harding McGrath, "The Patriotic Youngs," an essay, 1912, for the 200th Anniversary of the Town of Chatham, Mass., Chatham Historical Society

37 Smith, William C., *Op.cit.*, p.351

38 *Representative Women of New England,* New England Historical Publishing Company, 1904, account of descendent Helen C. Mumford, superintendent for nine years of the Women's Christian Temperance Union.

39 McGrath, *Op.cit.*

40 Ibid.

41 Mumford, *Op.cit.*; Smith, William C., *Op.cit.,* p.352

42 McGrath, *Op.cit.*

43 *Ibid.*

44 Mumford, *Op.cit.*

45 *Ibid*

46 Massachusetts State House Library and Archive

47 McGrath, *Op.cit.*

48 Simeon Deyo, *History of Barnstable County, 1890*, Chapter XIX.

49 Ernest John Knapton, *Chatham Since the American Revolution*, 1976, published by the Chatham Historical Society.

50 Smith, William C., *Op.cit.*, p.356

51 *Ibid*, p.357

52 Freeman, *Op.cit.*

53 Smith, William C., *Op.cit.*, p.358

54 United States Coast Guard, history curriculum

55 Freeman, *Op.cit.*

56 Cape Cod National Seashore history by the National Parks Service.

57 Jeremy D'Entremont, *Lighthouses of Massachusetts*, Commonwealth Editions, 2007

58 Smith, William C., *Op.cit.*, p.399

59 Freeman, *Op.cit.*

60 Smith, William C., *Op.cit.*, p.383

61 *Ibid*, p.400

62 *Ibid*, p.399

63 *Ibid*, p.400

64 *Ibid*

65 Leslie Ray Sears III, Sears Family Association.

66 *Ibid*

Chapter 4

1 The children of Sears Atwood and his wife Azubah Collins were Joseph, Solomon, David, John, Sears, James and Azubah. The homes of John, Joseph, David, and James still stand on the street, and when Azubah married Enathan Mayo in 1823, her father built a house for them, which until recently was the home of Sherrill Atwood and his family.

2 Sea weed was banked around the foundation of the house to help insulate it

3 *Two Hundred Anniversary Proceedings*, Chatham, Massachusetts Historical Society

4 Henry C. Kittredge, *Shipmasters of Cape Cod*, Archon Books 1971, pp.292-293

5 Hosea Starr Ballou. *Hosea Ballou, 2nd, His Origins,Life and Letters,* (Boston: E. P. Guild, 1896)

6 G. H. Ballou, "Monomoy", 1864, *Harper's New Monthly Magazine*, 28 (165):305-311. All quotations are from this article.

7 By-laws of the Chatham Mining Company are in the archives of the Atwood House Museum. All quotations from that document included here are from that document.

Chapter 5

1   Stauffer Miller, *Hoisting Their Colors: Cape Cod's Civil War Navy Officers* (Lexington, KY: Xlibris Corporation, 2008), p.233

2   Stauffer Miller, *Cape Cod and the Civil War* (Charleston, SC: The History Press, 2010), Appendix C, pp.121-133

3   According to the 1890 Veterans Schedules, Special Schedule of the Eleventh Census, common disabilities of the wounded were typhus and intermittent fevers, plaguing gunshot wounds that made them unable to work most of the time, recurring malarial fevers and chronic diarrhea. Barnstable County, Massachusetts, Chatham, enumeration district 5, pp. 3; NARA microfilm publication M123, roll 13; digital image by subscription, *Ancestry.com* (http://ancestry.com : accessed 4 September 2011)

4   Simeon L. Deyo, *History of Barnstable County, Massachusetts* (New York: H.W. Blake Co., 1890) digital archive, *Cape Cod History*, (http://capecodhistory.us/Deyo/Chatham-Deyo.htm : accessed 1 September 2011), Chapter XIX, Town of Chatham. p.598

5   A rapid perusal of the U.S. censuses enumerated in Massachusetts during this time will show that most residents of Chatham were born in Massachusetts, as were their parents. 1880 U.S. census, Barnstable County, Massachusetts, population schedule, Chatham, enumeration district 2, pp. 1-52; NARA microfilm publication T9, roll 519; digital image by subscription, *Ancestry.com* (http://ancestry.com : accessed 4 September 2011)

6   Jeremy D'Entremont, *The Lighthouses of Massachusetts* (Beverly, MA: Commonwealth Editions, 2007), p.155

7   Deyo, *Op.cit.*, p.591

8   *Ibid*, 582

9   William C. Smith, *Congregational Church in Chatham 1720-1920: Historical Address on the Two Hundredth Anniversary of the Organization of the Church* (Chatham: Chatham Monitor Print, 1920), p.24

10   Nancy Barr, *A Sense of Place by the Sea: The Legacy of Chatham's Historic Homes* (Bourne, MA: O'Brien & Company Printers, Inc., 2007), p.40

11   *The Barnstable Patriot*, February 12, 1867

12   *Ibid*, July 30, 1867

13   Morgan Morony, "Touring the New York City Obelisks," August 19, 2009, *Archaeology*, Archaeology Institute of America (http://www.archaeology.org/online/features/obelisk_tour/ : accessed 3 August 2011)

14   *Boston Daily Globe*, January 27, 1907

15   *Chatham Monitor*, May 11, 1886

16   *Ibid*, June 15, 1886.

17   Ellen St. Sure, *With a Passion for Brush and Palette: Giddings H. Ballou and His Cape Cod Portraits c. 1841-1861.* (East Greenwich, RI: Meridian Printing, 2003), pp.6, 9

18   *Chatham Monitor*, April 27, 1886.

19   Giddings Ballou's sister Harriet Eliza had married into another branch of the Ballou family. Adin Ballou, *An Elaborate History and Genealogy of the Ballous in America*, v. 2 (Ariel Ballou and Latimer W. Ballou, publishers, n.d.), pp.759-760

20   *Chatham Monitor*, May 11 and 18, 1886

21   1890 Veterans Schedules, Special Schedule of the Eleventh Census, Barnstable County, Massachusetts, Chatham, enumeration district 5, pp. 3, Henry M. Couden; NARA microfilm publication M123, roll 13; digital image by subscription, *Ancestry.com* (http://ancestry.com : accessed 4 September 2011)

22   Unattributed newspaper clipping, probably 1884

23   St. Sure, *Op.cit.*, 10

24   Smith, William C., *Congregational Church, Ibid,* p.25

25   1880 U.S. census, Barnstable County, Massachusetts, population schedule, Chatham, enumeration district 2, pp. 1-52; NARA microfilm publication T9, roll 519; digital image by subscription, *Ancestry.com* (http://ancestry.com : accessed 4 September 2011)

26   D'Entremont, *Ibid*, pp.171-173.

27 Ruth Howard Foley, *Some Chatham Neighbors of Yesterday* (Duxbury, MA: Thompson and Forbes Company, 1984), p.54

28 1890 Veterans Schedules, Special Schedule of the Eleventh Census, Barnstable County, Massachusetts, Harwich, enumeration district 10, pp. 1, Asa L. Jones; NARA microfilm publication M123, roll 13; digital image by subscription, *Ancestry.com* (http://ancestry.com : accessed 4 September 2011)

29 Maro Jones would travel far from Monomoy– not by sea, but by land. After studies at Boston University and several European universities, he became a college professor, rising to head of the Department of Romance Languages at Pomona College in Claremont, Calif. He died in May 1945. Theresa Mitchell Barbo, *True Accounts of Yankee Ingenuity and Grit from the Cape Cod Voice,* (Charleston, SC: The History Press, 2007), p.72

30 Giddings Ballou, "Monomoy," *Harper's New Monthly Magazine,* XXVIII, December 1863- May 1864, p.308

31 Elizabeth Reynard, *The Narrow Land: Folk Chronicles of Old Cape Cod,* 5th ed. (Chatham, MA: Chatham Historical Society, 1978), p.253

32 Ballou, *Op.cit.,* p.309

33 St. Sure, *Op.cit.,* p.9

34 *Barnstable Patriot,* April 8, 1912

35 *Chatham's Old Houses,* Book IV, p.21

36 *Chatham Monitor,* undated clipping

37 *Ibid,* June 15, 1886.

38 Lung ailments were rampant in the 19th century, according to contemporary necrologies and advertisements for patent medicines. Ballou apparently died of consumption; Capt. Taylor died of "congestion of the lungs." Dr. Atwood himself suffered from a cough every winter.

39 *Barnstable Patriot,* April 8, 1912

40 St. Sure, *Op.cit.,* p.7

41 Colleen Cowles Heslip, *Between the Rivers: Itinerant Painters from the Connecticut to the Hudson* (Williamstown, MA: Sterling and Francine Clark Art Institute, 1990), p.16

42 *Ibid,* p.26

43 *Barnstable Patriot,* June 18 and November 12, 1850

44 Todd Gustavson, *Camera: A History of Photography from Daguerreotype to Digital* (New York: Sterling Publishing Co., Inc., 2009), pp.70-71

45 *Chatham Monitor,* July 5, 1887

46 *Reports of the Town Officers of the Town of Chatham,* 1888

47 1880 U.S. Census, Barnstable County, Massachusetts, population schedule, Chatham, enumeration district 2, 38A (stamped), p. 49 (penned), dwelling 495, family 563, John K. Kendrick; NARA microfilm publication T9, roll 519; digital image by subscription, *Ancestry.com* (http://ancestry.com : accessed 4 September 2011)

48 Adam Gamble, ed. *1880 Atlas of Barnstable County, Massachusetts: Cape Cod's Earliest Atlas* (Yarmouth Port, MA.: 1998)

49 *Chatham Monitor,* March 28, 1888

50 *Reports of the Town Officers,* 1888

51 Josephine Buck Ivanoff, *Pieces of Old Cape Cod,* 1985, p.17

52 *Chatham Monitor,* March 7, 1888

53 *Chatham Monitor,* March 20, 1888

54 *Hyannis Patriot,* May 24, 1909

55 *Chatham Monitor,* November 1, 1871

56 Britton W. Crosby, *Cape Cod Firefighting* (Charleston, SC: Arcadia Publishing, 2003), p.21. In contrast to Chatham, Provincetown organized a fire department in 1869.

57 *Chatham Monitor,* July 5, 1887

58 Unattributed, undated newspaper clipping held by the Chatham Historical Society, 347 Stage Harbor Road, Chatham, Mass., 2011

59 Ibid., November 26, 1889

60 Ibid., December 3, 1889

61 Joseph A. Nickerson Jr. and Geraldine D. Nickerson, *Chatham Sea Captains in the Age of Sail* (Charleston, SC: The History Press, 2008), p.135

62 Josephine Atkins (Chatham, Massachusetts) invitation to birthday party, July 4, 1893; held by the Chatham Historical Society, 347 Stage Harbor Road, Chatham, Mass., 2011

63 *Chatham Monitor*, July 14, 1896

64 Unattributed newspaper article, March 1898

65 Historic Properties Inventory Form, filed in the Eldredge Public Library, 564 Main Street, Chatham, Mass., 2011

66 Spencerian System of Penmanship, work book held by the Chatham Historical Society, 347 Stage Harbor Road, Chatham, Mass., 2011

67 Deyo, *Op.cit.*, p.599

68 Lillie Osborn (Chatham, Massachusetts) to Josephine Atkins, red leather autograph album, July 25, 1900; held by the Chatham Historical Society, 347 Stage Harbor Road, Chatham, Mass., 2011

69 *Barnstable Patriot*, April 30, 1900

70 Nickerson and Nickerson, *Chatham Sea Captains*, pp.134-35

71 *Barnstable Patriot*, October 17, 1904

72 Almena Kent, notes held by the Chatham Historical Society, 347 Stage Harbor Road, Chatham, Mass., 2011

73 *The Two Hundredth Anniversary of the Incorporation of the Town of Chatham, Massachusetts*. Chatham, MA: Town Celebration Committee, 1913, p.86

74 *Ibid*, p.87

75 *Chatham Monitor*, November 22, 1887

76 *Chatham Monitor*, June 8, 1903

Chapter 6

1 Joseph D. Buckley, *Wings over Cape Cod: The Chatham Naval Air Station 1917-1922* (Orleans, Mass.: Lower Cape Publishing Co., 2000), p.71

2 *Ibid*, p.15

3 *Ibid*, p.15

4 *Ibid*, p.18

5 *Ibid*, p.17

6 Robert D. B. Carlisle, *Weathering A Century of Change: The Story of a Seaside Village 1900-2000* (Chatham, Mass.: Chatham Historical Society, 200) p.54

7 Interview with Edward C. Collins II, Chatham, Mass. July, September 2011

8 Interview with David C. Ryder, Brewster, Mass., April 2011

9 Interview with George Goodspeed, Chatham, Mass., April 2011

10 Carlisle, *Op.cit.*, p.99

11 *Ibid*, p.102

12 Interview with Barbara Townson Weller, Grosse Pointe, Mich., March 2011

13 Weller interview, March 2011

14 Goodspeed interview, April 2011

15 Buckley, *Op.cit.*, p.95

16 *Ibid*, p.95

17 *Ibid*, p.95

18 Collins interview, July 2011

19 Buckley, *Op.cit.*, pp.27-32

20 *Ibid*, pp.30-32

21 Collins interview, July 2011

22   Ryder interview, April 2011

23   Goodspeed interview, June 2011

24   Weller interview, March 2011

25   Collins interview, July 2011

26   Goodspeed interview, April 2011

27   Bernard C. Webber, *Chatham "The Lifeboatmen"* (Orleans, Mass. Lower Cape Publishing, 1985) p.40

28   *Ibid*, p.43

29   Ryder interview, April 2011

30   Massachusetts Office of Coastal Zone Management archives. www.mass.gov/czm/buar/shipwrecks/ua-pendleton.htm.

31   Webber, *Op.cit.*, p.46

32   *Ibid*, p.48

33   www.mass.gov/czm/buar/shipwrecks/ua-pendleton.htm

34   Webber, *Op.cit.*, pp.49-51

35   Ryder interview, April 2011

36   Weller interview, March 2011

37   Ryder interview, April 2011

38   Goodspeed interview, April 2011

39   Goodspeed interview, April 2011

Index